SOCIAL CUSTOMS

BY

FLORENCE HOWE HALL

Who does not delight in fine manners? Their charm cannot be predicted or overstated. — EMERSON

BOSTON
ESTES AND LAURIAT

𝕌𝕟𝕚𝕧𝕖𝕣𝕤𝕚𝕥𝕪 ℙ𝕣𝕖𝕤𝕤:
JOHN WILSON AND SON, CAMBRIDGE.

PREFACE.

THE man who made the first map of the earth's surface had a comparatively easy task to fulfil. Like Columbus, the world lay before him where to choose; he was not obliged to respect the prejudices nor the landmarks of any predecessor, but could draw freely upon his own imagination. The last maker of atlases has a very different work to do. His fancy can make no lofty flights; cold realities fence him in on every side. Not an island, not a wretched little cape can he omit; he must copy all his predecessors, and yet he must create a new work. "It is the last step which costs," he exclaims in the bitterness of his heart, and longs for those ancient days of geographical license when turtles, elephants, and serpents figured in place of North and South America.

It is with somewhat similar feelings that the writer of this little volume has entered upon her task. The difficulty of writing a new discourse upon so old a theme as manners is greater than might appear to one who had given the subject no thought. The old charts must constantly be consulted, and the general outlines

of the new must in great measure correspond with them.
The great social continents, the moral Baffin's Bays and
Hudson's Straits must be represented as they always
have been, in all essential particulars, and yet the whole
must be no servile copy, no mere reproduction. The
writer has attempted, therefore, to give a bird's-eye
view, as it were, of her subject, in order that she might
be enabled to depart a little from the beaten track,
and also because it has seemed to her that such a
view was the most correct one. One cannot judge of
the merits of a picture if one stands too near it; and
the theme of manners is one that admits of a moral
perspective.

It was the wish of the publishers, Messrs. Estes and
Lauriat, that this book should be something more than
a mere set of rules for behavior; that it should contain
some reflections on the reason and origin of social customs. To enter deeply into such a matter would of course
be impossible in a volume of this size and scope; but
it has been touched upon here and there as opportunity
offered. If the reader finds as much pleasure in reading
these little details of ancient customs as the writer has
enjoyed in collecting them, she will feel amply repaid
for her labor.

Another great difficulty which confronts all writers
upon American etiquette is, that many matters of detail
are not definitely settled in our social code. About the
great general principles upon which all really good manners are founded, no difference of opinion exists. But
we are pre-eminently a freedom-loving people, and every

man claims liberty of conscience in social as in other matters. For the rest, we have no person nor set of persons who have a right to dictate to us what our conduct shall be. In European countries it is a part of the privilege of the court to lay down an absolute law on all matters of etiquette, and the social culture and training, hereditary and traditional in a royal house for centuries, give its members a certain moral right to prescribe what shall and what shall not be considered good breeding. Whatever we may think of a monarchical and aristocratic form of government, we must at least acknowledge that in countries where it is allowed to exist at all it may reasonably claim the privilege of, and a special fitness for, social jurisdiction. The great standing armies, too, of European States, with their military discipline and strict subordination, no doubt have an important influence on public opinion. They inculcate obedience and uniformity of action with a silent influence which is difficult to estimate exactly.

Our own army may be just as well regulated, or perhaps even better; but it is so small, and so scattered over our Western frontiers, that its influence is scarcely perceptible. Our political rulers are often men of no especial culture or early advantages. Even those who set themselves up as our social rulers are often utterly deficient in the important social prerequisite of grandparents; and the man whose ancestors came over in the "Mayflower" will not submit to dictation in matters of conduct from the man who had a rag-picker for his grandfather.

Thus it will be seen that in treating of our etiquette one must necessarily avoid as far as possible *ex cathedra* or absolute statements, while one must also beware of confusing the reader by offering too many alternatives and showing too many possible paths. The writer has therefore striven to avoid dogmatism on the one hand and ambiguity on the other, giving decided opinions where it seemed best to do so, and in other cases mentioning the various views that are taken of those subjects upon which doctors disagree.

FLORENCE HOWE HALL.

September 21, 1887.

CONTENTS.

X CONTENTS.

SOCIAL CUSTOMS.

CHAPTER I.

THE EARLY ORIGIN OF MANNERS, AND THEIR FOUNDATION ON HUMAN REASON.

HERBERT SPENCER declares the earliest kind of government to be that of ceremonial institutions. Ceremonial control precedes religious and political control, and he finds an ingenious argument in favor of this hypothesis in the conduct of savage tribes. " Daily intercourse among the lowest savages, whose small, loose groups, scarcely to be called social, are without political or religious regulation, is under a considerable amount of ceremonial regulation."

In other words, ceremonies, manners, whatever you please to call them, are necessarily the first law which binds man, because they are personal and concrete. The earliest necessity for a savage is to show his fellow that he does not mean to fight him, but intends rather to live peaceably with him and give him his dues. Hence certain peaceful observances and signs are early established, such as salutations, doing homage, etc., and perhaps are the first tokens of order that appear out of the primeval chaos of mutual warfare and destruction.

The first bondage, then, is that of manners, and the last bondage is of manners also, and from it we need neither

1

wish nor hope to be set free.   If we live among civilized
men, we surely cannot be free from it; if we flee to savage
nations, we must still observe their code of manners.   Our
only hope of escape is to live the life of a hermit, and even
Robinson Crusoe was polite to his cat and his parrot!   And
why should we wish to escape from this easy-fitting yoke,
which surely protects far more than it hampers us?   Manners are, or should be, defensive, not offensive.   They have
undergone vast changes during all these ages, and the customs of the savage resemble little enough the polished ways
of the highly civilized man of the nineteenth century.   But
in this one point they must ever resemble each other, — that
they protect and defend the man who uses them.   Emerson
says of manners, "Their vast convenience I must always
admire.   The perfect defence and isolation which they effect
makes an insuperable protection."   And some one else has
said, "Etiquette is the barrier which society draws around
itself as a protection against offences the 'law' cannot
touch; it is a shield against the intrusion of the impertinent."

But what a vast difference between the old slavish customs
wherein the inferior tremblingly deprecated the wrath of his
superior, and the manners of to-day, with which equal greets
equal!   The fear of personal violence, or even of death, made
unfortunate wretches grovel in the earth, and place dirt upon
their heads, as a sign of their entire submission, a plea of
humility; whereas, with the liberty we of the Western
world now enjoy, we need not "crook the pregnant hinges
of the knee" to any man; and though we still use manners
as a defence, it is only to guard those innermost citadels of
privacy, the mind and heart, from unwarranted intrusion.

The history of manners is the history of civilization, and
in their study the wise man finds his account.   It is only the
fool who despises them, because he has not taken the time

and trouble to come at their real meaning and significance, and therefore begs the whole question by declaring that they have none.

It is a significant fact that manners, in old English, meant much the same thing as what we now call morals, — thus showing the ethical importance which our ancestors attached to a decent behavior. "Evil communications corrupt good manners," saith the Scripture, and the word is used elsewhere in the Bible in the same sense. In Shakespeare's "As You Like It," Touchstone makes a delightful pun on the word.

"Touch. Wast ever in court, shepherd?
Cor. No, truly.
Touch. Then thou art damned.

. . . . . .

Cor. For not being at court? Your reason.
Touch. Why, if thou never wast at court thou never sawest good manners; if thou never sawest good manners, then thy manners must be wicked; and wickedness is sin, and sin is damnation. Thou art in a parlous state, shepherd."

The word "morals" was not used by the old writers; but here again we have a proof of the identity, in the opinion of our forefathers at least, of morals and good manners. Politeness they considered as an essential element of good behavior, — a branch certainly of good morals. The word "moral" is derived from the Latin word *mos*, plural *mores*, meaning manners or customs; and while the English word has altogether lost the original Latin meaning, the French word *mœurs* (manners), derived from the same Latin root, is still used in the old sense.

Rev. Brooke Herford, in one of his recent sermons, called attention to the rigorous adherence to good manners, the use of a prescribed form of speech even under most trying and exciting circumstances, of which we find evidence in the Bible. Thus the Shunammite woman, hastening to Elisha, and full of anguish at the death of her only son, still answers, "It is well," when asked whether it is well with her child, although she has come to announce his death to the prophet. And the messenger who brought King David the tidings of that dreadful battle in which his beloved son Absalom was slain, prefaced his deadly message with the usual phrase, "All is well," though he knew that the dearest treasure of the king's heart, his favorite son, was lying dead on the bloody plain. The fear of seeming to doubt or deny in some way the providence of the Almighty, was perhaps one reason for the use of this phrase, as the preacher suggested.

As the state of society changes from one age to another, manners must necessarily change with it, otherwise they cease to be the true exponents of the thought and feeling of the time. Having once been fitting symbols, they become only dead letters when the thought they represented passes away, — mere empty forms, savoring of hypocrisy, and surviving their usefulness on account of the conservative nature of man, which tends to make him do always what he has done once.

Thus the phrase "your worship" no doubt had originally a more or less sincere meaning, in the time when inferiors were so low in the scale of civilization that they did in some sort worship those who were so high above them. When men really believed that a king could do no wrong, that he was a king by Divine right, and that his very touch could heal the diseases of ordinary mankind, — in such a time it would not be wonderful that one man should consider another as worthy even of worship. In the extremely enlightened and unbelieving state of mind of the present day we can scarcely believe that such superstitions as these ever existed; but it was only in the reign of Queen Anne that the royal touch for the king's evil was used for the last time, while the worship of heroes is not only as old as our race, but has not yet died out.

We do not worship them precisely as the old Greeks and Romans did, but rather after the fashion of mediævalism. We carefully preserve buttons from their coats, locks of their hair, the chairs in which they sat, and curious characters which they traced with a pointed instrument dipped in black fluid upon a material made of bleached and pounded rags,—— what we call autographs. And yet we think it was strange that the unlettered men of the Middle Ages should have treasured the bones of saints, and held as sacred, fragments of their garments! Verily the nature of man is ever the same, with all his boasted progress!

When customs no longer have a real meaning, when they become mere shams and pretences, then they will gradually disappear of themselves; and then the reformer is justified if he inveighs against them, although if he is a wise man he knows that customs "die hard," and will not expect to see them rapidly disappear. What a grand time they had in the French Revolution, when the whole order of society was changed, and the titles even of the old heathen months were taken away from them as savoring too much of ancient superstition! But somehow people did not take even to such sensible names as "Snowy," "Rainy," "Foggy." They clamored for the old names, and would have them back again; not because they cared for Janus or Maia, or even for Julius Cæsar, but because they were used to January and May and July, and liked the old nonsense better than the new sense.

Nay, it is to be feared that we have not quite outgrown a belief in the old nonsense yet; for while no living being now worships Maia, there are plenty of people who consider it unlucky to be married in May, —— a superstition which existed in the days of Ovid, and no one knows how long before. Its origin is a curious one. The Romans believed in good and evil spirits, and called the latter *Lemures*. These ancient ghosts were of a restless disposition, tormenting the good and haunting the wicked. With that common sense which ever distinguished the old Romans, they celebrated festivals in honor of the Lemures, which they called *Lemuria*, and held in the month of May. The solemnities lasted for three nights, during which *marriages were prohibited*, and the temples of the gods were shut. The populace burned black beans to drive away these bad spirits, and also beat on kettles and drums. It is said that Romulus first instituted the *Lemuria*, or *Lemuralia*, to appease the shade of Remus, and the word became corrupted from *Remuria* to *Lemuria*.

The manners peculiar to certain states of society pass away with them, and, despite the lamentations of some lovers of the past, it is best that it should be so. Though we may sometimes fall a little in the scale of our behavior, on the whole there is an improvement in the manners of the civilized world from one age to another.

Take for instance the beginning of the eighteenth century. Little as Thackeray liked the manners of his own day, and ruthlessly as he showed up their follies and foibles, he liked still less the manners of this older time, of which he made an especial study, to his great disgust. In his essay on Steele, he says : "We can't tell —— you would not bear to be told the whole truth regarding those men and manners. You could no more suffer in a British drawing-room, under the reign of Queen Victoria, a fine gentleman or fine lady of Queen Anne's time, or hear what they heard and said, than you would receive an ancient Briton. It is as one reads about savages, that one contemplates the wild ways, the barbarous feasts, the terrific pastimes of the men of pleasure of that age."

He then describes the career of a very rapid nobleman, who died while perpetrating his third murder, and a little farther on he continues in the same vein : "But things were done in that society, and names were named, which would make you shudder now. What would be the sensation of a polite youth of the present day, if at a ball he saw the object of his affections taking a box out of her pocket and a pinch of snuff; or if at dinner, by the charmer's side, she deliberately put her knife into her mouth? . . . Fancy the moral condition of that society in which a lady of fashion joked with a footman, and carved a sirloin, and provided besides a great shoulder of veal, a goose, hare, rabbit, chickens, partridges, black puddings, and a ham, for a dinner of eight Christians! What — what could have been the condition of that polite world in which people openly ate goose after almond-pudding, and took their soup in the middle of dinner? Fancy a Colonel in the Guards putting his hand into a dish of *beignets d'abricot*, and helping his neighbor, a young lady *du monde!* Fancy a noble lord calling out to the servants, before the ladies at his table, ' Hang expense, bring us a ha'porth of cheese ! ' "

Mankind do not change their manners from one epoch to another, as a snake sheds his skin; the transition is a very gradual one, and men cling so fondly to their old ways that they always incline to keep them, where it is possible to do so, changing the old form a little, to suit it to its new meaning. Thus, when heathen nations first become Christianized, their religious practices are a very queer jumble of the old and the new forms of worship. The history of Europe is full of records of these curious mixtures, some of which are very familiar to us all.

The old Scandinavians had no intention of giving up the custom so congenial to their tastes, that of drinking the "minni" (that is, love, memory, and the thought of the absent) of the objects of their worship; so upon their conversion to Christianity they arranged the matter very simply by abandoning their old favorites, Thor, Odin, and Freya, and drinking the "minne" of Mary and of Christ. "Minnying" or "mynde" days, on which the memory of the dead was celebrated by services or banquets, survived for a long time in England.

Many customs which now seem to us foolish and absurd had once their serious meaning; but in the course of long years, and perhaps of wanderings from far countries, that meaning has been utterly lost from sight. Again, we can often see plainly what significance certain observances once had, but we no longer believe in them. We still say "Bless you" from force of habit, when some one sneezes, but we have ceased to attach the slightest importance to the remark. It is rather curious to find that the ancient Greeks and Romans saluted one another in the same way, and two thousand years ago Pliny asked, "Why do we salute those who sneeze?"

When Guachoga, a native chief, came to pay a visit to Hernando de Soto, the former happened to sneeze; whereupon "the gentlemen who had come with him, and were lining the walls of the hall among the Spaniards there, all at once bowing their heads, opening their arms and closing them again, and making other gestures of great veneration and respect, saluted him with different words, all directed to one end, saying, 'The Sun guard thee, etc.,'" upon which the Spanish governor concluded that "all the world was one."

The petty superstitions of every-day life, which cultivated people laugh at and the uneducated still believe in, were once no doubt features of a serious though childish religious belief. All the superstitions about the moon point plainly in this direction, while those about Friday are of Christian origin, as all the world knows. Many servants firmly believe that it is unlucky to engage or take service on Saturday, although they cannot tell you why they think so. I have often seen women of this class entreat a child to get up if it happened to be lying in their path on the stairs or elsewhere, saying, "If I step over you, you will never grow, you know!"

For every superstition and every exploded belief there is, or has been, some argument in its favor, some train of reasoning more or less ingenious and well carried out. We smile at the curious scientific theories of Plato, for instance, although he presents arguments in their favor that are as good as many modern reasons. In the same way there is no small point of etiquette which has not its *raison d'être*, although the train of logic which brought it into being may be quite forgotten by living men.

It is with the law of etiquette as with the common law; both contain many absurdities, but nevertheless these very absurdities have all been carefully reasoned out. As the common law concerned the lives and safety of all men, its sayings were carefully preserved and accurately written down by learned men; but the law of etiquette has had comparatively few expounders to keep careful record of its vagaries. It certainly, however, contains no greater follies than those of its prototype, which gravely declared that a mother was not of kin to her own child, and proceeded to prove the same!

Despite its many imperfections, the common law surprises us with its accumulation of sound views and its exposition of true principles, — the result of the combined wisdom of many great minds during long centuries. In the same way the laws that govern manners contain many true and unchanging principles mingled with much that is untrue, unimportant, and transitory.

But this subject cannot well be treated of at the end of a chapter, and demands a new one for itself.

CHAPTER II.

PERMANENT AND TRANSIENT INSTITUTIONS IN SOCIETY.

"CRABBED age and youth cannot live together" says the old song, and the unregenerate heart of man repeats it. But modern civilization not only brings youth and age together, she accomplishes even greater wonders. Black and white, rich and poor, educated and ignorant, Christian and heathen, evil and good, powerful and weak, sick and well, civilized and savage, high and low, — all races, classes and ages of men she brings together pitilessly, and without hesitation. Nay, she does more than this, for she tells them that they must not only live together, but live peaceably — and on the whole they do so.

When you consider what a seething caldron of opposing nationalities, creeds, and views a modern city consists of, what widely differing people are thrown together in steamships, hotels, and railroads by the remorseless Cook and the wide-reaching Vanderbilt, the wonder is, not that somebody occasionally kills somebody else, but that men do not slay their tormentors daily. If we lived in those cheerful old times when the world was still young, we should do so, as a matter of course, just as those individuals among us whose civilization remains crude, slay one another for any slight difference of opinion, and promptly make an end of the female of the species whenever she does not have supper ready in time.

The composition of our modern society is not only cosmopolitan in the extreme, but another element of complexity is added to it in the vast and ever-increasing intricacy of the machinery of our daily life. We have become so highly and uncomfortably civilized, our surroundings are so artificial, that there is some danger of our all turning into so many machines, each one being a part of the great central Corliss engine of our civilization.

It is this, or the forest. In past ages every high state of civilization has wrought its own ruin, and vigorous barbarism has taken the place of effete luxury and corruption, just as the vacuum of idiocy succeeds to over-activity of the brain.

In our own time the fleeing to the country, the desertion of large cities by the very rich, during the greater part of the year is something more than a new whim of Fashion, a feature of Anglo-imitation. It is instinct which teaches such people to return — as far as is agreeable and comfortable — to Nature. Having plenty of leisure time in which to note their feelings, they find themselves suffocated with the fingers of iron whose grasp extends into every corner of a great city.

Was it not with some such blind instinct that poor Marie Antoinette strove to escape from the artificial life of the French court? Did she not have a foreboding of the dreadful fate that awaited her, the frightful collapse of that rotten state of society so soon to follow? Alas! the Little Trianon was a poor, weak substitute for the lap of great mother Nature, and could ill protect its votary from the nihilism of the eighteenth century, — the nihilism of the guillotine.

In such a complex state of society as ours at the present day, the code of manners must evidently be a complicated one. It is true that we have simplified forms wherever we could do so, and have abridged much of the ceremony that was once thought necessary. There is still much that we cannot abridge, and the variety of our life must involve a corresponding variety of customs.

Through all the meshes of these confused details, however, run certain unchanging principles, like the strong midribs in a delicate leaf. These great general truths are bodied forth in what may be called the permanent institutions in society as distinguished from those transient features which change with every generation, — one might almost say with every year.

The great truths on which our code of manners is founded are those of the Christian religion, — a due regard for others, humility, a sense of duty, and self-respect.

Humility may have existed before the Christian era, but it was not counted a virtue — in men. The old Romans, even in their most civilized days, believed in vaunting their own exploits. Cicero continually tells us of what prodigies he performed in saving the State, and Virgil makes his hero boast of his own prowess in a way to make a Harvard Sophomore blush. Savages of course proclaim their own great deeds and those of their ancestors ; and as Herbert Spencer points out, Egyptian and Assyrian inscriptions prove that this habit of self-praise long persists in some cases.

Self-respect cannot exist where there is not due humility, since it is inconsistent with boasting and self-flattery, just as a true respect for others is inconsistent with adulation and undue glorification of them. Respect implies a proper consideration for its object, — a right measuring of it.

Love for one's neighbor, at least in a modified form, — a due regard for him and his rights, — may be considered as the key-stone of our code of manners, which even the most selfish man does not dare wholly to ignore if he is well-bred and wishes to appear so.

The ancient Persians believed in treating their neighbors well, but from a rather singular motive. Herodotus says, "They honor above all those who live nearest to themselves ;

in the second degree, those that are second in nearness, and after that, as they go farther off, they honor in proportion; and least of all they honor those who live at the greatest distance; esteeming themselves to be by far the most excellent of men in every respect, and that others make approaches to excellence according to the foregoing gradations, but that they are the worst who live farthest from them."

The permanent institutions in society are those in which every one believes — at least theoretically — and whose primary importance no one is disposed to deny. Respect to elders and deference to superiors belong to this class of institutions, as does also courtesy to women and kindness to inferiors.

Who is my superior? He who is higher and greater than I am, — not in the mere accident of outward circumstances, but greater in himself, in his character, nature, talents, deeds.

Fortunately for ourselves we are not obliged by law and tradition in this country to look up to any set of men as our superiors; we have no aristocracy of birth, but we are in imminent danger of making for ourselves what is infinitely worse, a plutocracy whose only recommendation shall be that they have amassed vast wealth, — in what manner, we must not ask too curiously.

Not long ago a book agent called upon me, and with extraordinary volubility sang the praises of the volume for which she was canvassing. This was nothing more nor less than a compilation of the lives of all the very rich men of the present day, with an account of the ways in which their fortunes had been accumulated, the whole intended as a guiding star to the tender mind of youth, that should shine upon their path in the world, and help them in all troubles, with its noble golden light.

It seemed to me I had never seen Mammon-worship so openly recommended. Far be it from me to say that all rich men are bad, or their fortunes accumulated by ignoble means. All honor to the good and great, be they rich or be they poor; but for Heaven's sake let us not set apart as a class worthy of all praise and imitation a certain set of men whose claim to our attention is that they have amassed a large amount of shekels! Do not let us (yet awhile at least) say —

> " Lives of [rich] men all remind us
> We must make our lives sublime ;
> And, departing, leave behind us
> [Millions] on the sands of time."

The man who has made a large fortune must have talent of some sort, to have prevailed over his fellows in the Gold-race ; but often it is his only talent, and too often it has been helped out by unscrupulous means.

When we come to the question of respect to elders, there seems to be little danger of excess in this direction — among the present generation. If our young people feel a natural inclination to show excessive reverence to their superiors in age, why, they repress that inclination in a most surprising manner.

Our elders are always our superiors — in length of life and experience, if in nothing else. Magnanimity, too, bids us treat them always with a certain gentleness. Are we not their conquerors, to whom sooner or later they must abandon their inheritance, the earth? As conquerors, then, let us bear ourselves with becoming meekness, remembering always now hard it is to be old, — to be in the past tense instead of the present.

How touching is that story of Hans Andersen's, in which a young married couple are made to see how unfilial their conduct is, when it is imitated by their little child! They have put the old father in the corner and given him a wooden spoon to eat with ; whereupon the boy takes out his knife to carve a spoon for *his* parents to use when he shall be a grown man !

Courtesy to women we may surely claim as an American virtue ; not that our men are always perfectly polite, or that we may not hope to make further progress in this direction, but that on the whole, American women are better treated than any others on the face of the globe. In Dickens's "American Notes " he says, in commenting on our behavior at table, " But no man sat down until the ladies were seated ; or omitted any little act of politeness which could contribute to their comfort. Nor did I ever once, on any occasion, anywhere, during my rambles in America, see a woman exposed to the slightest act of rudeness, incivility, or even inattention."

The elegance of manner, the profound obeisances with which courtly Europeans honor the women whom they admire, we cannot perhaps rival in this new country ; but the spirit of true chivalry, the respect for women of all classes because they are women, and not because they are beautiful, young, or rich, prevails here to an extent of which we may well be proud.

How permanent the essential elements of good manners are, strikes one very forcibly in reading the books of bygone times that relate to courtesies, as well as the truths that great thinkers have uttered on this subject. Lord Chesterfield's wise and witty sayings may still be read with much profit, while the profound maxims of De la Rochefoucauld remain as true as ever. Hear what the former says of the treatment of inferiors : —

"You cannot, and I am sure you do not, think yourself superior by nature to the Savoyard who cleans your room, or the footman who cleans your shoes ; but you may rejoice, and with reason, at the difference which fortune has made in your favor. Enjoy all those advantages, but without insulting those who are unfortunate enough to want them, or even doing anything unnecessarily that may remind them of that want. For my own part, *I am more upon my guard as to my behavior to my servants, and others who are called my inferiors, than I am toward my equals;* for fear of being suspected of that mean and ungenerous sentiment of desiring to make others feel that difference which fortune has, and perhaps, too, undeservedly, made between us."

Haste is the natural enemy of politeness. A man who is in a hurry is seldom polite, and the constant high pressure under which we all live has had its legitimate effect on our manners.

A person who is in great haste necessarily appears selfish, because he cannot stop to consider any one else, all his energies being bent on his own business of the moment. That business may be in reality some deed of pure philanthropy or utter unselfishness; it will still make the doer appear selfish if he is pursuing it at headlong speed. People will avoid him, much as they get out of the way of a fire-engine running at full speed through the streets. They respect the mission of the tearing, rattling creature of steam, but they don't want to get in its way.

A wise man therefore apportions his affairs in such a manner as to leave a little leeway for possible contingencies, and allows himself a certain amount of leisure time which can be expended in speaking or listening to others if occasion shall require it. Thus a man who has allowed himself five minutes more time than he needs to catch a train, will be able to stop and speak a few words if he meets an old friend on his way; whereas if he has left no margin, he must rush on, with some hasty and half-heard apology, perhaps giving life-long offence, and all for want of five minutes!

What a picture Mrs. Stowe gives, in her "Oldtown Folks," of one of these ever-hurried philanthropists, — old Uncle

Fliakim ! His special mission is to drive around the country and bring all the forlorn and feeble old women " to meeting," — arriving late, of course.

"The benevolence of his motives was allowed ; but why, it was asked, must he always drive his wagon with a bang against the doorstep just as the congregation rose to the first prayer? It was a fact that the stillness which followed the words ' Let us pray ' was too often broken by the thump of the wagon and the sound ' Whoa, whoa ! take care, there !' from without, as Uncle Fly's blind steed rushed headlong against the meeting-house door, as if he were going straight in, wagon and all."

Lord Chesterfield says, " Whoever is in a hurry, shows that the thing he is about is too big for him."

The details of behavior and outward observance, what one might call transient or minor manners, are certainly of great importance, but of little real value unless they are founded upon a true spirit of politeness. Where an arrogant and brutal nature seeks to shield its essential qualities under a thin varnish of good manners, the disguise is a poor one, and deceives nobody permanently.

To master all the details of etiquette except by mingling in the society of well-bred people is obviously impossible. One cannot become polished unless by social friction, any more than you can make a piece of marble shine without rubbing it.

A wise Frenchman has said : " Politeness is a quality [qualité] which a man living in society should acquire first of all things. It is the key of all human relations, and gives them their charm. The man who possesses only the instruction of colleges may be but a sort of rustic in the midst of a city. . . . There is a great difference between civility and politeness. A man of the people, a simple peasant even, can be *civil ;* it is only the man of the world who can be *polite.*"

2

In democratic America we should not use quite such strong language as this, but we recognize in a measure the truth it contains. With us, it is but a half-truth, since the absence of all distinctions of class and caste, the diffusion of education, and the high level of general intelligence, unite to put us on a par with one another far more than can be the case in any European nation.

The manners of an American, imbued with the self-respect which is the birthright of all our citizens, have a dignity that would be sought vainly among a people who had grown up with the idea of their own social inferiority forever hanging over them. The danger with us is that the thoughtless and ill-educated sometimes forget the respect they owe to others, in their over-anxiety to claim what is due to themselves. Thus a Yankee coachman spoke of a gentleman who was visiting his master as "that man," but called the driver of the carriage "the gentleman." In the case of this Yankee, self-respect was so abnormally developed that it had become self-assertion, — a very different quality from self-respect, and resembling it as some grotesque caricature resembles the original.

It has been well said that the source of good manners to-day is found in respect for human nature, one's own and that of others, heightened by a sense of the value of life, and a desire to make the most of its opportunities for others as well as for ourselves.

CHAPTER III.

THE USES OF SOCIETY.

WHAT is the use of the thing called Society? What are the objects for which men come together in social meetings of various sorts? "Empty show and vulgar display, the wish to marry their daughters and to advance their own way in the world," cry the cynics. "Vanitas vanitatum" they say of it all, and deny that it has any real use or gives any real pleasure.

Yet these very same people who so decry what is technically called society in our great cities, usually have a society of their own, a circle of friends whom they enjoy meeting very much. Indeed, these carpers will often go themselves to balls and parties, when they are invited, and will, to all outward appearance, enjoy themselves as much as anybody. If you speak to them on the subject, however, they will say that it was all very great folly and nonsense, etc.; that they only went because So-and-so was kind enough to ask them.

There are comparatively few people who do not really enjoy society of some sort, though they may dislike that which seems to them too showy or too formal. Even the cynic Diogenes himself occasionally attended festive gatherings, and when asked what kind of wine he liked best, replied, "That which is drunk at the expense of others."

Man is eminently a gregarious animal. Is not condemning

him to pass his life in solitude the most terrible punishment that can be bestowed on him, — a punishment which has often driven its victims into hopeless madness?

It is true that Swift has said, "A wise man is never less alone than when he is alone;" but what a terrible commentary on this saying was the lonely, unhappy life of its author alone in the midst of crowds! Thackeray says of him, "It is awful to think of the great sufferings of this great man. Through life he always seems alone, somehow. . . . The giants must live apart. The kings can have no company. But this man suffered so, and deserved so to suffer." And again, "He was always alone; alone and gnashing in the darkness, except when Stella's sweet smile came and shone upon him." Swift was alone, not because he did not mingle with other men, but because he had little in common with them. His genius lifted him far above ordinary people, while his unhappy temper and disposition placed him far below them in the moral scale.

Whether society is of any use to us must depend largely on the spirit in which we go into it. If that spirit is purely mercenary or selfish, it is not probable that we shall do ourselves or any one else much good; but if we go into the world in the spirit of good-fellowship, meaning to have a good time and to help others to have a good time, to be amused, instructed, cheered, or moved, as the occasion may demand, then society will be both a pleasure and a benefit to us.

If you want to enjoy salt-water bathing, you don't go into the ocean clad in a waterproof garment; and if you wish to enjoy society, you must n't enter it clad in a cast-iron armor warranted sympathy-proof. If you enter it in the spirit which Swift too often showed, — the unamiable one of bullying and snubbing men and saying unkind things to women, — why, you will enjoy it about as much as he did, and quite as well as you deserve to.

Emerson says, "The delight in good company, in pure, brilliant, social atmosphere, the incomparable satisfaction of a society in which everything can be safely said, in which every member returns a true echo, in which a wise freedom, an ideal republic of sense, simplicity, knowledge, and thorough good-meaning abide, doubles the value of life; . . . the hunger for company is keen, but it must be discriminating, and must be economized." Would that we could all hope to enjoy often such society as is here described, and that we might be intellectually and morally capable of appreciating it!

One very positive use of society, though not the pleasantest one, is to teach us our own limitations, and to keep down that self-conceit which, like a cork, is forever bobbing up to the surface.

Narcissus met his foolish fate because he stayed alone, his eyes and thoughts fixed on himself; if he had been content to dwell with other men, he would never have been the victim of his own vanity.

Goldsmith says, "People seldom improve when they have no other model but themselves to copy after."

The chief use of society, it seems to me, is threefold: first, the amusement it affords, — the relaxation from care so necessary for every human being to have; second, the good-will and good-fellowship that it promotes between men and their fellows; and last, but not least, the sharpening of the wits, the intensification of the intellectual powers, which it brings to pass in many people. Even two chips of wood if rubbed together will produce flame; and even two dull wits brought in contact with one another, will throw out more light than either could do alone. And when you assemble in one company men of brilliant talents instead of dullards, how dazzling is the effect! The electric current of intellectual sympathy runs through the assembly, and flashes of wit, — the wit that is wisdom, — of brilliant satire, and of sparkling anecdote, delight the lookers-on at such a contest of intellectual giants!

Could we spare from our literature the brilliant things that have been *said* in this world, and said in society, though not always at court balls? Great as are the delights of the written word, we cannot live upon them alone. Deaf-and-dumb people are proverbially gloomy. All the treasures of literature may lie open before them, but the spoken word of their fellows, the social word, they can never hear nor know save in image and dumb-show.

In one of Plato's dialogues we have an exposition of the value of the spoken word that is truly wonderful. Through the mouth of Socrates he shows us how it may leaven the whole world of thought. This would not be an astounding discovery in our day, since the modern world knows that Christianity was taught orally ; but that a Greek philosopher of ancient times should have thought it out before the Christian Era, shows how profound was his reasoning, how keen his insight! These wonderful thoughts were worked out largely in solitude ; but one must prepare for social life in solitude, as one prepares for war in time of peace.

Madame de Staël said, " Fine society depraves the frivolous mind and braces the strong one." Those who live for society, to whom it is the end and object of their existence, instead of merely a means of agreeable relaxation, and a pleasant way of meeting their kind, — such people may fairly be considered frivolous, and incur the reproach of dissipation.

The poet Cowper says : —

> " Man in society is like a flower
> Blown in its native bed. 'T is there alone
> His faculties expanded in full bloom
> Shine out, there only reach their proper use."

Cynics like Byron may contend that society creates neither good-feeling nor mutual kindness, but mankind knows better than to believe them.

> " Society itself, which should create
> Kindness, destroys what little we had got :
> To feel for none is the true social art
> Of the world's stoics, — men without a heart."

These lines express only a half-truth, not a whole one.

Even worldlings give us unconsciously a proof that society promotes good-will among its members. Do not many of them mingle in it with the avowed purpose of bettering their fortunes or improving their business? Yet how could this be if it only promoted ill-will and contempt among its members? Do people help the fortunes of those whom they dislike, or intrust their business to those whom they despise?

The man who affects to despise society, and yet mingles in it to further his own ends, may or may not be a hypocrite, but he lays himself open to the charge of being a designing person, who makes other people his dupes and tools.

It would be foolish to deny that there is a vast amount of humbug and of empty pretence in society ; but there is something more, something that we can ill do without.

Every one who has lived for any length of time in the real country understands, as no dweller in towns can understand, what a blessing society is to mankind. Is not suicide especially common among farmers' wives, who cannot endure the dreary solitude and endless round of toil in which their lives are spent? Rustics coming to a great city are like men who taste wine for the first time, — the crowds, the life, the gayety, all intoxicate them ; they seem to be in a dream of fairy enchantment from which, alas! a rude wakening follows only too speedily.

It has been said that great men are born in the country and come to the city to live. This is not altogether true; but most great men, and may I not say *all* great women, have found their account in social rather than in solitary life, and have preferred for the most part to dwell in cities.

Mrs. Howe in her treatise on "Modern Society" distinguishes between "society of representation" and genuine society. The former is entirely a show-affair; and the extreme instance of it which she cites is found in the ministerial balls in Paris, where the guests are admitted by card, and do not necessarily know their host and hostess, nor need they make the latter's acquaintance. The whole is a grand pageant, but no introductions are given, and no social fusion takes place.

Mrs. Howe goes on to say, "Now, this I call society of representation. It bears about the same relation to genuine society that scene-painting bears to a carefully-finished picture. People of culture and education enjoy a peep at this spectacular drama of the social stage, but their idea of society would be something very different from this. Where this show-society monopolizes the resources of a community, it implies either a dearth of intellectual resources or a great misapprehension of what is really delightful and profitable in social intercourse. . . . No gift can make rich those who are poor in wisdom. The wealth which should build up society will pull it down if its possession lead to fatal luxury and indulgence."

CHAPTER IV.

THE FRANKNESS OF MODERN MANNERS.

RICHARD GRANT WHITE, who was a man not inclined to mince matters, boldly and calmly asserted that there was no such thing as English grammar! English grammar, in the opinion of this gentleman, was only a sort of old-fashioned myth, invented and kept alive by pedagogues for the torture of unoffending youth of both sexes.

It has occurred to me that if some departed worthy of the last century should again return to this earth and this country, it would strike him that our grammar was well enough, and our spelling really fine; but as regards our manners, would he be apt to observe that we had any in particular? I fear he would not; certainly he would find little to correspond with the manners of his own day. And yet he would be greatly mistaken if he supposed that manners had gone entirely out of fashion, lingering only in remote places in the country, and surviving in the cities merely among a few old-fashioned and conservative people.

The manners of the present day, despite a great deal that is said against them, have a certain merit that is all their own, — the merit of frankness and honesty. Furthermore, they fit the time, and suit the last quarter of the nineteenth century much better than if we masqueraded in the courtly and elaborate manners of our grandfathers, who were perhaps a little more sentimental, a little more ideal than we are, and whose ceremonies were not curtailed by the constant necessity of catching trains.

It seems to me that frankness is one of the most striking features of our modern manners. People have got tired of all the formality, all the ceremony that was once thought necessary to good breeding. The circumlocution office has gone out of fashion in good society, which has discovered that a straight line is the shortest distance between two points. Curves, no doubt, are more beautiful than straight lines; but what would you? Curves take time; and what a pity it would be to lose time that might be so much more profitably spent in the sacred business of amusement!

We have lost our belief in many things in these days, and among others, in lying, — that is, in polite lying. Whether this is from any access of virtue on our part is more than doubtful. Perhaps it is rather that people just now value the noble art of lying too highly to use it lightly. It is of course needed constantly in business, so why waste it on mere matters of ceremony? Besides, the truth, after all, is more direct, and easier to tell; so, since the polite world has agreed to tell it in many instances, what fashion is easier to follow?

Ceremony is in a great measure humbug; that is to say, it consists largely in saying and doing things one does not mean, and which the other side knows one doesnot mean. Take, for instance, the Spanish custom of bestowing any article that is admired, on the person who admires it. It is perhaps a pretty little piece of acting; but would it not be difficult for one of our Northern race to go through this polite humbug without a smile at the farce? Our directness may be brutal, but it has this advantage, — you know on what ground you are standing.

A good illustration of the greater frankness of manners in this day is, that it is no longer considered necessary to say that you have had a good time, when taking leave of your hostess after a dinner-party or other entertainment. What a saving of white lies would have been effected if this simple and self-evident rule had been adopted at the first primeval tea-party!

It is interesting to note that according to Buddhist tradition the first lie was told by a king, and was therefore no doubt a white, or society lie. The citizens who heard it were even more innocent than George Washington. He, at least, knew what a lie was, if he did n't know how to tell one; but these poor people were utterly ignorant on the subject, and asked whether a lie was white, black, or blue! It is to be feared that the blue lie has disappeared from the face of the earth, unless it survives in that kind of swearing which is said to turn the air blue.

It was the custom, not so many years ago, for a hostess, when bidding adieu to ladies calling upon her, to accompany them as far as the door of the house. This fashion, like so many others involving time and trouble, has gone out of style, though some people still keep it up. As it prolongs the agony of leave-taking indefinitely, and often keeps the hostess standing in the cold of the open doorway, it would seem to be a custom more honored in the breach than in the observance.

But how different was the old-fashioned view of the matter! How well do I remember a most polite old lady in New York, who has now been dead for many years! She always insisted upon opening the door for her visitors, — the door through which she herself had not ventured to pass for twenty years. She was over eighty years of age, and very rheumatic; but she *would* do what politeness required of her, as long as she could walk.

Another very noticeable change in manners is in the form of address. It is no longer considered necessary, or even the right thing, to say "Yes, madam," or "Yes, sir." The

"Mum" in which Uncle Pumblechook delighted is a thing
of the past, and with it "ma'am," or "m'm," is also departing from our midst.   This is certainly carrying out the
Scriptural injunction, "Let your communication be yea, yea;
nay, nay;" but it is very doubtful whether the change is
due to any religious feeling or scruple.   No, it is a simple
following of the English custom, though it fits well enough,
perhaps, with republican simplicity.

In the mouths of children, the simple monosyllables "yes"
and "no" certainly sound a little startling when addressed to
their elders; but what would you? *Autre temps, autres mœurs.*
It seems a pity to bring children up to use forms of expression that are fast becoming obsolete; and the child who has
been taught from its earliest infancy to speak thus, sees no
impropriety or disrespect to age in so doing.

After all, when we look into the matter, "sir" is short for
"sire," — a title savoring strongly of monarchies, and therefore to be avoided by good democrats, using the word in its
broad sense.   "Madame," French *Ma dame,* — "my lady," —
is a hardly more desirable title in these days, when the word
"lady" has been so abused that those who perhaps have
the best claim to it use it but little, preferring the broader
term "woman," and for young lady, "girl."

There is something quite delightful in this abandonment of
the much-abused words "lady" and "gentleman" by those
to whom, in the old sense, the words exclusively applied.
They make no protest against "washer-ladies," or gentlemen
who need to be told "not to spit on the cabin floor, out of
respect for the ladies;" but with quiet satire they are content
to call themselves simply men and women, as the English
nobleman signs himself "Argyle" or "Dufferin."

In this country, where all are free and equal, and where
our forms of address are so simple and democratic, we do not
realize the caste spirit, the degradation and corresponding

elevation implied in the use of different persons of the verb in European countries. An Italian — a political refugee in the old troublous times of Italy — explained to his pupils with considerable warmth that republicans in Italy repudiated as slavish the old mode of address, namely, the use of the third person singular feminine, *lei*, or, as we should say, "she." He said it meant *sa majestà* — "her majesty" — and of course was a really servile mode of address not to be tolerated by freedom-loving republicans. In the same way, in Germany, only servants or inferiors are spoken to in the second person plural. All others are addressed in the third person plural, — "they," — save relatives and intimates, who are called "thou."

Many of the changes in social customs that have taken place in this country are owing to the great growth of society itself. Formerly, when the country was comparatively small, and people of good breeding comparatively rare, society, so called, was very much smaller than it is now, and the relations of those belonging to it were necessarily more personal, even if more formal. The hostess felt more responsibility for the entertainment of her guests, and took more pains to see that they were amused and comfortable, than it is now customary to take. The lady of the house was temporarily a social queen, and her guests were her subjects ; now a party or a ball is simply a republic where all are equal, — at least, where the fact of being hostess gives little title to distinction or prominence.

As a logical result of these new theories the uncomfortable custom of pressing your guests to eat, has been happily relegated to past ages. It is assumed, and very properly, that a guest is not, or ought not to be, afraid to eat as much as he wants; so while everything on the table should be handed to him, he should not be urged to eat this, that, or the other.

This idea of the propriety of pressing guests to eat or drink, evidently had its origin in a more primitive state of society, and in times when social gatherings were not so numerous as now. The regular society habitué of these days goes too constantly into the gay world, to stand in the slightest awe of his hostess, or of any one else, and is quite to be trusted to look after his own interests.

Another custom in which we have improved on the ways of our forefathers is that of allowing each person to pay for himself, whether in public conveyances, or at the theatre and other places of amusement. Of course this does not apply to formal opera or theatre parties, where the invitations all come from one person, who buys and pays for all the tickets himself. But the theory that a lady is never to be allowed to pay anything for herself, even in a horse-car, is obsolescent, if not obsolete. A gentleman should certainly offer to pay for a lady on such occasions, but he should not insist upon doing so. If she evidently prefers to pay her own way, she should be allowed that privilege, without a prolonged discussion. It is no longer "good form" for two people to vie with each other in politeness.

Still another evidence of the greater frankness and directness of modern society, of the fact that matters are placed more nearly on a business footing now than formerly, is to be found in the change in methods of shopping. No one now has the time or the inclination to haggle over prices when on a shopping tour; nor would it be of any use, in most cases, to do so. And yet, in the times of our mothers and grandmothers, "cheapening" was a necessary part of the art of purchasing.

Of course in the wholesale business it still prevails almost without exception; but let us rejoice that in ordinary shopping, at least, we no longer need to fight these wordy and long-winded battles where one party or the other surrenders from sheer exhaustion.

There are some people who still persist in cutting down every bill that is rendered to them; but it is to be more than suspected that their tradespeople soon come to understand this little weakness, and make the accounts out to meet it.

CHAPTER V.

VISITING CARDS AND THEIR USES.

WE do not often associate in our minds the famous Magna Charta of English history, the source of so great a part of our modern liberty, and the insignificant bits of pasteboard which constitute modern visiting cards. Nevertheless, they come from the same Greek root, signifying paper; or, to speak more exactly, *card* is derived from *charta* (Greek χάρτης). Thus the sword is beat into the ploughshare, and the formal instrument for fettering the caprices of tyrants softens into the peaceful emblem of social recognition.

In the ancient " cartel of defiance " we find a more directly hostile meaning to our word — with a slight change in its form — than in charter. A cartel means, among other things, a challenge to single combat. Ben Jonson says, " You shall cartel him." Where two strangers quarrel, the one who has reason to expect a challenge presents his opponent with his card, so that the latter may know where to find him, — a pleasant little courteous preliminary to the most polite form of murder, the duel.

Under ordinary circumstances, however, the exchange of visiting cards is an eminently peaceful act, and would at the first blush seem to be a very simple affair. But with the perverse ingenuity in which the human mind delights, mankind, or rather womankind, has involved even this ap-

parently innocent ceremony in a large amount of red tape
and confusion. Nothing would appear to be simpler than
for one neighbor to leave her card upon another; but it is
just such apparently insignificant acts, such "first steps,"
that have embroiled nations in countless wars.

> "Oh, what a tangled web we weave,
> When first we practise *cards to leave !*"

The following somewhat detailed account of visiting cards
and their chief uses is submitted, in the hope that it may
prove of use. It has been compiled from three sources, —
personal experience ; the works on the subject written by the
best and most recent authorities ; and last, but not least, from
consultations with divers wise, witty, and fashionable women,
to whom all the "newest fads" on both sides of the water
are as familiar as *A, B, C*.

Visiting cards should be engraved in script, fine rather
than large, and should be of unglazed cardboard. They
should be perfectly plain, that is, without ornamentation of
any sort ; a fine, rather thin pasteboard is usually preferred
for them. Indeed, very little room for individual taste is
allowed in the matter of cards, which resemble each other
much as one dress-suit resembles the next. German text is
sometimes used for engraving the names, but it is more apt
to go out of style than plain script. Very fine lettering,
like any other singularity, is in bad taste. Gentlemen's
cards are smaller than ladies', and are also narrower in proportion to their length. It was formerly a mooted point
whether a gentleman's visiting card looked better with or
without "Mr." prefixed to his name. Almost all young men
of fashion now use the "Mr.," which is considered to be in
better form.

For a lady there is no room for choice in the matter. She
must always use "Miss" or "Mrs." on her visiting card. If

3

a young lady, she may use either her initials or her full name, but never a nickname. "Miss Mamie Smith" on a card is in very bad form. Nicknames are all very well at home, or among intimate friends, but they are out of place on a visiting card because they are too familiar; and a card is, or should be, a formal matter. It is now the fashion for young ladies to have their names printed in full, thus :—

> *Miss Mary Stuart Phelps.*

Indeed, every one who has a middle name, now displays it on his or her card.

An army or navy officer, a physician, a judge, or a minister may use his title on his card. For a physician, "M. D." is preferable to "Dr.," because the latter is such a very vague term, and means so many different things. Militia or complimentary titles are not used on visiting cards, nor are coats-of-arms. In this republican country it is considered an affectation and in bad taste thus to make use of them.

Husband and wife do not often now have their names engraved on the same card, except for wedding cards, or for sending wedding presents, etc. For visiting, each gentleman of the family has his own card, although, sooth to say, he seldom leaves it himself, intrusting that duty to his wife, his mother, or his sisters.

Every one's card should have the address of the owner engraved in the right-hand corner; that is to say, the street and the number where he lives, but not the name of the city. If a lady has a reception day, it is engraved usually in the left-hand corner. The address is often omitted from the cards of very young ladies, and sometimes from those of married ladies, in which case the card of the husband, with the address, must always be left. Young men belonging to a fashionable or well-known club often put its name, instead of their residence, on their cards. This is especially the case where they do not live at home, but board or have rooms in the city.

A married lady should have her husband's full name or his initials on her card, and not her own. Even where a woman occupies a prominent position in the world of art or letters she usually follows this rule, especially if she is at the same time what is technically termed "a society woman." Where the last name is not a very common one, a lady sometimes compromises the matter by using no initials, and calling herself simply "Mrs. Dunbar." But she has not, strictly speaking, a right to put "Mrs. Dunbar" on her card, unless her husband is the eldest married man of his family, or belongs to the eldest branch of it. Thus, where there are two brothers who are both married, the wife of the elder one only can use "Mrs. Dunbar" on her card. But if her husband has an uncle, even though he may be a younger man than his nephew, this right belongs to his (the uncle's) wife.

The same rule holds good for unmarried ladies. The eldest single daughter of the eldest brother, and she alone, has a right to use "Miss Cavendish" on her card, although she may have a cousin who is much older than herself but who is the daughter of a younger brother of the same family.

The existence of an aged aunt, or cousin belonging to an elder branch, will deprive both young ladies of this coveted privilege.

In this country, where we are considered by foreigners as being so very radical, we are in reality more conservative in the matter of merging a married woman's name in that of her husband than are most European nations. An Englishwoman of rank keeps her own title, where she marries a man of inferior station. If Lady Evelina Stuart marries Mr. John

Smith, she becomes Lady Evelina Smith, and *not* Mrs. John Smith.   So, on the Continent, it is quite common for a married woman to keep her maiden name in addition to her husband's, the husband's name being placed first.

A widow has no legal right to use her husband's initials ; but she often prefers to retain them on her card, and it is entirely proper for her to do so, the question being one of sentiment and feeling alone.   Where a widow has a son who is married, and whose name is the same as his father's, there may arise some confusion, however, between the two " Mrs. T. R. Jones," unless the elder lady puts " Sr." on her cards, as she sometimes does.   Widows often use their own names or initials, as " Mrs. Mary Jones," and it is perhaps less confusing for them to do so.

The custom of having the names of the daughter or daughters engraved below that of their mother is growing in favor.   Thus : —

> *Mrs. Stuart Mill.*
> *Miss Mill.*

or

> *Mrs. T. R. Jones.*
> *The Misses Jones.*

Indeed, those who are strict in the matter of etiquette say that a young lady should not leave her own card without that of her mother or chaperone during her first year in society. English etiquette is much stricter; according to its rules a young lady has no card of her own, her name being engraved on that of her mother.

When must one call personally, and when will it suffice to send cards by a servant or through the post? These are questions not so thoroughly settled in this country as in Europe, where the social treadmill has been so long in full operation that as a matter of necessity its laws have become definitely fixed.

As society increases in size, there is a growing tendency in our large cities toward simplifying the burden of social duties. It is not now considered necessary to call in person under various circumstances where formerly the rule was that one must do so. Even the post-office is coming gradually into requisition as an agent for discharging social obligations; but as yet it is only sparingly used, and with definite limitations.

Thus P. P. C. cards may be sent by mail, where the person leaving town has not the time to make a personal visit. Also, where one is unable to attend a reception, or an afternoon tea, cards may be sent by mail (it is better to send them by a messenger), to arrive on the day of the entertainment. This relieves the sender from the necessity of making a subsequent call; indeed, the unspeakable advantage of afternoon teas, kettledrums, and receptions is, that you enjoy your party and make your visit all at the same time. It is an economic device worthy the brain of a John Stuart Mill, and possibly secretly invented by him. The great popularity of afternoon teas no doubt arises from the fact that they are time-saving institutions.

Usually the servant who opens the door on these occasions has a little silver salver in his hand for the cards of guests; otherwise, guests leave their cards on the hall table, as a reminder to their hostess, who can hardly be expected to remember, after a large reception, every one who has been there.

When should P. P. C. cards be left or sent? P. P. C., it is hardly necessary to say, means Pour Prendre Congé (to take one's leave). Sometimes it is abbreviated thus, P. p. c., or p. p. c., but the capitals are used oftener than the small letters. These cards are used when one is going away from a place either permanently or for quite a length of time; and "P. P. C." is written in a corner of the card, usually the lower right-hand one, to emphasize this fact. One does not leave them, however, when about to go out of town for the summer, since this is only a brief absence, and an absence that is made by most people. On the other hand, it is quite proper to send or leave P. P. C. cards when one goes away from a watering-place or other summer resort, especially if the people to whom you send them do not live in the same city or town with yourself during the rest of the year. The obvious reason for the propriety of sending these cards in lieu of making a personal visit is, that when people go away they are almost always hurried; indeed, they are often obliged to leave very suddenly, and under such circumstances that making visits would be an impossibility.

Gentlemen in New York often send their cards by post, instead of calling, on New Year's Day, now that New Year's calls are going so rapidly out of fashion there. Some people do not approve of this custom, and think that a gentleman should either call, or take no notice of the day.

But there are certain visits which must be made personally if one does not wish to break the rules of good society and perhaps deeply offend people. After one has been invited to a dinner-party, one must call within a week after the occasion, — call in person, and ask if the hostess is at home. A dinner-party is one of the most solemn obligations of society;

if you accept an invitation to one, only death or mortal illness is a legitimate excuse for not attending it, and you must have nearly as good a reason for not calling promptly after it.

According to the strict rule, one should also call within a week after any entertainment to which one has been invited ; but this is often impossible, and resembles one of those rules in the Latin Grammar which have such a long list of "exceptions" that the rule itself seems quite dwarfed and insignificant beside them.   The actual or "working" rule is that one calls, after every invitation, as soon as is practicable.   In New York, it is allowable to send your card, although people of the old-fashioned sort would hardly think it the right thing to do.   In Boston, it is more the custom to call in person, and very properly, because Boston is a smaller city, and the distances are not so immense as in New York, whose extreme narrowness of shape increases the effect of its great size.   A pious subterfuge is practised, however, in the Puritan City and elsewhere, by which you send your empty carriage, the footman accompanying it and leaving cards.

Society holds young people, and people who have plenty of leisure time, much more strictly to account in the matter of visiting than it does elderly persons, or those whose hands are so full that they have comparatively little time to give to the claims of social life.   A young mother with a nursery full of little ones, a literary woman, an artist, a professional woman, — all these are allowed a certain immunity from social duties.   But no young lady must expect to find herself excused from paying calls because she is "too busy having a good time."   If she can go to a party to amuse herself, she must call afterwards to acknowledge the attention her hostess has paid her by the invitation.

How often is it necessary to pay formal calls?   Where no invitations have been received, once a year is all that the strict rules of society require in large cities. According to some authorities it is sufficient for such a formal call to leave cards at the door, or even to send them in an envelope; but it certainly seems more cordial and friendly to make the yearly call in person, and to ask at the door if the ladies are receiving, if one can possibly spare the time to do so.

As many servants in this country cannot reconcile it to their consciences to say a lady is "not at home" when she is in the house, it is often a wise precaution for the visitor to ask if the ladies are receiving on that day. Thus the conscience of Betty, which is curiously tender on this one point, considering her habitual views of truth, is spared, and the caller is often relieved from the necessity of making a formal call for which she perhaps has not really time. The servant too, from the form of the inquiry, and from seeing cards in the visitor's hands, is enabled to distinguish between a ceremonious caller and a friend of her mistress who really wishes to see the lady of the house.

Where there are several ladies in the house, it is usual for a caller to leave two cards; even three are sometimes left, where there is some stranger also staying in the house. But do not be too prodigal with your pasteboard, because that would seem a little ostentatious, — a little like "overdoing." It is said that one lady should never leave more than three of her own cards at the same house; she may of course leave cards for the other members of her family, in moderation. It is becoming quite customary for a wife to leave her husband's cards, and indeed for any lady to leave the cards of the gentlemen of her family even when she herself is admitted and pays her visit. In this case she leaves them on the hall table.

The custom of receiving on a certain day in the week is a sensible and hospitable one, but alas! it takes up a great deal of time. Where a lady thus sets apart a certain day for receiving her friends, it is much more polite to call on that day of the week when it is possible to do so. Especially is this the case when the ladies of one neighborhood or of one street fix on the same day for receiving friends. But the case is quite otherwise when a lady sends out cards announcing that she is "at home" on "Wednesdays in January and February." If one knows that a lady has thus issued cards for a series of receptions, even though they be quite informal occasions, one should avoid calling on those particular days unless one has received a card with the necessary invitation.

The custom of sending out cards for a certain day throughout one month is a very good one; a lady is thus enabled to receive her friends very informally, without giving up a great deal of her time, and she also avoids the "crush" that is apt to ensue if she gives only a single afternoon tea or reception.

The custom of cornering cards or turning them down at one end is going out of fashion. This is certainly cause for rejoicing, because the exact meanings of the various turnings have never been clearly established and understood in this country, as they are in Europe.

According to the doctrine that is usually received here, the turning down of one end (ordinarily the right end) indicates that you have called in person, while turning down one corner, usually the right upper one, means that the card is left for more than one person. Old-fashioned authorities insist that a card ought always to be turned down across the whole end, or else the recipient will suppose that the visitor has not called in person. This may have been true ten or fifteen years ago; it certainly is not true now. The custom of to-day is to leave the cards without any turnings, unless in calling upon people of the old school, in which case a lady would be apt to turn down her card, lest it might be supposed that she had not come in person.

If she happened to have only one card remaining, and there was a visitor staying in the house, she would impress on the servant's mind that the card was meant for both ladies, or she might write on it "For Mrs. Jenckes and Mrs. Appleton." Where only one card is left, it is always held to be for the lady of the house.

After a removal from one part of a city to another, it is now becoming customary for ladies to send cards engraved with their new address to all their circle of acquaintance. These cards serve instead of a personal visit, as people evidently cannot make calls in the confusion consequent upon moving, and settling in a new house.

Although authorities differ on many subjects connected with manners, they all agree in saying that first calls should be promptly returned, — within a week, under ordinary circumstances. Brides who upon their marriage go to live in another city sometimes give great offence by neglecting to return visits of this sort; and it is entirely reasonable and natural that those who pay a first call, which is equivalent to an offer to make one's acquaintance, should feel hurt if their advance is not recognized and reciprocated.

In America, it is the usual custom for residents of a city or town to call first upon new-comers. Washington is a well-known exception to this rule, the strangers calling first, as indeed they do in most European cities.

It is also the custom in some cities for the older residents in a certain street or neighborhood to call upon those who have recently moved to that part; I need hardly say that these latter should by all means return such calls. The good old custom of interchanging neighborly civilities should certainly not be allowed to die out. It is not necessary to become intimate with your neighbors if they are not people who are sympathetic to you; but for two families to live next door to one another year after year, and never to show any token of mutual good-will, or perhaps even of mutual recognition, argues that their civilization is below that of rustics. Indeed, it would probably be considered as bad form even in Ashantee.

Except in the case of neighbors, a lady needs however to be very cautious about making first calls unless she is certain that her acquaintance will be considered desirable by those whom she visits in this way. Thus if Mrs. A. is a woman of greater wealth or higher social position than Mrs. B., the latter will hesitate to call first upon the former unless she is asked to do so, for fear she may be thought pushing.

Where society is divided into certain cliques or sets, as is too often the case in our cities, a lady belonging to the less fashionable clique should hesitate long before calling upon one of a more fashionable circle, even though she may have been introduced to the other lady, and may have met her a number of times on social or other occasions.

It is simply a question of the Golden Rule, which applies more to social customs than the unthinking realize or perceive. Do not call first on any one who your common sense tells you would in all probability prefer not to make your acquaintance, or, if that is already made, not to add you to her visiting list. True, this is mortifying to one's vanity, but it does one's vanity good to trample on it occasionally; and if we do this unpleasant office for ourselves, others will be less likely to do it for us. Vanity, moreover, can be well repressed without in the least injuring self-respect, which is a very different quality.

First calls must be returned personally as well as promptly, in order that you may not appear to slight those who have made the first demonstration of courtesy. A lady does not wish to be outdone in politeness even by some one whose acquaintance she may not especially desire.

But if the lady who calls first only leaves her card, then the second lady responds by leaving her card in like manner; or if the first merely sends her card through the post, then the second does likewise.

An important exception to this rule is made where the lady who sends her cards through the post sends at the same time an invitation to some entertainment at her house. As this expresses more good-will and is a greater compliment than the making of a formal call, the second lady should receive the courtesy in the spirit in which it was meant. She should call very soon after the entertainment, and in person, since a first invitation is a more formal matter than subsequent ones, just as a first call is; and both must be responded to with special formality.

In making a first call, a card should be left for each lady of the family; where there are several young ladies who are sisters, and their mother is living, it suffices to leave two cards, — one for the mother and one for the daughters. A lady also leaves the cards of her own immediate family, in making the first call of the season, including those of her husband.

One married lady in calling upon another leaves two of her husband's cards, — one for the lady of the house and the other for the husband. Even if admitted, the caller leaves these cards on the hall table.

People who are in mourning should have a black border on their visiting cards; it is *en règle* to leave cards for people in affliction, though one should make inquiries at the door, and not ask for admittance, where one is not an intimate friend of the family. These cards of condolence are answered by enclosing mourning cards and sending them to people who have called in this way, after a proper lapse of time; that is, when the mourners feel ready to receive visits once more.

One should also call, or at least send cards, when an engagement is announced, or when a marriage has taken place, in the family of an acquaintance. When a friend or acquaintance has made a prolonged absence, in Europe or elsewhere, it is usual to call upon her; but it is equally proper for the person who has been absent to make the first call if she prefers to do so. Society is growing so large in our great cities, and is likewise so self-absorbed, that the latter course is the wiser one if a lady wishes to recall herself to people's minds. She may naturally expect her intimate friends to make the first call; but she should not feel hurt if others neglect to do so.

It is the custom in New York, if not elsewhere, for people who are temporarily staying in the city to send their cards, with address upon them, to those whom they wish to have call; otherwise they might remain for weeks without their friends being at all aware of their presence in the city. Cards should not be sent in this way to mere acquaintances, however, unless they have especially expressed the desire to be informed of one's arrival.

Where one is invited to any entertainment by a new acquaintance, one should leave cards without delay, according to rule; but this is a canon which is certainly often violated. At least one should be very particular to call within a week after the event, even if one has also left cards upon receiving the invitation.

Those who send invitations to people to whom they owe calls which they have been unable to pay, sometimes enclose their cards with the invitation, thus showing that the call has been omitted from the pressure of time and circumstances, but not with intention to neglect. This should always be done when inviting those on whom one has never called, although the better way would be to call before sending the invitation.

The hours for formal calling differ in different cities, though there seems to be a growing tendency in New York and Boston to make the calling hours later and later. A recent authority says that from four to six is the proper time to make ceremonious calls in New York; but many people call earlier than this, and in the short winter days it is surely allowable to make visits at least as early as three o'clock.

One should carefully avoid the lunch or dinner hour in calling even upon friends, and of course much more in the case of acquaintances. Where one has been told, however, to call at the lunch-hour, one is naturally at liberty to do so. People sometimes say, "Our lunch-hour is so-and-so; come and see me then, and you will be sure to find me at home." In such a case it is perfectly proper to go at the hour named; but if the friend is at lunch it is not polite to detain her. Word should be sent in that one will wait till the meal is over. If the friend comes out and asks you to the lunch-table, you should go in without peradventure, or else take your leave at once. It is very thoughtless, if not positively ill-bred, to play the part of dog-in-the-manger, and by refusing to comply with your friend's request, compel her to delay or go without her meal; and yet it is a thing that is often done, from want of thought.

Calling has become so ceremonious, and has grown to consist so largely of a simple exchange of cards, that a practice of making informal calls in the morning upon friends and intimates is coming much into vogue in our large cities. For these unceremonious visits a lady should not wear an elaborate toilette. Unless one is extremely intimate with a friend, however, it is best not to call at a very early hour, before twelve or one o'clock for instance.

A lady should always carefully consider her friends' occupations, habits, and ways of life, and should avoid making even a very friendly visit at an hour when she knows the person in question will probably be otherwise engaged. It may seem perhaps superfluous to mention such self-evident facts as these; but the truth is that it is just such rules that are often violated by well-bred people who are either thoughtless or selfish. "Save me from my friends" is a saying whose use is not yet accomplished and done with. Many people who would start back in horror at the mere thought of committing any breach of certain conventional rules, will wantonly violate the ethical and unwritten laws of good breeding without hesitation.

Thus, ladies in the country will make calls upon a friend in the morning hours, when they are well aware that the said friend has only one, or perhaps no servant, and is obliged to be busied over her housework. If the thoughtless caller happens to be rich in the goods of this world, and drives up to the friend's door in her carriage, she will be almost certain to mortify the other's feelings by her untimely arrival.

There is a certain gentleman in New York who moves in what is considered the best society, and who is very punctilious in most matters of ceremony; but he frequently enters the houses of his friends without first paying his respects to the door-mat. Well, possibly such men are to be found out of New York too. Other gentlemen endeavor to "sit each other out" when calling, although they know perfectly well that according to the laws of good manners the first-comer should be the first to take his leave.

According to strict rules, a gentleman should never call upon a young lady without asking also for her mother or chaperone; but where a young man knows a young lady very well this formality is apt to be dispensed with. Society in America is growing more strict on this subject, however, than it used to be, and the chaperone is gradually assuming larger and larger powers, and taking more and more the position of an English or Continental matron. It is a question upon which there is a wide difference of opinion, and of which more will be said in another chapter.

Certainly in making a formal call a gentleman should ask for the lady of the house as well as for the young ladies, and should leave cards for her and also for the gentlemen of the family. Although business men seldom make calls in person and cannot reasonably be expected to do so, a young man of leisure or a college student is not so easily excused for thus neglecting his social duties.

A gentleman should never call on a lady unless she has asked him to do so, or he has asked and received her leave to come. If he brings a letter of introduction, he may of course call, or if an intimate friend of the house — one who has a right to introduce people there — brings him. A lady is at liberty to ask a gentleman to call if she wishes to do so, although a young lady should not give such an invitation until she knows him quite well, and should always phrase it in such a way as to show that not she alone but her mother also would be pleased to receive the visit. "We should be glad to see you on any Wednesday afternoon," or, "I hope we shall see you at our house." Strictly speaking, *such an invitation should come from the chaperone*, and not from the young lady.

A gentleman is required to call at once upon receiving an invitation from a new acquaintance or a stranger, and also to call after the entertainment. But if he answers the invitation promptly, and calls soon after the gay event, whatever it may be, he does as well as most American gentlemen do; foreign etiquette is more stringent than ours on this, as on many other points.

It is quite permissible to leave cards without asking for the ladies of the house, where one is much pressed for time or has any special reason for not doing so; but it is not allowable on a lady's regular reception day, since this would imply that you did not care to see her.

This does not conflict with the rule in accordance with which one sends cards when invited to a special reception if unable to attend it. In this latter case the card is sent in acknowledgment of the invitation, serving also as a substitute for personal attendance. But while one may very easily be prevented from attending special receptions, one has not the same excuse where a lady has a regular day for receiving her friends throughout the season.

When one lady calls upon another whom she already knows, and when she finds the latter at home, she should not send up her card, but should merely give her name to the servant. This is English etiquette, and is also according to strict rule in this country. Nevertheless, cards often are sent up, either through a blunder of the servant or because that functionary looks so hopelessly stupid as to show that no name would be safe in his keeping for two minutes. In very stylish houses the servant announces the name of each visitor, where the lady of the house is already in the drawing-room.

It is not strictly necessary to leave cards upon the hall table where one is admitted to pay a visit, but it is very customary to do so, especially in New York. A card so left is intended merely as a reminder to the lady of the house that she may not forget who have called upon her. When calling upon a stranger, a lady should send in her card, but she must never, under any circumstances, hand it to her hostess.

It is considered uncivil not to see a caller who has once been admitted to the house, unless there is some very strong reason for not doing so ; hence it is very desirable to give servants clear directions as to what they shall say to visitors, so that no one shall be admitted by mistake. But it is also

4

very unpleasant to people who are making calls if they are obliged to wait a long time before seeing the hostess; therefore where one cannot appear for some little time, it is better to send word to the visitor that Mrs. So-and-so will be very happy to see her if she can wait five or ten minutes, as the case may be.

It is certainly very uncivil to keep a caller waiting for any length of time; if one cannot make one's appearance promptly, it is usually best not to detain a visitor. I have known elderly ladies to be very much annoyed when kept waiting in this way.

Where a caller has been admitted by mistake, and one cannot come down to receive the visit, the servant should be told to apologize for her mistress, and if the latter is just going out, or is lying down, the servant may very properly say so. Where the servant is uncertain whether or not her mistress is at home to visitors, it is usual to send up a card, although it is perhaps better form to send up the name only.

It is not considered polite to call upon a friend who is staying at another person's house, without leaving cards for the hostess also, even if the latter is a stranger to you; otherwise you appear to be making a convenience of some one else's house.

If admitted, it is usual for the caller in the course of her visit to ask whether or not the lady of the house will see her. While one must be careful to pay all due consideration to the hostess of a friend, one must also avoid forcing one's acquaintanceship upon her if she appears not to desire it, or if there is reason to suppose that she will not desire it.

The Countess * * * says in her book, "If there are visitors staying in the house, it is better to distinguish the cards intended for them by writing their names above your own."

This could only be done when the ladies were not at home; and in America it is considered in better form *not* to write the names thus, unless when calling at a hotel. Still, it is sometimes done, "For Mrs. Roderick," or whoever the visitor may be, being written on the upper part of the card with a black lead-pencil. It is considered inelegant to write with a colored pencil, just as it is to use colored ink.

There should always be a special place — the hall table usually — for the cards of the day, and the servant should be instructed to leave them there until his mistress has seen them. She can then tell by their number whether the calls were intended for her visitor as well as for herself.

A young lady who is visiting at the house of a friend should not invite gentlemen to call upon her, without asking her hostess whether it will be convenient and agreeable to have them do so. She should also ask the ladies of the house to come down and have the gentlemen presented to them, lest she may appear to be selfish in receiving her callers, or to be doing so in a clandestine way.

Gentlemen leave their umbrellas in the hall, but bring their canes and hats into the drawing-room with them, in making morning calls, unless in houses where they are on the footing of friends. As a gentleman is not allowed to deposit these cumbrances anywhere save on the floor close to his chair, their management requires some little tact, or else the awkward man may step into his hat, and the forgetful one may depart without his cane. In making evening calls in New York, gentlemen now wear evening dress.

A lady rises when visitors enter, but need not cross the room to receive them unless she wishes to do so. If they are old friends, or people much older than herself, if they are persons of distinction, or if the lady who is receiving is of a very cordial disposition, she will be apt to go to meet them.

But there is no universal rule on this point, and a lady may fitly follow the promptings of her own nature in the matter, taking care that she errs neither on the side of too great effusiveness nor, still worse, on that of over-formality. She should endeavor to pay equal attention to all her guests as far as is possible, and to have a few words at least with each of them.

Where a second visitor arrives after the first has already made a call of sufficient length, the visitor who came first should take her leave soon after the arrival of the second comer, but not instantly.

For a formal call, about fifteen minutes is usually considered the proper length of time ; one may prolong it to half an hour occasionally, but only under "favorable circumstances," since it is far better to take one's leave before people begin to wish that one would go. Emerson says : "'T is a defect in our manners, that they have not reached the prescribing a limit to visits. That every well dressed lady or gentleman should be at liberty to exceed ten minutes in his or her call on serious people shows a civilization still rude."

CHAPTER VI.

INVITATIONS.

In writing an invitation, it is an excellent plan to "make the punishment fit the crime," or, in plain English, to write your invitation in such terms that the recipient shall understand just what it means, just what sort and size of occasion he is invited to attend.

This does not go against the fact that there are certain prescribed modes and forms in which it is customary, and therefore best, to write invitations. But some people, wishing to make a party as informal as possible, invite their guests with less formality than the size of the occasion warrants; hence there is often a great diversity of dress, some of the guests learning beforehand how large the party will really be, and others supposing it will be limited to a very few persons. Hence heart-burnings and mortification often ensue, since most ladies, particularly very young ladies, prefer to be dressed neither with more nor with less elaborateness than others who are present with them.

Another cause for the *undervaluation* which people used to put on their entertainments more than they do now, was the old-fashioned idea of humility as being a necessary adjunct of politeness. All this has been much modified in the manners of to-day, whose frankness I have spoken of elsewhere as being one of their pronounced features. Still, even now it requires some knowledge of the uses of society to know just what a form of invitation means; and a society habitué himself often cannot tell just what the size or form of an entertainment will be.

Be explicit, therefore, within the bounds of politeness, in your invitations; let them all be uniform,—not some verbal and others written,—and write them, or have them engraved, in plenty of time. Some hostesses do not send out their invitations until the eleventh hour, and are then disappointed because people do not come.

The length of time beforehand that an invitation should be sent, depends on the formality and size of the occasion. For a ball, two weeks is the usual time, and it is the same with any very ceremonious occasion,—a large dinner-party or a formal luncheon.

People judge a little, and properly, of the size and formality of an entertainment from this "lapsed time" between the receipt of the invitation and the occasion itself, but it is not an infallible guide. If you invite your guests a long time in advance of the event, they naturally infer that it is one for which you yourself will make elaborate preparations, or one that they will specially wish to attend, and that therefore they are notified of it in good season.

Engraved cards and note-paper are very much used at the present day, both as being more elegant (in the true sense of the word) and more convenient than writing so many invitations. Per contra, for dinners it is quite fashionable to write notes in the first person, even where one has only a slight acquaintance with the person invited. This is the vogue of the present moment, and does not apply to very large and ceremonious dinner-parties.

In writing invitations, be very careful to write names and dates distinctly. I have known some unhappy instances where the guest arrived "the day after the fair" because he mistook "Tuesday" for "Monday" in the note of invitation.

It need hardly be said that these notes should be written very carefully in all respects, notably that of spacing correctly, where the invitation is a formal one, written in the third person. Thus, "Mr. and Mrs. Thomas Jenks" must not be separated, even in a note of invitation; the whole phrase must be written on the same line.

Another point to be observed in writing is, not to mix up your second and third persons. Thus, it would not be allowable to write

Mrs. Simon Montfort

requests the pleasure of your company.

It is permitted to employ this form in engraved invitations, although it is not correct, grammatically speaking. No doubt the use of it is considered allowable in engraved invitations for large parties or balls, because it is so convenient, and saves the trouble of filling in the names.

Mrs. Simon Montfort
requests the pleasure of the company of
Mr. and Mrs. Thomas Newcome
on Friday evening, December twenty-ninth,
at nine o'clock.
Dancing.   *R. S. V. P.*

is a correct form for an invitation to a large party or ball; the R. S. V. P. is often omitted. The name of the hostess only should be used for all occasions save weddings and dinners. For these, the invitations should always run in the name of both host and hostess.

No matter how large or grand a ball you contemplate giving, you must not mention the word "ball" in your invitations; neither must you invite people to "a party," using that word. Some of the English books on manners give express permission to use the phrase "evening party" in invitations, but it is not done in these United States. We all know, to be sure, that "Hans Breitman gave a party," but the lamentable consequences which followed it prevent us from doing likewise. No doubt the reason we do not use these objectionable words is from an old notion that it is well to assume the forms at least of modesty and humility, even if we do not possess the virtues themselves.

For public balls it is allowable and usual to call a spade a spade, and to use the word "ball," because the affair being a public one, no arrogance is displayed by any individual in using the proper term. Instead of "Dancing," "Cotillon" may be engraved in the left-hand corner when there is to be a german ; or the hour may be added, "Cotillon at ten."

> *Mrs. Caleb Sartoris*
> *At Home*
> *Tuesday evening, January twenty-third.*
> *Cotillon.*

This form is preferred very often to the one given on the preceding page, and saves the trouble of writing in the names. It is always easy to learn from first-class stationers what are the customary forms to be used for invitations for various occasions, and to have the cards or note-paper engraved either in whole or in part. It is quite a convenience for ladies who entertain frequently, to have these forms engraved, with spaces left for the date and the names of guests.

Invitation cards should be perfectly plain, and engraved in plain script. The same is true of the engraved note-paper which is now used largely instead of cards. This paper is always white, and rather heavy. It may have a coat-of-arms, or monogram, or both, embossed in white, but colored designs have gone out of fashion for this purpose. Perfectly plain envelopes also are now used for invitations. If they are sent by post, two envelopes should always be sent.

In England, it is entirely proper to send invitations through the post-office, and the custom is such a sensible and excellent one that it is growing in favor in this country. When we remember how often messenger boys "post letters in a snow-bank," in case of any difficulty about finding the address, we ought to be more willing to trust to the paternal Government, with its efficient public servants especially trained to solve riddles in the way of addresses.

The English, who ape French customs less than we do, use the phrase "The favor of an answer is requested," instead of R. S. V. P. (Répondez S'il Vous Plaît).

Never use ruled paper either for writing or answering invitations, or indeed for any letters save business communications. Probably the reasons in accordance with which ruled paper is considered to be in such bad style are: First, because it seems commercial, and our society, like the English, still has a horror of anything that smacks of trade. When it is considered how largely our aristocracy, so far as we have any, is founded upon trade, and composed of people whose fortunes were all made in business, this little prejudice appears somewhat unreasonable. But beware of trifling with prejudices! It is more dangerous than meddling with principles, as all men of the world know. The second reason for which ruled paper is tabooed as a part of the furniture of the writing-desk, is because its use implies that the writer does not know how to write straight without lines, and every lady and gentleman ought to be able to do that. Then, ruled paper looks cheap, and "is used by everybody."

An English gentleman, a scion of the nobility, quite horrified the inhabitants of Boston some years ago, by answering his invitations on this same ruled paper, enclosed in a yellow envelope, which he found at the Somerset Club, if I remember rightly. Of course society was in a state of collapse over this British eccentricity; but perhaps the truth of the matter was that the Hon. Mr. —— supposed the use of the stationery in question was permissible in this country, since he found it at one of our most fashionable clubs.[1]

For dinner-parties, the invitations should be in the name of both husband and wife.

> *Mr. and Mrs. John Morley*
> *request the pleasure of*
> *Mr. and Mrs. John Fisk's company at dinner,*
> *November twenty-seventh, at six o'clock.*
> *23 Beacon Street.*

[1] Since writing the above, I have read, in Mr. Adam Badeau's "Aristocracy in England," that this same noble gentleman shakes hands with the domestics of his friends — on democratic principles; so

An invitation to dinner must be answered without loss of time and without prevarication. If you have any reason to suppose that you will not be able to attend the dinner-party, there is no alternative but to refuse, since it may spoil the whole occasion if the hostess does not know exactly who is coming, and if she does not know it in good season.

Hence it is not unusual for the messenger who brings an invitation to a dinner, to wait and see if there is any answer.

> *Mr. and Mrs. John Morley*
>
> *regret extremely that a previous engagement*
>
> *must deprive them of the pleasure of accepting*
>
> *Mr. and Mrs. John Fisk's*
>
> *polite invitation for dinner*
>
> *on November twenty-seventh.*
>
> *7 Arlington St.,*
> *Thursday.*

is a proper form of refusal. Or if you accept, "accept with pleasure the polite invitation," etc. Always mention the hour, when accepting a dinner invitation, so as to be sure that

the natural inference is that the yellow envelope was used "malice prepense," and that the Somerset Club should be acquitted from any responsibility in so grave a matter.

there is no mistake about it. One should be careful also to express one's self in courteous terms in answering a note of invitation. If the note is a refusal, it is better, if possible, to state the reason which has compelled one to refuse; as,

---

Mrs. Samuel Jones

regrets extremely that a previous engagement

prevents her accepting

Mrs. Wm. L. Sloane's

polite invitation for

Thursday evening next.

Or, "must deprive her of the pleasure of accepting," etc. If you are to be out of town, "absence from the city" will be the excuse proper to send. Of course the form "regrets extremely her inability to accept" is often used; but the other form seems more courteous, especially in answering a first invitation, or any one where the entertainer will be apt to suppose that there is an intention to slight her if no reason for the refusal is given.

All invitations should be answered promptly, except those to afternoon teas and receptions and "At Homes," which are usually not answered at all. It is manifestly illogical to answer a card which says merely "Mrs. Breeze At Home Friday, January thirtieth," because the invitation is not worded in such a way that it can be answered. Sometimes R. S. V. P. is appended to an "At Home" card; but this is an incorrect form of invitation, though used occasionally to save time and trouble.

I find it stated in one book on manners, — and a very good book in many respects,— that one should never write "polite" invitation, but always "kind" or "very kind." The writer adds that it — the latter form — "is English, you know," and states also that "polite" is no longer used in this way in good society in America.

It is to be feared in this case that the wish was father to the thought; for however charming it might be in the eyes of many people to have our social manners and customs become mere duplicates of English forms, we certainly have not yet reached that delightful apotheosis of Anglomania, perfect similarity. "Kind" is certainly often used in answering notes of invitation, but "polite" is still a proper and quite usual form of expression in New York and Boston.

The same authority points out the incorrectness of such forms of expression as "will have the pleasure of accepting," "will prevent his acceptance," "will accept," etc. You accept or are prevented from accepting in the present tense, —that is, when you write the note, — therefore it is incorrect to use "will," which is in the future tense. Neither is it polite to "decline" an invitation; the refusal must be worded in a more courteous form. One should never abbreviate, in writing either acceptances or regrets. They should always correspond in style with the invitation, which should be referred to in order that the answer may be exact.

Where a lady sends her visiting card with "At Home" and the day and hour written upon it, no answer is necessary. In sending your card in acknowledgment of such an invitation, do not write "regrets" or anything else on it, as it would be very impolite to do so.

If an invitation is issued in the name of "Mr. and Mrs. Folsom," then one must accept or refuse Mr. and Mrs.

Folsom's kind invitation; or if Mrs. F. alone invites the guests, then they send their answers to Mrs. F.

It is necessary to be explicit on this point, since some people imagine that if they are not personally acquainted with the hostess, they ought to send their answers to her invitation not to her, but to whatever member of the family they happen to know personally.

This is both illogical and absurd. Indeed, it would be extremely rude to send to the daughter, for instance, an answer to an invitation received from the mother. It would imply that you thought the hostess had committed a breach of etiquette in the form of her invitation. If a lady does you the honor of asking you to her house, the least you can do is to respond courteously, whether she is a stranger to you or not.

A student at Harvard College, a few years ago, was somewhat surprised at receiving an invitation for a dancing party at the house of a lady in Cambridge whom he did not know. As he was a great favorite in society, and a good dancer, he concluded that he had been invited in the character of an eligible partner, and went to the ball.

The hostess and her family treated him with such marked politeness and courtesy that he began to fear something was wrong. Subsequent inquiry revealed the fact that the invitation had been intended for a classmate who bore the same name and surname; and the hostess was so much afraid that her guest would discover the mistake, and would be mortified to think he had come where he had not been invited, that she showed him, by special attentions, that she was pleased to receive him as her guest. *Verb. sat. sap.*

Married people can never be invited separately, unless on some occasion where ladies only or gentlemen only are asked to be present. But if any gentlemen are invited, all — that is, all husbands — must be. Even where it is well known that a lady or a gentleman never goes into society, you must still pay the stay-at-home member the compliment of asking him or her. In the case of very informal occasions, or where another person is suddenly wanted to fill a vacant seat at a dinner-table, this rule is sometimes waived among intimate friends; otherwise it is strictly adhered to, being one of the active laws, as opposed to the dead letters of social observances.

If a person finds that he cannot go to an entertainment after he has accepted the invitation, he should write before the occasion and send his "regrets." This is in accordance with European custom, it is stated, but it is not usually done here, except in the case of dinners, "sit-down" lunches, or other occasions where the host needs to know the exact number of people who will be present, such as tea-parties, "sit-down" suppers, etc. If only a few guests are invited, even to an informal occasion, any one who finds that he cannot go, after he has written that he will do so, should certainly write and let his host know of his change of plan, because the absence of one makes a great difference when only a small number are invited.

Once in a while a very polite person will write to a hostess who is about to give a party, and say that he is at the last moment prevented from coming. But for balls or large parties it is not customary to do so in America, unless one is to be the guest of honor, or unless there is some other special reason for writing.

Should one send invitations to people who are in mourning? It is considered to be more polite to do so, except in case of a recent bereavement. While a family is plunged in deep sorrow and affliction, it is certainly more delicate and considerate not to do anything which would jar upon their feelings, and invitations coming at such a time would almost certainly have that effect. But to people in the later periods of mourning it is quite in order to send general invitations ; that is, invitations to large parties, weddings, etc. Of course they do not go ; but one should pay them the compliment of asking them.

People who are in mourning do not plead a previous engagement when declining an invitation, but regret simply, without giving any reason. They then send by mail their visiting cards with black borders, thus showing clearly why they cannot accept the invitation, the cards also serving instead of a personal visit. These cards should be mailed on the day when the ball or wedding takes place, and should be enclosed in two envelopes. The same number should be sent as if one were calling in person ; the lady would send one card, and her husband would send two, — one for the host and one for the hostess.

"Avail" and "preclude" are words not thought to be in good form for the answers to invitations. "An invite" for "an invitation" is slang of the worst description.

In sending invitations to a family of several members, the most approved method is to send one to the husband and wife, a separate one to the daughters, be they few or many, directed to the Misses Brown, and a third to the brothers, addressed to Messrs. Brown. If there is only one son and one daughter, an invitation may be sent to "Miss Brown and brother ; " but "Misses Brown and brothers " is not advisable, although on these minor and less important points people often follow their own convenience.

"Dr. Brown and family," however, is a form of invitation not favored by those who are careful in such matters. Quite as bad, or worse, is the other extreme, — that of sending a separate card of invitation to each member of a large family. This looks ostentatious, and society dislikes rather particularly ostentation of the sort.

CHAPTER VII.

DINNER-PARTIES, AND HOW TO GIVE THEM.

THE extravagance of our modern dinner-table has grown to be so great that it rivals those ancient Roman feasts where dowries were expended on a single meal, and almost surpasses Cleopatra's famed and costly beverage. But let not the poor imagine that endless dainties bring continual pleasure to the palate ; or that all these fine dishes, with high-sounding French names, taste any better than plain, homely fare, carefully seasoned and well prepared, eaten with the best sauce, hunger, and served hot ! Epicurism is apt to bring its own reward — in the very unpleasant shape of dyspepsia ; and many a millionnaire sits at his richly-furnished table eating gruel or drinking milk ! Sir —— ——, an English nobleman who is thus unfortunately reduced to "spoon food," eats nothing else at his own elaborate dinner-parties ; but, with a truly noble spirit, he still points out to others the best pieces on the dish, his eyes glistening at the sight of the forbidden dainties.

Other more prudent bon-vivants live very simply when at home, eating always of the best, but also of the simplest, and reserving the full force of their appetite for grand occasions. "I get dreadfully tired," said a well-known society woman recently, "of these swell lunches, where you have a little bit of this, and a scrap of the other, and nothing that amounts to anything, — a little chicken-bone in a silver saucepan, a

5

few truffles, lots of empty nothings; and I come home hungry
and eat a good dinner." One certainly tires of elaborate
"made dishes" much sooner than of plain ones. People who
go often to restaurants know that the plain roast and boiled,
a good steak, or a hot chop are best; it is dangerous to try
made dishes unless you are sure of the capacity of the cook
who made them.

Another great objection to formal banquets is the impossibility of having the food really hot, in the long and elaborate
succession of hands through which the dishes have to pass
before reaching the diners. Thomas Hazard, in his "Johnny-
cake" papers, tells how, in his grandfather's time, eels were
broiled on a gridiron and brought in from the kitchen on the
same utensil "smoking hot;" and he intimates that the
result was ambrosial.

Even "hotter" were the old-fashioned blazers, or chafing-
dishes, on which each person at table broiled his own oysters
or his own venison. Some New England ladies use them to
this day for luncheon; and scrambled eggs cooked in this
way are superior to all others.

Rich people, too, get very tired of the formality and show
which accompany their daily meals, and enjoy a plain, good
dinner at a friend's house, because it is a novelty to them.

The famous dinner in the "Book of Snobs" is entirely true
to human nature, and will be remembered for its kindly and
humane sentiment long after Thackeray's more bitter utterances shall have been laid on the shelf. Let no one hesitate,
therefore, to invite his friends to dinner merely because he
will be obliged to entertain them simply. Let the dinner be
plain, but good of its kind; and remember that for people of
small means, quite as much as for the rich, it is important
to make a study of gastronomy, — to combine those articles
of food which go well together. A small circle is still as
perfect as a large one.

Often, with a little thought, some dish can be devised which will be at once unusual, good, and cheap. Thus, flounders go for almost nothing in our markets, and yet are really very delicious fish. Some of the French-made dishes are economical — of everything but labor. The French are a thrifty people, and the style of dishes that they have invented can be made to suit a light as well as a heavy purse.

It is not well to attempt any elaborate dishes, however, unless one has a really competent cook ; and above all, never try any entirely new dish when you are going to have company. Culinary and other experiments should be tried only in the bosom of one's own family.

Let the attendance, even at a very simple dinner, be good. If your own servants are not efficient waiters, by all means hire good ones, who are always to be found in cities of any size. If you cannot afford to do so, or if you live in the country, your only resource is to train your own servants, —— remembering always that they must be trained daily, especially if hitherto they have been undisciplined. You cannot expect raw troops to stand the fire of the enemy ; and servants who are not trained to wait well every day, will do even worse than usual with the excitement of company.

The son of an English earl, Hon. Mr. ——, being possessed only of small means, has two maid-servants to wait on his table, who perform the services expected of them quite as skilfully as men, and at much lower wages. They wear a species of uniform ; that is, dresses of dark blue cloth, made very plainly, with gilt buttons like a page.

The same plan, that of employing women as first-class waiters, has been adopted in this country, all but the uniform. No American woman, even if her citizenship was but a week old, would consent to appear as a female Buttons. The baptism of Castle Garden has a wonderfully liberalizing effect, especially on womankind. At very elegant houses, however, maid-servants often wait upon the table, and when well drilled are fully equal to the best men-servants. They usually wear black dresses made perfectly plain, without overskirt or trimmings, plain white aprons, and white collars and cuffs. Occasionally they wear white caps, although these have become so common that many people do not care to have their servants wear them.

The social enjoyment, the conversation, ought to be the best part of any entertainment, even of that very carnal feast a dinner-party. Crœsus will come all the more willingly to your simple table if he is to meet there some brilliant and agreeable guest. No dinner-party can be really successful at which only dull wits are present, — unless it be that if they are *all* dull they will not notice the difference.

There are certain brilliant talkers who are monopolists of conversation ; they charm with their wit, but no one else has a "show." Such people should be invited "one at a time," and in company with those who will be content to admire and listen to them in silence. I was present at a dinner once where Emerson, William R. Alger, and other men of mark were guests, all of us listening, with charmed attention it must be confessed, to the scintillating flow of speech of one witty and delightful autocrat !

It is a cruel rule that altogether excludes very old and very young people from dinners; but the "dumb" are out of place at them as much as the over-loquacious. Very literal people, too, who cannot take a joke, do not add to the general enjoyment of a feast.

With the English, it is an almost invariable custom that social position should regulate the order in which people go in to dinner, the host taking in the lady of highest rank, and the guests following in couples assorted according to Burke's peerage, very much as children arrange a Noah's Ark procession, the hostess meekly bringing up the rear with the gentleman of highest rank !

Fortunately for us in these United States we have no nobility to dictate our places to us ; and while a host often takes in the lady of highest social position, he quite as often does not. If a distinguished woman is present, he usually pays this honor to her, or perhaps he pays it to the wife of a distinguished man. Where a dinner has been given for a married couple, the host and hostess respectively go in with them. A bride, too, is privileged in this respect, often taking precedence of older ladies ; so also does a distinguished stranger.

But while, *ceteris paribus*, the host takes in the lady of the highest distinction, social, literary, or political, etc., the other couples intermediate between the host and the hostess (who comes last *always*) do not go in in any especial order. Young people naturally give the *pas* to elder ones, or to persons of note, but there is no law on the subject.

The squabbles for precedence in European courts seem to us very undignified. The Countesses of Egmont and Horn used to pass through a doorway arm in arm, as it could not be decided which should go first !

The host and hostess should decide with due deliberation beforehand the order in which the guests are to sit at table, since it may "make or mar" a dinner. Indeed, they should be careful to invite only people who will harmonize well together. Tradition tells about dreadful dinner-parties to which deadly enemies were asked, and where they sat glaring mutually and refusing to speak to one another, like two Banquos at a feast. Certainly this was ill-bred on the part of the guests. Private animosities should be sunk on such occasions ; but one would prefer not to invite the Capulets and Montagues to dine together.

The lady of the house informs each gentleman which lady

he is to take in to dinner, or sometimes cards are placed on the hall table giving this information. If the gentleman does not know the lady, he should ask for an introduction. At small and informal dinners, where all are acquainted, the lady of the house, if she prefers, can say to each gentleman, "Mr. So-and-so, will you take down Miss Blank," just before going down to dinner.

It is perhaps needless to say that a bell should never be rung to announce any formal meal; indeed, it is better form to dispense with the bell-summons for *all* meals, even when no guests are present.

The servant should enter the drawing-room and should say, "Dinner is served," or simply bow, as soon as he catches the eye of his mistress.

The host and hostess may sit at each end of the table or in the middle of each side. The lady who is to be specially honored is placed on the host's right, and the second place of distinction is on his left. In the same way the gentleman who has taken the hostess down to dinner sits on her right, and the "next best man" on her left.

Neither a dining-room nor a table should ever be overcrowded. Brillat-Savarin said that the number of people at a dinner should not be less than the Graces nor more than the Muses; though at some very brilliant dinners this limit has been exceeded. The objection to certain even numbers is, that in the case of four, eight, twelve, sixteen, and twenty (in fact, any number divisible by four), two ladies and two gentlemen will have to sit next each other, when the host and hostess sit at the head and foot of the table. But when a table is wide enough for two people to sit at one end this difficulty may be overcome; and it is certainly pleasanter to have an even number, as otherwise one person is obliged to go in to dinner alone. With the numbers, six, ten, fourteen, eighteen, etc., there is no trouble in arranging the guests.

The host and hostess at a dinner-party stand in need of a great deal of tact; for they must watch the conversation carefully, skilfully starting it when it flags, suggesting new topics, etc., and yet not talking too much. Let the host beware of bringing out his old stories; and let the hostess remember that though her heart may be in the kitchen, her *head* must be with her guests. No matter how much anxiety she may feel, she must betray none, or she will be sure to dampen every one's pleasure.

Hence it is much wiser not to attempt a dinner-party on such an unaccustomed scale that you are worried to death lest your servants should commit some blunder.

The folly of over-pretentious dinners Thackeray has shown up so thoroughly that he has exhausted the subject; while Dickens's description of the Veneering banquets is an equally good piece of satire directed at the solemn and burdensome pomp of stupid *nouveaux-riches*.

CHAPTER VIII.

DINNER-PARTIES; SERVICE AND ARRANGEMENTS OF THE TABLE.

"SCRATCH a Russian, and you will find a Tartar," says the old proverb; intimating, in language more plain than elegant, that a Russian is only a sort of half-savage. And yet these same people, savage or not, control in large measure the diplomacy of Europe, invent wonderful and dreadful forms of modern liberalism, write our best contemporary novels, and last but not least, lay down the law which regulates the tables of every civilized land.

Clearly these Russians are not effete, whatever else they may be; and we have adopted the *dîner à la Russe* from them, just as in an earlier state of civilization the Romans adopted trousers from their savage conquerors, who were *brachati*, or "breeches-wearing." And to the bondage of the trouser mankind has remained a slave all these fourteen hundred years since Rome fell.

How long our bondage to the *dîner à la Russe* will last it is difficult to imagine; probably as long as the present epoch of luxury and æstheticism lasts, for this method of serving meals is as pleasing to the eye as it is agreeable to that natural laziness which abides in the hearts of most men.

A table covered with fruit and flowers, exquisite glass, china, and silver, graceful candelabra, — bonbons and candied fruits perhaps at the corners, — these are all that the modern guest sees when he sits down to the table; but to the eye of faith much more is present, especially if menu-cards, placed in pretty holders, rehearse the catalogue of tempting dainties that are to come.

The table-cloth, the foundation for all this gorgeous display, may be of plain damask, or it may consist of the most costly and elaborate drawn-work, dainty and lace-like in effect; but let it be always white. While some people place a colored cloth beneath the embroidered one in order to show the effect of the work, this arrangement is in questionable taste, and is thought by many persons to be wanting in refinement.

A few years ago dinner-tables were lighted by gas only; but we have borrowed a leaf from Europeans, and as they consider gas vulgar, we begin to think we must do so too, although gas in America is superior in quality to that manufactured abroad. Handsome branching candelabra, usually of silver, filled with white or colored wax-candles, the light softened by colored shades, are now considered the most elegant way of lighting the table; although lamps — which are now made of such beautiful patterns — are often used.

There must not be too great a glare of light on the table, as that would be trying to the eyes of many guests; it is better to have some of the light come from side-branches or chandeliers projecting from the wall, or hanging from the ceiling.

Too much light means also too much heat, and above all things a dining-room should not be overheated; neither should it be full of draughts from open windows. The best way is to keep it pretty cool during the day, instead of neglecting to pay any attention to the temperature until the last moment, and then throwing open windows and doors in every direction. A dining-room should always have a carpet on it to deaden the sound of feet.

The decoration of the table is largely a matter of individual taste, limited by certain rules which do not vary. One of the most important of these is that mere ornament must not be allowed to take too prominent a place at the feast; it must never be arranged so as to interfere with conversation across the table, or to intercept the view of the guests. The decorations should be high enough for people to see under them, or so low that one can look over them.

An ingenious gentleman of Boston has lofty palm-trees, which seem to spring from the centre of his festive board and wave above the heads of his guests with true tropical luxuriance. They really have their roots in large pots placed under the table, through which holes are bored to admit the passage of the stems.

Low, flat centre-pieces of flowers, round or oblong in shape, are often used, and are much liked, because they afford no barrier to sight or to conversation. With this style four smaller bouquets for the corners of the table are very pretty, the flowers in the latter corresponding with the central design. Blue hydrangea interspersed with sprays of lily of the valley and bordered with maiden's-hair ferns makes a very effective decoration used in this way, and has also the good quality of not emitting too strong an odor. Flowers for the dinner-table may be sweet, but should not be oppressive with their fragrance. A centre-piece of blush roses, with hand bouquets to match, is an old-time favorite. These bouquets may be tied with broad pink satin ribbon and laid beside each lady's plate.

The "blue" and "pink" dinners — in which china, table ornaments, etc., were all of the chosen color — are no longer as fashionable as they were. The same is true of "silver" and "glass" dinners, at which the guests marvelled at the gorgeous display of plate or admired the beautiful shape and endless variety of crystal vessels, — now of cut glass, sparkling like diamonds, now of delicate glass engraved with exquisite designs, and as brittle as the heart of an old-fashioned heroine of romance. These "fancies in china" are all very well occasionally; but the greatest beauty is found in harmony, not in monotone, and the most æsthetically adorned tables encourage variety rather than oddity.

Where the giver of a dinner does not wish to go to much expense for flowers, a very graceful ornament can be made by placing a pot of maiden-hair fern in the centre of the table, the pot being covered by pieces of bark or moss, tied on with fine thread or wire. Or pretty little majolica and china ornaments in all sorts of odd shapes may be placed about the table, filled with cut flowers.

A very effective centre-piece can be made by arranging fruit and flowers together, or even with fruit alone. Very pretty gilt baskets low and flat in shape have now come into vogue, with pans fitted in the centre and filled with growing ferns. Wild-flowers artistically arranged make exquisite table ornaments. It would doubtless surprise some farmers to see the weeds which they so detest, and wage a life-long warfare with, set in the place of honor on the rich man's table. Yet there the sturdy weeds stand to-day, pretty, saucy, and graceful, like country beauties newly come to Court.

In England, where tropical fruit is so much more expensive than with us, pineapples, etc., are sometimes hired to ornament the table with, and are returned intact when the feast is over.

The lofty épergnes for fruit and flowers are very imposing and showy; they correspond with the candelabra or lamps, and are preferred by many people. A tall centre-piece (whether of silver or glass — the latter is more modern) should stand on a silver tray, or on a flat mirror made for the purpose. Beneath may be a sort of large mat of bright-colored velvet, which is often used to give a good bit of color to the table. *Carafes* or water-bottles of cut or engraved glass should be placed at each corner, and for a large dinner-party in the middle of each side also. This is not done in England, where "tumblers are placed on the sideboard and not on the table," and where they are inclined to laugh good-naturedly at our American habit of perpetually drinking ice-water.

A "cover" signifies the place laid at table for each person, and should consist of two large knives, a small silver knife and fork for fish, three large forks, a table-spoon for soup, a small "oyster-fork" for eating oysters on the half-shell, a goblet for water, and claret, hock, champagne, and sherry glasses, which are placed around it. The knives and forks should always be placed on the right and left of the plate, and never across the table.

In England, where raw oysters are not usually given at dinner, the dinner-napkin, with the bread folded in it, is placed between the knives and forks. But with us, the napkin and bread are placed on the left, as raw oysters, served on a majolica oyster-plate, with a piece of lemon in the centre, are set at each place before the guests enter. The oyster-fork is usually placed at the right side of the plate, but the other forks should be on the left.

The napkin, as has been said elsewhere, should be simply folded, either standing upright, like a sort of triangle, with the ends drawn together to hold the bread, or folded square, with the top part creased and turned back diagonally; and the bread, which should be cut in small thick pieces, and not in slices, tucked under this fold — or in any other simple way.

The glasses are placed on the right. For champagne glasses a broad, low, flaring shape is now in vogue, although the old-fashioned long slender ones are much more graceful. For hock, green glass, and for claret or Burgundy, deep red glass should be used ; for sherry, a white wine-glass, of conventional form, the old unchanging pattern, remains always essentially the same.

Seven and even nine wine-glasses are sometimes put beside each plate, but most of us would not approve of such a profusion of wine as this would imply. At other tables, two extra glasses, one for sherry or Madeira, and the other for claret or Burgundy, are put on with the dessert. These late-coming glasses are usually very delicate, as they accompany choice wines. No table-spoons (save those for soup) or other extra silver are placed on table for *diner à la Russe*, and no cruets or casters.

After the raw oysters soup is served. At very stylish dinners it is customary to serve two soups, — white and brown, or white and clear. A thick soup is *purée*, and a clear soup is *consommé*. The soup, like the rest of the dinner, is served from the sideboard.

Fish is the next course, and is followed by the entrées, or "those dishes which are served in the first course after the fish." It is well to serve two entrées at once at a very elaborate dinner, and thus save time. To these succeed the roast, followed by Roman punch, and this in turn is followed by game and salad. Roman punch should only be given with a dinner of many courses ; it is quite out of place at a simple dinner, where there is only one course of meat. It is properly an "entremêt," or "dish coming after the roast, in the second course."

Salad is sometimes served with the game, or again, it is served as a separate course, accompanied with cheese and with bread and butter. The bread should be cut very thin and nicely buttered, although sometimes the butter and bread are served separately.

Cheese is often made a course by itself ; indeed, the general tendency of the modern dinner is to have each dish "all alone by itself," like the one fishball of classic memory. This style, however, may be carried too far. Only one or at most two vegetables are served with one course, and many vegetables make a course by themselves, as asparagus, sweet corn, macaroni, etc.

Some people think it is very barbarous to eat corn from the cob, but many others consider it entirely allowable to do so. A lady who gives many elegant dinners at Newport causes to be laid beside the plate of each guest two little silver-gilt spike-like arrangements. Each person then places these in either end of the corn-cob, and eats his corn holding it by two silver handles as it were.

After the salad and cheese come the ices and sweet dishes, then the fruit, then the bonbons. Coffee is usually served in the drawing-room, although it may be handed around in the dining-room if the guests have not already sat too long at the table.

Gentlemen stay at table a short time after the ladies have left it, discussing wine, cigars, and liqueurs (or cordials), and no doubt indulging in the most improving conversation. After dinner coffee should always be *café noir*, or strong black coffee. It should be poured out in the kitchen or butler's pantry and handed round on a salver in tiny cups, with tiny gold or silver spoons and lump sugar, but no cream or milk.

For all the hot-meat courses, entrées, etc., the guests are provided with hot plates; but these are not used for salads nor cold meats, nor for hot puddings, which keep their own heat too well to need any artificial aid.

For a dinner of many courses the knives and forks laid beside the plates will not be sufficient. Therefore at a later stage of the entertainment a fresh fork, or fork and knife, as the course may require, is set before each person on a fresh plate.

Before the dessert everything is of course cleared from the table except the table-cloth, which is never taken away now, for two reasons : first, because this would disturb too much the many decorations which adorn a modern feast; second, because, with the new methods of serving, there is little danger of soiling the cloth.

For the dessert, a silver dessert knife and fork and a gold or silver dessert spoon are put at each place. To these is often added an ice-spoon, — a compromise between a fork and a spoon. The finger-bowl comes with the fruit; it is set on the plate (usually a glass one or a handsomely decorated china one), a fruit napkin or one of the embroidered doilies now so fashionable being placed between.

As these dainty trifles often cost twenty-five or thirty dollars a dozen, it would be an act of Vandalism to do more than look at them; the guest, therefore, must fall back on his dinner-napkin for real use. For peaches, a genuine fruit napkin should be provided, as they stain white ones very badly.

Sherry is the proper wine to accompany soup. Chablis, hock, or sauterne go with the fish course, claret and champagne with the roast. If Madeira and port are used, they should come after the game. Sherry and claret, or Burgundy, are again offered with the dessert, the after-dinner wines being of a superior quality to those served during the meal.

Cordials or liqueurs come after the dessert. These are poured out by the butler into tiny glasses and passed around the table on a small salver. Champagne and other sparkling wines should be set in an ice-pail to cool until just before they are served. They are never decanted, but poured out as quickly as possible after they are opened.

It is customary in this country to pass around a silver or china ice-bowl containing broken ice before the champagne is offered ; but the servant should never put ice in any one's glass without first asking if he wishes it, as some people object decidedly to having their wine thus weakened. Claret is not usually decanted in America. It should never be iced, but, on the contrary, is sometimes warmed slightly; it should be about the same temperature as the room. The same is true of Burgundy.

Sherry, Madeira, and port are always decanted, and are placed on the sideboard ready for use. No wine should be put on the dinner-table at first. At a later stage decanters may be set before the host, who sends them to his guests. When these are placed on the table gentlemen help themselves and the ladies next to them.

Champagne is passed many a time and oft during the dinner, being a favorite wine; but it is not usually handed with the dessert in this country, whereas on the Continent it is served with the sweets. A napkin should always be fastened around a champagne bottle, as it is almost necessarily wet from recent contact with the ice.

For a small dinner it is quite sufficient to have two or three wines; in this case, sherry with the soup, and claret or champagne with the roast, would be the best selection. Wine should be offered on the right hand, thus making an exception to the rule in accordance with which all dishes are handed on the left hand.

The washing of plates, silver, etc., at a dinner-party should if possible be performed at such a distance from the dining-room that the clatter will be inaudible to those seated at table. In order to give an elaborate dinner it is almost indispensable that one should have a large quantity of china and plate, otherwise the delay from washing the dishes will be endless. Those that have been used should be at once removed from the dining-room, a page or maid-servant carrying them away; and one or two servants should be employed in washing them.

When one plate is taken away at the end of a course another is at once substituted for it. If a knife and fork are laid on this, the guest should take them off promptly, otherwise he may delay the serving of the next course. For the same reason the finger-bowl and doily should be at once removed from the plate.

The entrées are generally passed to guests in order that they may help themselves. Sometimes, however, all the courses are helped from the side-table. It is considered to be in better style for the servant to have a small napkin wrapped around his hand, so that it shall not come in contact with the dishes as he passes them, rather than that he should wear gloves. Only hired waiters wear gloves.

The number of servants required to wait on a dinner depends largely on their efficiency. At a large dinner one waiter to every three guests, or even to every two guests, is sometimes employed ; *per contra*, one thoroughly trained and efficient waiter can attend to eight or ten people.

At large and ceremonious dinners a card with each person's name is usually placed on or beside each plate. If a menu or bill of fare is used it may be laid beside the other card, or it may be placed in the pretty and fanciful menu-holders that are now easily obtainable. Where these holders are used there should be at least one to every two guests, or still better one to each person ; but many people do not consider menu-cards appropriate in a private house.

As the custom is now abolished of waiting till every one is helped before beginning to eat, it should be one servant's duty to pass the proper sauce or vegetables to each person just after he has been helped by another servant to the meat. This greatly expedites matters, besides enabling every one to begin to eat his dinner while it is still hot.

The order in which the guests should be helped depends somewhat on the number of servants who wait on the table.

6

Where there are a number in attendance, one servant should begin on each side of the table, helping first the lady sitting next the host, and then the other ladies, in the order in which they sit. The gentlemen should be helped afterward, the host always receiving his plate last.

Where, however, the attendance is limited, and it is desirable to expedite matters, the servant may first help the lady on the host's right (the guest of honor), then the one on his left, and then the guests as they sit, ladies and gentlemen, leaving the host to be helped last. But it is always desirable to help all the ladies first.

The butler or head waiter is much too grand a person to wear any man's livery. He wears full evening dress, — dress-coat, white tie, etc., for late dinners. Earlier in the day he appears in dark morning costume. The second man wears livery, and where more than two men are kept, the others wear livery also.

The drinking of toasts is going out of fashion ; people still occasionally drink one another's health. In order to do so it is merely necessary to bow, when the other person bows in return. Each one then drinks a few drops of wine and sets down his glass, bowing once more.

CHAPTER IX.

"EAT at your table as you would eat at the table of the king," said Confucius; and the advice is as good now as when it was given nearly three thousand years ago. If you would learn to behave well in company you must behave well at home; otherwise the polite manners which you assume when you are abroad will fit you much as a workman's Sunday suit fits him. He wears it with an unaccustomed air which shows far more plainly than words that this is not his habitual dress; and behavior that is kept for high days and holidays betrays itself in a like manner.

A still better reason for uniformity in one's manners is, that it savors of hypocrisy to behave in one way at home and in a totally different way in society. A greater amount of ease and freedom may certainly be permitted in one's own house; but the keynote of a person's behavior should always be the same: self-respect and respect for others must never be forgotten.

What an excellent custom of the old French monarchy it was, that of breakfasting in public, and giving the people every day a lesson from the very best authorities on the proper way to behave at the table! Whether the French king who first set this fashion had read Confucius is more than doubtful; but as great minds think alike, he was probably actuated by the same general idea, and determined to show his subjects a good example in the way of manners, whatever his views of morals may have been.

Too much stress cannot be laid on the importance of refinement at the table, both in manners and in the laying and service of the table itself. The habit of eating together and at stated times is one of the distinguishing marks that separate civilized men from savages, and a man's behavior at table is a pretty sure indication of his social status.

The negroes on the old Southern plantations could hardly be induced to eat their meals save irregularly and by snatches. To them the idea of sitting down to a regularly set table at a formal meal was extremely irksome. As extremes meet, the first gentleman in England, the Prince of Wales, has also found the customs of society too formal, and he has very wisely shortened the length of a fashionable dinner from three or four hours to an hour or an hour and a half, two hours being the very outside limit now allowed.

In a subsequent chapter, "Children, and how they should behave at the Table," many *gaucheries* of which grown people as well as children are often guilty are mentioned. Still, the catalogue there given is not an exhaustive one, and a few hints on the etiquette of the table will not be out of place here. *Imprimis*, one should never speak, unless in jest, of "table manners;" the expression is tabooed in good society, as are also the kindred ones, "parlor manners," "company manners," etc.

Never come late to a dinner-party. The old rule was that guests should arrive within five minutes of the appointed hour, either before or after. Some people say that the etiquette on this point is not as strict as formerly, but it is much wiser to be on the safe side. Gentlemen should not take their seats until the ladies are seated, and each gentleman should pull out the chair for the lady next him, and assist her to draw it up to the table before seating himself. This is not always necessary, as the servants assume the duty where there are a number of them in attendance.

It is not the easiest thing in the world to assume a proper attitude at table, for it is very awkward to bend over your plate or to lean over between each mouthful. On the other hand, it does not look well to lean back in one's chair when eating, or to sit up as stiffly as if one had just swallowed a ramrod.

It is not allowable to ask for a second helping of soup or fish, and the reason of the rule is that these courses are preliminary to the *pièces de résistance* of the dinner; therefore most people prefer not to delay over them, and in asking for a second plate of soup you keep the whole assemblage waiting for one person.

There is a story of the Revolution, however, which shows that this law was not then held in such sacred esteem as it is now. According to the tradition, a number of French officers were invited to dine with an aristocratic family at Newport, and the soup was so rich and so good that the French chevaliers never got beyond that course!

Soup is a terrible snare to the unwary, especially if the unwary happens to have a moustache! For it is one of the unpardonable sins of the social decalogue to eat soup noisily. Neither, however, can you save yourself by refusing soup, since this also would be bad form. If it is of a sort which you especially dislike, simply let it alone. In helping to soup, do not fill the plate; half a ladleful suffices, where the ladle is large.

The old rule, never to use a knife with fish, was so very inconvenient, especially in eating shad, that it has been abandoned. Silver fish-knives are now provided at all ceremonious dinners. They are of a peculiar shape and of small size, as also are the forks that accompany them.

It used to be a standing reproach to Americans that they ate so rapidly; but we have improved in this respect as we have grown more luxurious. Still, every one should remember that haste in eating is inelegant as well as very unwholesome.

If any competent person should institute a knife, fork, and spoon drill, and should offer to give private lessons in the use of these formidable weapons, he might easily make a fortune. The knife is the easiest of the dread trio to manage, if you can successfully resist the temptation to thrust it into the mouth, that besets so many people.

Everybody ate with their knives before the invention of the four-pronged fork, because with the old two-pronged instrument it was manifestly impossible to eat pease, rice, and many other articles of food. All English-speaking nations, however, as well as the French, now absolutely forbid the use of the knife except to cut with. On the Continent, society is not so strictly divided by the "knife line;" and it would not be safe in Germany, for instance, to judge of a man's social position by his method of using his knife.

It is an awkward trick to raise and spread out the elbows when cutting up the food. It also looks very badly to seize the knife too far down on the blade or to grasp it too vigorously.

Every one ought to know how to carve, otherwise he may be placed in the predicament of the Boston lady who had chicken for dinner but was utterly ignorant of how to cut it up. "Mother took hold of one drumstick and I took hold of the other, and we *ran* till we pulled it apart," — so she told the story!

The modern custom of having the butler do all the carving on the sideboard saves the master of the house a great deal of trouble; but there are still many occasions on which it is very important to be able to carve, — at luncheon, at informal suppers, dinners in the country, picnics, etc.

Charles James Fox, who made it a point to do everything well and vigorously that he once undertook, was an excellent carver. It is related in Trevelyan's life of him that he used to have a book giving special directions about carving by his side at table, so that he might be sure to carve in the best possible manner.

It is not well to emphasize one's conversation by waving about one's knife or fork, even in an entirely peaceful and friendly manner.

The fork has now become the favorite and fashionable utensil for conveying food to the mouth. First it crowded out the knife, and now in its pride it has invaded the domain of the once powerful spoon. The spoon is now pretty well subdued also, and the fork, insolent and triumphant, has become a sumptuary tyrant. The true devotee of fashion does not dare to use a spoon except to stir his tea or to eat his soup with, and meekly eats his ice-cream with a fork and pretends to like it.

Vegetables are always eaten with a fork now, save asparagus, which may be held in the fingers by the butt and eaten without other assistance. Where it is much covered with sauce it is certainly the part of discretion to use a fork.

Olives are eaten with the fingers, as being a species of fruit. For salad, good authorities sanction the use of both knife and fork, unless the salad has been cut up beforehand. One should use a knife as little as possible, however, and only where the lettuce leaves are so large that they cannot be managed with the aid of a silver fork and a piece of bread. To cut up salad very fine on one's plate, until it is like mincemeat, is in decidedly bad taste. This should be done before the dish comes to table, if at all.

Croquettes, patties, and most of the made dishes which now are so much in vogue should be eaten with a fork;

indeed, at a modern fashionable lunch or dinner a large proportion of the courses require no other implement. Of course a knife must be used for plain beef and mutton, chops, cutlets, game, etc. Cheese should be eaten with a fork where it is at all soft, and so should most fruits, as has been said elsewhere. Celery is usually held in the fingers and eaten *au naturel*.

Another use for the fork is to convey back to the plate fish-bones and other *reliquiæ* which one cannot swallow; these objects should be got rid of, by means of the fork, in the most quiet and unobtrusive manner possible.

The spoon is used for water-ices, Roman punch, soup, puddings, tea and coffee, preserves and canned fruits, for all berries, especially if cream is served with them, for custards, — in fact, for whatever dishes are too liquid to be managed with a fork. A spoon should never be left standing in a teacup, but should be laid on the saucer.

Never look as if you were trying to swallow either a spoon or a fork; it has been done, and though the man did not die he came very near it. Do not, either, adopt the childish habit of turning your spoon upside down in your mouth like an abandoned boat at sea. This looks as badly, nay worse than eating bread with the butter-side down.

It is better to break bread into pieces before buttering it, instead of buttering the whole slice at once. Indeed, only children should take "bites" out of a whole slice of bread. Grown people break off pieces of dry bread with their fingers and eat them, for bread, muffins, biscuits, etc., should never be cut apart, but merely broken. This does not apply, of course, to cutting the bread from the loaf.

It is very difficult to describe on paper the correct way of carrying the fork or spoon to the mouth. Mrs. Sherwood says: "The fork should be raised laterally to the mouth with the right hand; the elbow should never be crooked, so as to bring the hand round at a right angle, or the fork directly opposite the mouth." In other words, the fork should be nearly parallel with the mouth, and not at right angles with it.

Seeing, however, is better than hearing in such a case. For dwellers in cities, a simple recipe would be, Go to the Brevoort or Delmonico's in New York, or to Young's in Boston, and bribe the head waiter to point out to you any "real old families" that may be present, and watch their operations. Alas! even then you may be disappointed. There are men of old family and high degree who eat unpleasantly, — champing the end of the fork, perhaps, as if it were a curb bit.

While it is very undesirable to appear greedy or in too much haste, still it is always proper to ask to have things handed to you after waiting a suitable length of time. Ask the servant, however, if one is present; a word or sign will bring an efficient waiter to your side, and you can then quietly tell him what you need.

At a ceremonious dinner one does not need to ask for anything, unless perhaps for a fresh knife or fork (if one's own has fallen upon the floor), a piece of bread, salt, etc. Some people, however, even when staying at the house of an intimate friend, will starve rather than ask to have any dish passed to them. This is not in accordance with good manners. While it is the part of the host, either personally or through well-trained servants, to see that his guest wants for nothing, it is also the part of the guest to assist his entertainer in the matter, and to mention anything that has been forgotten.

At a dinner one must not neglect one's next-door neighbors. While it is often pleasanter to listen to some witty and agreeable person opposite than to talk platitudes to the person next you, still one must not appear neglectful; above

all a gentleman must not.   At a small dinner it is very
pleasant occasionally to have the conversation become general; at a large dinner, of course it is impossible.

The old-fashioned custom of thanking your hostess for a
meal is now unhappily obsolete.[1]   It always seemed such
a pretty, primitive, quaint fashion, that one would like to
revive it, together with the old colonial mansions which are
now once more beginning to adorn our land. As Byron
said, —

> "Ye have the Pyrrhic dance as yet;
> Where has the Pyrrhic phalanx gone ?
> Of two such lessons, why forget
> The nobler and the manlier one ?"

So might one now ask why we could not go back to the
courtly ways of our ancestors, as well as adopt their houses,
their dress — alas ! we pay little heed to their manners.

Gentlemen always rise when ladies leave the table, and
often now accompany them back to the drawing-room. More
often, however, they seat themselves again after the ladies
have left the room, and enjoy that cigar which is so indispensable to the good-nature of most men, and those other
favorites, — wines and liqueurs.   They do not linger long,
however. The old and barbarous British custom of indulging in deep after-dinner potations is now universally
condemned.

At a dinner-party, if you feel uncertain what to do, observe your neighbors, and do as they do. But above all,

---

[1] Since writing the above I have received a note from a friend,
who suggests that this custom has been very recently revived, in a
modified form, the guest saying when she takes her departure, " I
have had such a pleasant time ; thank you for asking me." All which
proves that great minds think alike, and that the revived colonial
architecture, with its white trimmings, is already beginning to have an
effect on our manners.

endeavor to be calm outwardly and inwardly. Remember that no one is thinking about what you are doing half as much as you are yourself, and if you seem quiet and at ease, people will notice your actions much less than if you seem flurried and troubled.

If you upset anything on the cloth, or break anything, don't apologize; and don't be overwhelmed with confusion if you drop your knife or fork. Such accidents have happened before, and will again. If you are too precise and prim, if you are like Dickens's woman, who continually said "Papa, potatoes, poultry, prunes, and prisms," you will not appear nearly as well as with a quiet, natural manner.

Be careful, however, not to talk across people, and not to turn your back to those who sit next you; be sure also to take off your gloves as soon as you sit down at the table.

While it is not customary to refuse soup, it is perfectly proper to refuse one or more courses at a long and elaborate dinner. Menu-cards are very desirable on such occasions, since it is impossible to eat everything without being greedy, and it is pleasant to be able to make one's choice; but as I have said elsewhere, their day of popularity is rapidly passing away.

One should not imitate the candor of a distinguished Englishman who dined in Washington with a former Minister to St. James, and who declined canvas-back ducks. His host pressed him to take some, saying that the dish was considered a great delicacy in America. "Thank you, I never eat raw meat," replied the Briton. Nothing daunted, his courteous entertainer sent the ducks back to the kitchen to be more thoroughly cooked. This time the Englishman tried a piece of the meat, and speaking to his wife across the table said, "My dear, try a piece. *It is not nearly as nasty as it looks!*"

To refuse wine, place your hand against the rim of the wine-glass; it is never necessary to take wine if you do not wish to, but in this case it is better not to allow the servant to fill your glass. A wine-glass should be held by the stem and not by the bowl, and the very last drops from it should not be drunk.

There is some question as to the best method of disposing of one's knife and fork when sending one's plate back for a second helping. Some people say that they should be left on the plate (placed carefully together, with the handles pointing the same way, so that they may not fall off), others contend that they should be retained in the hand; modern custom strongly inclines to sanction leaving them on the plate, while formerly it was thought proper to remove them.

This change in sentiment, like so many others of the kind, arises from the different way in which food is now served; in these days we eat fewer things at a time, therefore our plates are not so much encumbered, and the carver can put a second supply on them without as much difficulty as under the old régime. The carver, too, is often the butler; whereas formerly he was always the master of the house, whose convenience was of more importance.

Where dinner is served in the old-fashioned way, the gentleman who sits next to the hostess should always offer to relieve her from the duty of carving; although some ladies, who do it well, prefer to carve themselves.

Fish should always be cut up with a silver fish knife and fork, as steel should never come in contact with it.

It is now considered more polite not to pass a plate that has been handed to you, but to keep it yourself. In acting thus you simply accede to the arrangements of your hostess, and make less disturbance, than by endeavoring to make a new order of things. As has been said elsewhere, one does not now wait for other people to be helped before beginning to eat; the old rule — of waiting — certainly seemed more polite.

Not to take the last piece on a dish when it is handed to you is also a rule which has been relegated to the children's table. This old rule must have had its origin in more frugal days than the present; the reason of the new rule is, that if you refuse to take the last piece you imply a doubt of the existence of a further supply in the larder, and such a doubt is a reflection on your host! This is merely one of the many straws which tend to show what an epoch of luxury and wealth ours is.

The lady of the house should not allow her plate to be removed until all her guests have finished eating.

CHAPTER X.

THE FAMILY DINNER—TABLE; ITS FURNITURE AND EQUIPMENT.

THE service and arrangement of one's table must of course vary largely with one's income, but it is a mistake to let all the expenditure be for the food alone; part of it should be reserved for refined appointments of the table, — fine linen, napkins of generous size, pretty china and glass, and well-polished silver.

A lady whose generous and well-ordered table was always a pleasure merely to look at, said to the writer, " We have decided to have flowers on table every day this winter, and to make up for the additional expense by having one dish less in our bill of fare;" a very pretty idea, and a sanitary one too, for a rich man's table. We cannot all afford to have hot-house flowers in winter; but we *can* afford to have spotless table-linen, and to keep the silver bright and shining, — two very important adjuncts to a well-ordered dinner-table.

It is the decree of Fashion now that the same napkin must never appear twice on table without being washed in the interim ; hence napkin-rings have gone out of favor, and are not considered in good style. Of course this fashion makes great demands upon the laundress, and cannot well be adopted by large families of moderate means; but for every one who can afford it, for every one who wishes to have her table appointed with elegance, it is indispensable that the napkins should be changed at every meal and the table-cloths very frequently.

Large napkins spread on the table-cloth underneath the dishes containing meat are a great protection, as they prevent the spattering of the cloth by the carver. Indeed, fancy napkins made of linen or crash, fringed and embroidered, "carver's cloths," are used by some people.

A white table-cloth should always be used for dinner; the pretty tinted cloths and napkins that look so tempting in the windows of the linen draper may be used for breakfast or luncheon, but are not *en règle* for dinner.

A table-cloth should not only be snowy-white and perfectly fresh, it should also be very carefully ironed, and carefully folded before it is ironed, in order that it may lie smooth and even on the table. Where one has been poorly ironed, or has been too stiffly starched, it will hump up in wrinkles in a way that is very unseemly. There should always be an undercloth, not only to make the table-cloth lie smooth, but also to prevent the heat of the dishes from marring the table. White canton flannel of extra width is the best material for this purpose.

Table-cloths should be of fine linen; a coarse cloth is almost certain to offend a delicate taste. Double damask is thought to wear better than single, though it is more expensive, and very pretty fine cloths can be bought in single damask. It is now fashionable to embroider table-linen with the cipher (that is, interlaced initials) or crest of the family; the latter may be placed on the napkins, and should be very delicately worked, and made of small size, in white thread, since nothing is more vulgar than a loud and obtrusive coat-of-arms, especially in this republican country.

For the table-cloths the cipher should be two or three inches deep, and may be marked in the middle of each end of the cloth, so as to show beyond the dishes.

For dinner, very large napkins are now used; for breakfast, they should be rather smaller; for luncheon, they should be of the same size as dinner napkins. For tea, breakfast napkins are of the right size to use, although the little fringed doilies are liked better by some people. A napkin should never be stiff; very little starch should be put in it. It should also be perfectly dry, and simply folded, lying beside the plate, with a roll or thick short piece of bread enclosed, or placed upon it. Bread should never be put on the table at dinner save in this fashion. There should always be a reserve supply ready on the side-table for those who like a great deal of the staff of life.

How should a napkin be arranged? According to strict etiquette, it should not be fully unfolded and spread out, but should be laid across the knees, partially opened, to be used as a towel only; that is to say, to wipe the fingers and mouth.

The master of ceremonies in the time of Louis Napoleon considered it a decided breach of the etiquette of the table to unfold the napkin entirely and spread it out. But this is a very absurd and unpractical custom, especially for people who are apt to drop their food; and almost every one does so occasionally. I merely give it as the strict rule for formal occasions — and for very careful eaters.

For every-day use, and for ordinary people, the proper and usual way is to spread the napkin over the knees; it should never be placed at the neck, save for children, nor should it be tucked into a buttonhole.

Should the napkin be folded on leaving the table? It should never be, at a formal or ceremonious meal. At a dinner-party, for instance, no one thinks now-a-days of folding up a napkin; indeed, the custom is going out of favor generally, as a logical corollary of the fashion of having fresh napkins at every meal. Still, if one is staying at another person's house, and is uncertain what its customs may be, the best way is to watch the hostess and to do as she does in the matter ; because if the lady of the house does not intend to provide clean napery at every meal, her guests must conform to her usages, otherwise they will appear careless and underbred.

Fruit napkins should be brought in with the dessert, placed on the dessert-plate beneath the finger-bowl. They are indispensable on any formal occasion, unless ornamental doilies are used ; indeed, it is well to use them even at the simplest meal, where fruit is on the table, because they prevent the staining of the white napkins. Some hostesses provide them in addition to the ornamental doilies. In this case the fruit napkin is placed on top of the finger-bowl, or beside it on the plate.

The large caster-stands which were formerly placed in the centre of the table have now gone entirely out of style, and are replaced by small silver stands for pepper — an owl is a favorite shape for them — placed at the four corners of the table, or one at each plate.

Oil and vinegar are usually placed on the sideboard only, but may be placed on the table if preferred, in little ornamental glass bottles or jugs. Mustard also is relegated to the sideboard by most people. At a very formal dinner, pepper, oil, vinegar, etc., are not permitted on the table. To tell the truth, they are seldom required at such a meal, where every dish has its proper seasoning and sauce ready provided.

The old-fashioned caster-stand was such an ugly and awkward thing that it certainly deserved sentence of banishment. Nor can one regret the exile of the spoon-tumbler, which is now rarely used.

The truth is that the æsthetic movement in this country is nowhere more visible than in the arrangement and appointments of the table. We have made wonderful advances in

7

this matter during the last ten years, and the changes that have taken place are all in the direction of greater elegance and refinement.

We have grown more indolent too in proportion as we have grown more luxurious, and the appointments of the table are not only more elegant in themselves, they are also such as to obviate the necessity of any passing of dishes save by the servants. We require these to be better trained now than formerly, and to wait more quietly and more constantly.

The use of a little silver or brass tray or waiter, on which a servant now hands all the dishes, is a very great improvement upon the old-fashioned method by which the servant grasped the dish in her hand, often placing her thumbs unpleasantly near the food.

On the other hand, the banishment of mats from the table polite is not an unmixed blessing. Many servants find great difficulty in replacing the dishes in their exact places ; and the mat was a great assistance to them in this respect, besides the saving of the cloth that it effected.

Individual salt-cellars are much used now, and from these it is entirely proper to help yourself with your knife if no salt-spoon has been provided. But housekeepers should remember that where salt-spoons are not used, the salt should be thrown out and replaced by fresh at every meal.

The crumb-brush is not used nearly as much as was formerly the case, for the very good reason that it must almost necessarily be somewhat soiled, since it cannot be washed easily and often, like a crumb-scraper or napkin. A silver crumb-scraper with a plate or tray is much used for clearing the table, though a folded napkin is preferable on formal occasions because it makes less noise.

It has been said in another chapter that separate plates for vegetables are not considered to be in good style. An exception to this rule is made in the case of salad. Where this is served at the same time with vegetables and meat or fish, it is always proper to have a second plate for it, about the size of a tea-plate. The reason is an obvious one; namely, the unpleasant mixture that would ensue if the oil and vinegar from the dressing should mingle with the vegetables.

Where no vegetable is served with the salad, a second plate is not needed. Thus fish, with cucumber salad, calls for one plate only; but if potato is served in addition, then a second is required. It is better, however, to serve the fish with only one accompaniment, either salad or potato, instead of both. No vegetable except potato can be served with fish.

Butter is now banished even from the family dinner-table by people who follow the new customs. It should be placed upon the sideboard and passed around when sweet potatoes, sweet corn, etc., are served. If butter is used at dinner, butter-plates should always be provided for each person, as otherwise the combination of hot dinner-plates with melting butter slipping down their edges is far from agreeable.

CHAPTER XI.

CHILDREN, AND HOW THEY SHOULD BEHAVE AT THE TABLE.

THE parents who bring their children up well and carefully, who furnish them with an adequate physical, mental, and moral training, truly deserve the gratitude of the State, as well as that of their offspring.

In the mad struggle for wealth which now pervades all classes of society, this homely, old-fashioned truth is quite lost sight of. Men strain every nerve to amass great fortunes for themselves and their children, and forget that the wealth of Midas himself would not long benefit the man who had not been taught to use it aright. We all know what becomes of a beggar who is set on horseback; and most of us have seen the ill consequences that too often ensue when a great amount of money is suddenly put into the hands of some gilded and foolish youth, college-bred perhaps, but wanting in all practical training and discipline, nevertheless.

Golden armor is a great help; but to fight the battle of life successfully one needs above all to be a skilful soldier.

Great attention is certainly given now-a-days to education in certain forms, — education in schools and colleges; but even here there is a constant effort to make everything easy and pleasant, — to do away with or conceal discipline as far as is possible. All the rough corners are carefully smoothed away, and "the royal road to learning" is the philosopher's stone for which we of the nineteenth century search with constant and unabating ardor.

But how about the home training which should supplement all these "outside aids" to education and harmonious development? It is too often neglected; our children are left to imbibe from chance the sound principles and gentle manners which our forefathers so zealously and faithfully inculcated in the hearts and minds of their offspring. We have a pleasant theory that our young people will go right of themselves, and that they will "pick up" good-breeding somehow or other as they grow older!

The morals of our bank cashiers and our great army of embezzlers in general show what are the results of the want of proper moral training; while the thoughtlessness, selfishness, and rudeness of too many young men and women attest the folly of supposing that true good manners will form themselves.

Of morals it is not the province of this work to treat, except as they are connected with manners. Suffice it to say that before one can rear a fair and comely superstructure of good manners, one must lay deep in the heart their necessary foundation, namely, kindness and good-will toward others, and due consideration for their feelings. Just as Latin and Greek are the roots from which spring most of the modern languages of Europe, so are these sentiments of kindliness and thoughtfulness the substantial basis on which rests the good-breeding of the civilized world.

Hence even from a worldly and superficial point of view the importance cannot be over-estimated, of early impressing on the plastic minds of children the right principles which shall govern their minds and manners through life.

The unfortunate Catharine Howard, fifth wife of Henry VIII., is one of the saddest instances furnished by history of the results of parental neglect. We are told that she was left to the care of servants who so corrupted her morals from her girlhood, that when the royal Bluebeard sought a pretext for cutting off her young and beautiful head, the immorality of her past life readily afforded him one.

The natural savage is visibly present in most children, and nowhere more than at the table. They dislike extremely the necessary restraints that are imposed on them there, as well as the ablutions and general "tidying processes" which precede their meals. It is usually wiser, however, for their parents to endure the inconveniences entailed by their presence at the table, except in families where competent nursery governesses are kept, who can and will train the children properly.

Some people allow the little ones to take a short recess while the table is being cleared off for dessert; this is a much better way than keeping them so long at table that they become restless, and wriggle in a very trying manner.

Do not allow your children to sit sideways, or on the edge of their chairs, or to lean back in them, or to put their elbows on the table. Neither should they be permitted to crumble up and play with their bread, or to make playthings of the stray silver or napkin rings that may be on the table. Bread should always be broken, and not cut, in eating it; but it need not be pulverized into crumbs, in the favorite fashion of childhood.

Caution your children, too, always to wipe their mouths both before and after drinking, and not to drink until they have swallowed what they may be eating. Do not let them turn up their glasses or mugs on their noses while drinking, or look at people either through the glass or over the top of it.

They must be taught how to break a potato with a fork (since it is considered ill-bred to touch that vegetable with a knife), and how to use a bread fork as a necessary accompaniment to the silver fork, and not to pack the food on the back of it with the help of the knife, which is an ugly and awkward fashion. The fork should always be carried to the mouth with the tines curving down, like a bowl; that is, in just the reverse fashion from that employed when carving.

Teach them to take their soup quietly from the side of the spoon, and not to thrust this instrument into their mouths, pointed end foremost, as if they were making an attack with it! Dessert-spoons should be substituted for full-sized table-spoons for little children to eat soup with, as the latter are uncomfortably large for them to manage.

Watch your children, and see that they do not lean over the table too far in eating, or put their spoons and forks farther into their mouths than is necessary, or leave them there too long.

One unpleasant childish trick is to fill the fork full along its whole length, and then to "eat off" part at a time, instead of putting just enough on the end of the fork to make a proper-sized mouthful; another trick is to double up a large slice of meat into a comparatively small compass and then *bolt* it; still another is to tip the plate to get the last drop of soup, or to polish it in a most surprising manner by scraping up the last possible remnant of pudding or sweetmeats instead of leaving a little "for manners."

Little separate plates — "sauce-plates" — for different vegetables are not allowable except at a boarding-house table; do not therefore accustom your children to the use of them. And I trust it will be superfluous to add that neither they nor any one else, should ever see toothpicks placed on any private table, or used anywhere save in the solitude of one's own apartment.

Children sometimes have a depraved tendency to put the

skins of baked potatoes, bits of fat, or pieces of eggshell on the table-cloth; and if you cannot induce them to place these *reliquiæ* on the sides of their plates, let them have a saucer in which to lay them.

They should be taught, as soon as they are old enough, to eat an egg from the shell, instead of taking it out into a cup or glass, since this is a point of good-breeding which many people insist upon very strongly.

They should be told, also, not to dip cake or bread into a glass of water, and by all means never to put their knives in their mouths, nor to help themselves to any dish with their own knives, forks, or spoons, nor to reach and stretch across the table after some distant goal of their ambition and appetite, nor to reach in front of another person.

I know one little girl three years of age who is so well trained that she will not help herself from any dish passed to her by the servant unless it is handed *secundum artem*, on the left side! Indeed, very little children, after they have once been trained to hold the spoon and fork properly, etc., commit fewer breaches of etiquette than their older brethren and sisters; hence the importance of watching them carefully at the table, and checking any bad tendencies as fast as these may arise.

Picking out the largest piece of cake or the under slice of toast, or taking first one biscuit from the plate and then putting that back to exchange it for another, are familiar instances of childish "bad manners."

Poor little souls! What a long indictment I have made out against them, and of how many terrific misdemeanors do they stand charged!

Far be it from me to say anything that shall make the lot of any little one harsh or uncomfortable! If children stand in need of constant correction, we their parents need also a constant lesson of patience lest we hurt their feelings by querulous fault-finding, or wound their pride by setting them right when there is company present.

But if children see their parents and elders always careful to observe the rules of good manners, and if their little careless or greedy tricks are checked in the very beginning, the task of setting them right will be a comparatively easy one.

Children are extremely imitative; and if they see others hand the dishes politely, instead of shoving them along the table, and lay their knives and forks properly on the plate side by side, with the handles together, instead of sprawled about, so that the servant will be apt to drop them when she removes the dishes in clearing off the table, why, the children will be very apt to pay attention to these little points themselves.

Do not use expressions at table which are now thought extremely inelegant, whatever their former status may have been, in the constantly varying language of polite society. Thus, never ask any one to "dish out" the food.   "Will you be kind enough," or "Will you please help to the berries?" is the proper phrase.

The old rule was to help children after the grown people, and the youngest child last; but a more modern and humane way is to help little children first, if they are present at table. Girls should be helped before boys, just as ladies should invariably be served before gentlemen.   Thus all the ladies of the house should be helped before any of the gentlemen are served, even if among the latter there may be some distinguished guest.

While children should be accustomed to great punctuality at meals, they should not be allowed to hurry and annoy their elders by their own impatience and desire to get through.   Children who are of this impatient turn of mind sometimes make every one else uncomfortable through an entire meal, constantly complaining that they shall be late to school, or that they will have no time left for play, etc. They tip their chairs, jump up and down on their seats, brandish their napkins, and lament the time that is lost in removing the crumbs, — all to the great annoyance of every one else at table.

It is certainly a breach of etiquette to ask what kind of dessert there is to be, before it appears on the table ; but it is one that is often forgiven to children, as it is hard for them to sit for a long time and then see some dish appear that they especially dislike.

While children should be brought up for the most part on plain, substantial food, they ought also to be taught as they grow older to eat different kinds of food, and to overcome the prejudices of extreme youth against tomatoes and other vegetables, oysters, etc. It is a small misfortune in this life not to be able to eat what other people do ; not only does it make the fastidious person uncomfortable, but it grieves or mortifies his hosts to find that they have provided nothing that he can eat.

Of course a thoroughly well-bred person will make no complaints under these circumstances, or allude in any way to his dislike of the food before him ; he will be content with something else that is on the table, or console himself with the next course.

Children should be especially cautioned, when they are about to dine away from home, not to ask for what is not upon the table, like the Southern children who cried out in amazement, "Where is *the* rice ?" — a dish to which they had always been accustomed at home ; or like those other very exact infants who asked, " Is this home-made sponge-cake, or baker's, — because we are not allowed to eat baker's," etc. Of course a considerate hostess who entertains children will inquire carefully about their tastes, and what they are allowed to eat at home.

Children are usually extremely fond of fruit, and they should be taught how to prepare and eat the different kinds, and above all, never to spit the seeds and stones out, but to remove them quietly and carefully with the thumb and fingers, or with the fork.   Oranges are very difficult for young people to manage, and it is well to have some older person peel them and divide them into pegs, which is the best way for children to eat them.   Grown people who are skilful have various pretty ways of cutting up this very juicy fruit; but many persons not thus dexterous avoid eating oranges in public.   English people often pare them with a spoon.

A steel knife should never be used with fruit of any sort, for the very good reason that the acid in the juice stains the steel, giving it an unpleasant appearance, as well as imparting an unpleasant taste to the fruit.

All fruit requires great nicety of management in order that the person eating it may not make himself disagreeable to his neighbors.   Thus, one who is delicate in his way of eating may very properly eat apples or pears with his fingers after he has nicely peeled and quartered them.   But for many people it is safer to eat these fruits with a fork, especially in the case of a very juicy pear.

The first rule at the table is not to do anything that is unpleasant.   Hence it is better to use a fork, even if it may seem affected to do so, rather than to use the fingers and be disagreeable.   With very juicy fruits a fork is necessary in order that the fingers may not become soiled.   Thus a pineapple requires a knife and fork both.   Bananas should be peeled and sliced with a knife and eaten with a fork.

Children should also be taught the use of the finger-bowl; that is, to dip the tips of their fingers in it nicely, and to pass the fingers thus moistened across the mouth, then wiping both the mouth and fingers delicately on the napkin, — a fruit napkin, if one has been provided.

One childish trick I had nearly forgotten to enumerate, — that of eating or drinking from one hand while passing a dish or plate with the other. This should never be done ; the child should put down its glass or fork, or whatever it holds in its hand, before attempting to pass anything. Indeed, where the servants who wait are efficient, there is little need of the handing of dishes by those who are sitting at table.

Children must not be allowed to dip bread in any sauce that may be on their plates, nor to drain off a goblet at a single draught. This is a favorite expression in romance, but is not considered to be in "good form" at the present day. Children like to do it, and then gasp for breath — a natural but unpleasant result — afterward. Some of them, also, need to be cautioned against speaking when their mouths are full, keeping their mouths open when they are eating, bolting their food, etc.

Many of them like to read at table ; but this is a most unsocial habit, and is also bad for the digestion, in the opinion of some doctors. If there is any reading at all at a meal, it should be reading aloud, — a custom at the table of that noble and learned man, Sir Thomas More.

But our Sybaritic age does not favor any form of instruction at meals, unless of the mild and doubtful kind which is shed upon us in after-dinner speeches. The elder Pliny not only read at his meals, but when he was going along in the streets ; indeed, reading would appear to have been his normal condition when he was awake.

A pitcher should be handed with the handle toward the person to whom it is passed. Spoons and forks should be held by the middle, and knives by the lower part of the shaft, the handles always turned toward the recipient.

Should children be allowed to talk at the table ? Yes, and no. It is cruel to follow the rules of our ancestors and expect the little ones to preserve perfect silence through a long meal. On the other hand, children's tongues are dangerous gear to set in motion, and should never be allowed to gain full headway at the table, especially if any guests are present. Children should never be allowed to appear at a dinner-party, unless the occasion is a very friendly and informal one. Even then it is better to place them at a side-table.

If they are allowed to talk at all they must be cautioned not to do so while they are eating, not to interrupt other people, not to make personal remarks about any one at the table, and not to argue or find fault.

It seems to me that the theme, or main and initiative part of the conversation, should be left to the "grown-ups;" while the younger members of the family may strike in occasionally with a "piano" accompaniment, or some variations of moderate length only.

CHAPTER XII.

LUNCHEONS.

A DINNER-PARTY has become in these days such an elaborate and formal affair that the timid and modest entertainer, or one who shrinks from ceremony, no longer invites people to dine with him. An invitation to dinner seems such a solemn thing, even if you protest and declare that the dinner will be strictly *en famille!* The word "dinner" implies of necessity a certain degree of formality; "luncheon," on the other hand, may imply anything or nothing; it is a delightfully elastic meal — and name, and includes every sort of repast, from a bowl of bread and milk to a grand banquet of seventeen courses!

If your friend lunches with you and finds everything on a simple and unpretending scale, he may still imagine that at your dinner-table all is very different. But if you are "found wanting" in the preparations for your dinner, then indeed have you given away your last stronghold; beyond this can no imagination go.

To avoid this unhappy result many people invite their friends to take luncheon, or "stout tea," and you go and eat what is virtually a dinner in all but the name.

Between a formal lunch-party and a dinner there is really very little difference. Bouillon is usually served in cups, instead of soup in soup-plates, at luncheon. When the guests enter the dining-room they find these cups already filled, and set at each place on a plate.

Tea and coffee, if served at all, are handed around in the dining-room, and never in the drawing-room, as they often are at a dinner-party. Menu-cards should never be used at luncheon; indeed, many people consider them as inelegant, and declare that they are only in place on public occasions or at stag parties. At a lunch only a few wines are given, and the courses are rather less substantial in character than at a dinner. But where the occasion is a ceremonious one, the table is set very much as it would be for a dinner-party — minus the lights; and even these are not wanting at some luncheons. There is the same profusion of flowers, silver, glass, and china ware, and the dishes are all served from the sideboard and handed around by the servants.

The guests go into the dining-room separately instead of arm-in-arm, — the ladies going first, and the gentlemen following them. The ladies' toilets, though sometimes elaborate, are never such as are worn at dinner or in the evening. Often there is a great variety of dress on these occasions, some ladies wearing very elegant reception dresses, others appearing in tailor-made street costumes. Bonnets are usually worn, but gloves are of course removed before sitting down to table. Gentlemen appear in morning dress, if they appear at all; but most lunch-parties in America are given for ladies alone. Sometimes, where quite a number of guests are present, many little tables are used, three or four guests sitting at each; or again, at a very large lunch, no one sits at table, the refreshments being handed around in the dining-room.

Among the very pleasantest lunches are the informal familiar occasions where six or eight friends meet together and enjoy a plain but substantial meal spiced with plenty of bright and witty talk. If a suburban friend or a gentleman of leisure accidentally arrives, he is warmly welcomed to the elastic meal, and many a charitable project, many a pleasant excursion or summer trip, is planned and arranged in this leisure moment of a busy day.　In short, lunch-time is the kaleidoscopic part of the twenty-four hours; the combinations that then arise charm us, because they are unforeseen. Old friends who have not met for years, perhaps, and busy people with "just a moment" to spare, all may meet at this enchanted hour, — meet and part as bubbles do, the bright prismatic colors of the rainbow flashing for a moment in their friendly talk; and then, presto! all is silence.　One guest has gone to a concert, another to a committee meeting, a third to her studio, and a fourth to offer up the constantly-recurring sacrifice of her time demanded by that insatiable Moloch, Family Shopping!

For such a lunch-table as I have just described, a great latitude in the matter of the bill of fare is allowable, though meat in some form, or soup, should certainly be found upon it.　Cold meats and salads are always appropriate, but most people prefer some hot dishes even at lunch.　Fried oysters, croquettes, French chops, fish, even a plain beefsteak or a dish of minced meat, if nicely cooked and served, may be placed on the lunch-table.

Chocolate is a favorite beverage with many people, and is more suitable for the middle of the day than for the evening, being a rather heavy and not very digestible form of food.

The plates should be changed for dessert, and for each course where there are several courses.

In England it is quite customary at informal luncheons for the servants to leave the dining-room after they have helped the guests to the joint (which is an inevitable feature of English luncheons) and handed around the vegetables and the wine, leaving the host and hostess to help to the entrées, where there are any, and to the sweets.　The same informality is allowable in this country; but in most American houses a hostess prefers to have the assistance of a servant, unless at a very simple lunch.　It is to be feared that we are lazier about waiting upon ourselves than our English brethren; and we also dislike less than they do the presence of servants at table, and the restraint that it entails.

The usual cover for lunch consists of two knives, two forks, one or two spoons, a water-goblet, and if wine is given, two wine-glasses, — one for sherry and one for claret. The bread is folded in the napkin, as at dinner. With bouillon, a large teaspoon is provided. Where the lunch is a very elaborate one, three knives and forks may be set at each place, or two knives and three forks, a fork for raw oysters also, etc.

According to English custom, tea and coffee are not given at luncheon, wine taking their place. But in America we cannot do without our tea and coffee even when wine is served. As we have no leisure class of men to stay at home and take lunch with us, it has become quite a feminine meal, and American ladies do not care much for wine, except possibly for champagne.

At an informal occasion the hostess pours out the tea and coffee; at a formal one, they are passed around on a waiter by the servant, two or three cups at a time, a second servant following with cream and sugar, also on a salver. The coffee must be served as it would be after dinner; that is, strong black coffee (*café noir*) in small cups, accompanied with tiny coffee-spoons. Strict etiquette forbids the use of milk with this beverage in its after-dinner form; but although Americans dearly love to copy foreign etiquette, they also love to be comfortable and to make other people so; hence the presence of the cream-jug is connived at by many hostesses. It is not necessary to give both tea and coffee at luncheon; either one may be given alone, or chocolate may be substituted for them both. Coffee is usually preferred to tea, especially by young people.

The wine may be set on table in decanters, — either sherry or claret, or both. Light sparkling wines are sometimes pre-

8

ferred for luncheon, or champagne, where the occasion is a formal one.

In setting the table the fruit and the dessert are often placed on it, and the meats either served from a side-table or set before the lady of the house, who helps her guests. With this arrangement the vegetables are handed from the buffet. In England finger-bowls are not used at luncheon; with us they often are, and are set on table just as they would be at dinner.

At elegant lunch-parties the service is usually *à la Russe*, and each lady finds a bouquet of flowers or some pretty painted trifle or other favor beside her plate. It is not usual to remain very long after luncheon, as the hostess may have other engagements for the afternoon; half an hour is long enough to stay unless where music is given, or unless in the case of intimate friends, who are privileged to linger.

What is the difference between lunch and luncheon? Just about as much as between tweedledum and tweedledee. The English call the meal luncheon, and we are beginning to do the same thing in this country. Some people consider it very affected to speak of the meal otherwise than as "lunch" or a "lunch-party;" but these are rather conservative individuals. According to present use in this country "lunch" and "luncheon" are practically synonymous; the terms "a ladies' lunch," "lunch-party" may be thought more euphonious than "a ladies' luncheon," etc., and are certainly very often used.

Lunch affords a good opportunity for housekeeper and cook to display their ingenuity, many excellent dishes suitable for this meal being in one form or another *réchauffés* from the previous day's dinner. At the family lunch-table many little odds and ends can be used which would be unsuitable for any more formal meal, but which fill up the gaps very conveniently at this delightfully unceremonious repast.

Invitations for lunch are formal or informal according to the nature of the occasion. They are usually written in the first person, or even given verbally, but are sometimes engraved for a very ceremonious entertainment. They should be answered promptly where one has reason to suppose the lunch will be a "sit down" affair; since the hostess ought to know which of her guests are coming, although it will not make so much difference in her arrangements as in the case of a dinner. In the same way a little more indulgence is shown to late comers at luncheon; though, as has been said above, much depends upon whether the occasion is to be a ceremonious one. If any unforeseen occurrence should prevent a guest from attending a formal luncheon, she should send her hostess word at once, that her place may if possible be filled.

Those who follow English customs closely never permit a butler (or head-waiter) to wear full dress when waiting at a lunch-party, even if it be of a very formal character. "Dark morning costume" is the correct dress for a butler until the magic hour for dinner arrives; he may wear dark but not black trousers, a black coat, and black necktie. Where two men-servants wait on table the second wears livery, unless the head of the house disapproves of the costume on principle.

Gentlemen sometimes ask whether ladies' lunches are not very tame and tiresome; very dull affairs, in short, without the great masculine element to give them tone. Alas for the vanity of men! How sad it is that they can *never* know (unless they hide themselves in the wine-cooler or behind the buffet) what a jolly time women can have together, or how fast feminine tongues can wag when unrestricted by the presence of lords and masters!

There is another great pleasure that ladies derive from these feminine lunches apart from the never-ending delight of unremitting conversation. This is the gratification of the æsthetic taste, with a hundred dainty devices and delicate articles of food whose beauty and value would be thrown away on the coarser masculine mind and palate.

Where but at a ladies' lunch or a fairy revel would you expect to find a course of calla lilies, each lady having on her plate one of these white blossoms with a few early strawberries tucked away in its delicate cup? Where else would you find your sherbet lying cold at the heart of a "truly" tulip, or frozen in the form of a candle and candlestick, with real wick burning at the end, a dainty shade surmounting the whole? Would you or could you reasonably expect, at any other meal, to find your rolls tied up with ribbon, and green (paper) frogs hopping about on your plate under the shade of most unpleasantly realistic ice-cream toadstools?

We hope not; the mania for blending is all very well, but some things do not mingle, and it is useless trying to make them do so. Ribbons are lovely in themselves, and for many centuries have appealed direct to the feminine heart; but why should they be mingled with our food? What possible connection can there be between ribbons and bread? It would look perfectly ridiculous to see the family loaf adorned with a wide ribbon bow on its broad brow; and why does not little bread look just as absurd garnished with narrow ribbon?

How pleasant were the old times when we could eat out of china, when we thought plates were good enough for us, and did not consider it necessary to take our food out of pasteboard boxes, silken bags, and paper cups, nor to have stationery and haberdashery hopelessly mixed up with our viands! Ribbon is now the serpent whose trail is over all. If I found it in my soup, I should not murmur at the all-pervading decrees of Decorative Art, but should meekly draw it out as an article not calculated to assist digestion.

Despite these little incongruities and fanciful extravagances, there is much to admire in and on the lunch-table of to-day. The table-cloth, to begin with, is a poem in linen, — a poem, alas ! which, with its elaborate drawn-work and wondrous lace-like effects, may have cost some poor woman her eyesight. The color which a stern good taste forbids in a dinner-cloth is considered quite allowable in a lunch-cloth. The handsomest ones are white, however, with a dash of color here and there. A beautiful set of table linen which sold recently for the moderate sum of fifty dollars, showed a bunch of grapes worked solid in fine gold-colored silk at each corner of the cloth ; this was bordered with elaborate drawn-work, finished with knotted white fringe. The large doilies, six in number, matched the cloth, save that the design was made smaller. The solid masses of golden berries clustered at each corner of the table and nestled beside the plate of each guest gave a rich golden effect that reminded the beholder of King Midas's famous meal. But the reminder was a delicate and artistic one, — a shadowy likeness in soft silk, not a bold copy in gross metal.

At some ladies' lunches one must begin before the table-cloth, because the ceremonies of ornamentation commence in the dressing-room. Here the ladies find enormous cards, each one decorated with a bow of different-colored satin ribbon (the inevitable serpent), pink, blue, orange, lilac, etc., while the legend beneath sets forth that the ladies whose names are written on the orange card will please sit at the orange table, and so on, through all the colors.

At the lunch-party of which I am now writing, assurance was made doubly sure, each lady's name being painted in gold letters on the wide streamer which flowed from her basket of flowers. The end of this ribbon was caught around the napkin so as to bring the name uppermost, thus forming a novel sort of dinner-card. The yellow ladies had golden baskets containing yellow flowers, the pink ladies had pink roses, etc. On each table was a handsome candelabrum con-

taining lighted candles of the color to match the prevailing
decoration, with shades of the same hue; smilax and delicate
flowers were wreathed about these candelabra, still maintain-
ing the harmony of color.   This dainty feast was called "a
rainbow lunch."

At a luncheon there is an excellent opportunity for the display of beautiful china, the daylight showing the beauty of
the ware to great advantage.   Where people have well-filled
china-closets, a complete change of design and color is made
for each course.   The delicacy of some of these courses is
almost exaggerated, and recalls to mind the nightingales'
tongues of ancient Rome.   If a countryman with a hearty,
healthy appetite were set down in the midst of one of these
feasts, what would he think?   Probably he would be of the
opinion that he had seen no real and actual luncheon, but
"samples" merely of several large repasts that were going on
elsewhere.   Certainly a *pâté* no larger than a silver dollar
looks like nothing but a sample of some more adequate pie,
even if the *pâté* is composed, as it usually is, of the most
rich and mysterious ingredients.

One of the new fancies is to eat off dainty little metal spits,
or skewers, each one ornamented with a butterfly by way of
a handle.   On these spits may be strung delicate morsels of
chicken liver, infinitesimal scraps of nicely browned pork, etc.
Each skewer is brought in erect, being firmly planted in a
groundwork of some æsthetic paste.

No, I am not speaking of the days of Heliogabalus, although for the moment it seemed as if I must be.   Where all
this luxury will end is hard to say.   As our people are in the
main very sensible, they will probably get tired of this extreme frippery in the course of a few years, just as they have
abandoned the Queen Anne style of architecture.   After out-
gabling gables, and indulging in a perfect frenzy of peaked
roofs, balconies, and loggias, they suddenly made the amazing

discovery that the inside of the house was the part actually lived in (at least in our climate), and that perhaps it would be well to have the dwelling-rooms large enough for comfort, instead of being chopped up into mince-meat, sacrificed for the appearance of the exterior. So Americans have soberly returned to building houses with simple outlines, and that contain large rooms, and they have hung the pumpkin, or its color, on the outer wall, to show that we still believe in the Puritans and in their favorite vegetable.

In the same way the ladies' lunches, with their twenty courses of china and glass, will no doubt subside before long as suddenly as a lofty and imposing but empty card-house tumbles to the ground. We may not perhaps return to the plain roast and boiled, the simple fare in which old George III. delighted, but rather to that safe middle path, the golden mean, which avoids all excesses alike, whether of luxury or of simplicity.

It has become the fashion now to speak of any meal taken between or after the regular meals as a luncheon. Thus sandwiches and beer, or any other light refreshments, if eaten at two o'clock in the morning, on returning from a ball, constitute a "luncheon," and not a supper.

The French *déjeûner à la fourchette* does not differ materially from what we call luncheon. It is now becoming the fashion to invite people to late breakfast, instead of to lunch ; but few of the guests would know the difference between the two meals, except from the wording of the invitation. A "French breakfast" takes place somewhat earlier than a lunch, — at twelve o'clock instead of one, for instance.

The first course usually consists of fruit, — strawberries, melons, or whatever fruit is in season. In the succeeding courses there are often various preparations of eggs, since these belong more distinctively to breakfast than to luncheon. At some houses every meal begins with a course of fruit.

CHAPTER XIII.

AFTERNOON TEAS AND RECEPTIONS.

With the ever-increasing luxury of the present day a new fashion has grown up; namely, that of giving frequent and expensive entertainments for a few people rather than large parties for society in general. Thus many ladies now give a dozen handsome lunches and dinners to repay their social obligations and entertain their friends, where fifteen or twenty years ago they would have given three or four large soirées.

There are many advantages in the new system, and many drawbacks as well. The beauty, æsthetic and gustatory, of a modern feast is not to be denied, and has been described at some length in another part of this volume. But the tendency of these comparatively small reunions is to divide people into cliques and sets, to encourage the animal within us, to make us selfish, and to do away with the larger and more catholic gatherings which have their own charm, — a charm apart from the æsthetic gratification of the senses which the modern dinner-table affords.

Let us lunch and dine, by all means, but let us also entertain in a more general way; otherwise we shall be apt to invite and be invited by the same people over and over again, excluding from our feasts the lame and halt whom the Bible bids us ask as our guests. The lame and halt, socially speaking, — who does not know them? Mr. ——, a man with the divine spark of poetry in him, is one of them. He shall write verses when his heart is touched, *œre perennius*; and his talk how full of thought, his wit how subtle and delicate! But he lives in a small old-fashioned house, and dines not, neither is he dined.

Mrs. —— is another of this fraternity. She has a large house and a sufficient income, but does not know how to entertain people, and fears to invite them lest they should be bored. Younger brothers and older sisters belong to those who are socially disabled as far as dinner-parties are concerned. A dinner-party is necessarily very limited as to the number of guests; hence, only two, or at the utmost three, can be invited out of the same family. These will usually be the most eligible members of it; the handsomest daughter and the most agreeable son will be asked over and over again; papa and mamma, if they are quiet dull people, will be "left out in the cold" altogether, unless they defend themselves by giving dull dinners of their own to those who may be counted upon to invite them in return.

Luckily there is one form of general entertainment which is still very popular, and in which even suburban lame ducks can find their account. "Afternoon teas," revived in England about twenty years ago, and imported to this country soon afterward, are certainly a most admirable institution. What if the dissipation they afford is of the mildest type? It may be mild, but it is perennial. An afternoon tea is so cheap that anybody can afford to give one, and involves so little trouble and formality that even the most timid or most lazy hostess need not shrink before the very diminutive lions it brings into her path. She need only provide tea, coffee, or chocolate, with thin slices of bread and butter or sandwiches, fancy biscuits, and cake.

Indeed, some of the pleasantest five-o'clock teas are the most informal ones, where the lady of the house has all the tea-equipage in the drawing-room, placed on a little table beside her, and where she pours out the fragrant beverage for her friends as they drop in, two or three at a time. For an occasion of this sort it would be sufficient to provide fancy biscuits or cake to accompany the tea, and the invitations would be given out quite informally. They might either be verbal, or written or engraved on a lady's visiting-card; thus, —

Mrs. Tracy Trevelyan,

Fridays in January
and February.

3 Gramercy Park.

If the hostess intends to receive on that day throughout the season, "Fridays" or "Friday" would be sufficient. Where a lady gives only one or two "afternoon teas," the refreshments are on a somewhat more elaborate scale, but may still be simple if she prefers to have them so.

Many people who dine late in our large cities have five-o'clock tea served every day, and are almost always at home to friends at that hour. But what a difference is there between the reception you will meet at various houses, even where the invitations are precisely alike and the preparations for receiving guests made on just the same scale!

Some people are so formal in their very natures, that they impart frigidity to all who approach them. Your backbone begins to straighten itself up at the very aspect of the servant who opens the door, whether he is a wooden footman or one of those preternaturally prim maid-servants who seem to have caught an inward starch from long contact with their grim mistresses.

If on entering the parlor you find the furniture upholstered in blue satin of a more than usual degree of slipperiness, it will all seem part of one general plan. You will only sit on the very edge of your chair, and as you receive your tea from the hands of another frozen menial you will wonder how the tea *can* keep hot under such chilling influences!

Of course the conversation will turn upon the weather (on looking out of the window you observe that it has suddenly begun to snow), and will be extremely limited, for the guests will not be introduced to one another, and they will feel the *gêne* of their austere surroundings. The hostess is robed in satin, like her chairs, and her hair has been dressed by a hair-dresser. The solemn servant passes around *marrons glacés*, or candied rose-leaves; but how can one insult his dignity by receiving such childish trifles at his hands? None but the most candy-hardened school-girl would dare to touch the little trifling bonbon tongs which surmount the sugary heap.

Slipping away from the congealing hospitality of this house, you go to another only a few blocks distant, and the sound of merry laughter greets your ear the moment that the door opens to admit you. Within, you find yourself in a wide spacious hall, through which you pass to a *suite* of three parlors. In each an open fire gives a cheerful look to the apartment, but the farthest is the centre of attraction. Here stands the tea-table, with a pretty girl sitting at either end pouring out tea and coffee. In this room also is the hostess, handsome, cordial, hospitable. Her hair, to be sure, is gray, but her heart does not match it, — *à la Byron*. She receives every guest with a cordial grasp of the hand, and her face is so beaming with kindliness and the true spirit of hospitality that every one feels himself sincerely welcomed.

The busy hostess hardly sits still for a moment; she wishes to be sure that all her guests are amused and happy, that they are provided with tea and cake, and, what is more important, that they have some one to talk to. Perhaps she has several lions among her company of the afternoon, and she wishes to see that all have a fair chance to make the acquaintance of these distinguished visitors.

This lady does not believe in the modern theory of non-introduction, although you will find in her *salon* fashionable women and distinguished men, a brilliant and charming assembly, where every one feels at home, and accepts cordially the hostess's parting invitation to "come next time." No, she does not live in Boston, this particular hostess, though no doubt the Hub can boast of some ladies who entertain with the same cordiality and grace.

The refreshments at an afternoon tea are so few and simple that they ought without peradventure to be the very best of their kind. The tea should be properly steeped in absolutely boiling water, but never allowed to boil on the stove, and ought to be accompanied with cream, and not milk. Where a large number of guests are expected, the tea and coffee should be in urns, kept warm by alcohol lamps.

Some people have the servants hand around cups of tea and coffee on a waiter, instead of pouring out these beverages themselves; but this method takes away half the charm and air of reality of the tea-drinking. The hostess herself cannot undertake to entertain her guests and pour tea too, except where very few people are present. She can usually, however, depute the duty to a daughter of the house, or bespeak beforehand the services of some other friend.

In the time of good Queen Anne they even went so far as to grind the coffee in public when the august sovereign gave an afternoon tea.

For lo ! the board with cups and spoons is crown'd,
The berries crackle, and the mill turns round;
On shining altars of Japan they raise
The silver lamp ; the fiery spirits blaze ;
From silver spouts the grateful liquors glide,
While China's earth receives the smoking tide:
At once they gratify their scent and taste,
And frequent cups prolong the rich repast.

POPE : Rape of the Lock.

The good queen evidently liked her beverages hot ; and
the modern hostess should remember that not only the tea
and coffee but the boiled milk as well should be hot, and
not lukewarm.   Cream makes a wonderful improvement in
the flavor of both tea and coffee.

If bread and butter are provided, the bread must be of wafer-
like thinness, spread nicely with "the best of butter" and
arranged sandwich fashion, with the crusts trimmed off.   In
summer, iced tea flavored with lemon and served without
cream or milk is sometimes substituted for hot tea.   English Breakfast is now the favorite and fashionable variety of
tea, though Oolong and Japan teas still have their faithful
adherents.

The little low five-o'clock tea-tables, with their dainty embroidered cloths, are so pretty and picturesque that it seems
a thousand pities not to use them.   But they will be found
inconvenient, except on very small occasions, not only on
account of their diminutive size, but because they are so low.
A rather small table of the ordinary height, placed against
the wall, may be substituted for the regulation five-o'clock
tea-table ; at this the hostess is not obliged to sit down every
time that she pours out tea.

When cards are issued for only one or two afternoon teas,
the refreshments are usually on a more elaborate scale, and
often comprise bouillon, ice-cream, lemonade, punch, and even
oysters and salads.   The latter belong more properly to a

reception; but afternoon teas, receptions, and kettledrums melt into one another by imperceptible gradations, and the names are often used interchangeably. Strictly speaking, the five-o'clock or afternoon tea is the least formal occasion of the three, the kettledrum coming next in order, while the afternoon reception, or "at home," is the most ceremonious of them all.

For a reception the hostess usually wears a handsome demi-toilet, silk, satin, or velvet, made with a train, and cut down at the throat if the wearer chooses. But she never wears full evening dress, as this would be in very bad taste. The house is often handsomely decorated with flowers, and a dressing-room is thrown open for those ladies who may prefer to take off their outside wraps, a second room being provided for the accommodation of gentlemen. The guests may, if they choose, wear handsome reception toilets, but never remove their bonnets unless they have been previously invited to receive with the hostess. As the same people often attend several receptions, teas, etc., in the same afternoon, quite a variety of dress is worn, many ladies preferring to appear in the plain tailor-made street costumes that are now so fashionable.

Gentlemen wear morning dress on all afternoon occasions; namely, black or dark frock-coat, with high waistcoat to match, dark or gray trousers, and scarf or necktie.

They leave their overcoats, umbrellas, etc., in the hall, or in the dressing-room if one has been provided for their use. Their hats they may bring with them into the drawing-room if they prefer to do so.

For a very handsome reception the rooms are sometimes lighted by artificial light, the windows being darkened by shutters or blinds, and a band of musicians is placed behind a leafy screen where it can discourse sweet music without being seen. The hostess stands near the door, so that she can readily welcome her guests as they enter the drawing-room. People do not usually remain very long at an occasion of this sort; half an hour's stay is sufficient to meet the requirements of politeness, but this is often prolonged to an hour or more, according to whether the guest is amused or not, and to the number of friends and acquaintances whom he happens to meet.

Mrs. Abbott Barclay,

At Home

Tuesday, January eighteenth,

from four to six o'clock,

342 Beacon Street.

The above is a proper form for an invitation to a reception. The whole card may be engraved, or the invitation may be written on a visiting card. It was formerly considered proper to use figures in an invitation, for the day of the month, the hour, etc.; but the new fashion is to have all the numbers except that of the street engraved in full, as in the card given above. If the invitation is written on a visiting card, it is still allowable to use figures.

As has been said elsewhere, it is not strictly correct to put either "R. S. V. P." or "to meet Miss So and so" on an "at home" card; but it is often done now, custom and convenience sanctioning the solecism.

Mrs. Abbott Barclay,

At Home

Tuesday, January thirtieth,

from three to five o'clock,

to meet

Mrs. Jennings Smith,

342 Beacon Street.

R. S. V. P.

This card means, if it means anything, that Mrs. Barclay intends to stay at home to give *herself* the pleasure of meeting Mrs. Smith, and that your views of her conduct on this occasion are respectfully requested, as those of an impartial third person. But it is useless to sneer at the decrees of fashion. By and by some leader of the social world will invent a different form of invitation, and we shall all follow his lead like so many well-bred sheep.

Kettledrums are said to have received their name from the fact that they were originally given by the wives of officers at the headquarters of the latter, a drum making an impromptu stand for the tea-equipage.

It is more likely, however, that the name is a survival or *re*vival of the old English "drum," a word which was constantly used in Queen Anne's time and later, to describe fashionable gatherings.   Smollett says : "This is a riotous assembly of fashionable people of both sexes at a private house, consisting of some hundreds ; not unaptly styled a *drum*, from the noise and emptiness of the entertainment."

The word "kettledrum" is not often used in invitations now, though for a time it was quite the rage to call every afternoon occasion by this name.   A *kaffee-klatsch* is the newest name for afternoon tea — or rather coffee drinking.   It certainly has an admirably descriptive sound, — this title, — and conveys the idea of boundless talk, clatter of spoons, and the harmless (?) scratch of gossip better than any of its predecessors.

The following is a form often used for invitations to afternoon teas.

Mrs. Evelyn Brooks,

Friday, February sixth,
Tea at five o'clock.

37 Newbury Street.

CHAPTER XIV.

BALLS AND DANCING-PARTIES, THEIR ARRANGEMENTS, ETC.

FORMULAS for invitations to balls and dances have been already given in the chapter on Invitations. For a large ball, especially if it be given at a very gay season, when people will be apt to have numerous engagements, the invitations are sometimes sent out three or four weeks beforehand. This is notably the case in London, where the short season of gayety is crowded with social events.

In America, we have few houses that are large enough to give balls in with any comfort to the dancers. Indeed, not many of them can boast a regular ball-room; and yet Americans are extremely fond of dancing, and dance extremely well. We have therefore adopted the custom of giving private balls at public assembly-rooms; and for the dancers this is infinitely more agreeable than trying to dance in crowded parlors, where the heat and the great crowd of non-combatants destroy all the pleasure for the young people.

It is in vain that the hospitable host and hostess at a private ball throw open their mansion from top to bottom, and arrange card-tables in the hope that the elderly will be lured away from the main scene of action. They will not be; every one wants to hear the music and see the dancing, save perhaps a few flirtatious couples who wander away to deserted nooks and corners.

But in the assembly-rooms at Delmonico's in New York, or at Pierce's Hall in Boston, there is room for every one. The elders can sit in comfort, without the danger of anybody's trampling on their feet or crushing their dresses, and the dancers have a delightful floor, spacious, smooth, and not too slippery. The music, too, can be placed and heard to much better advantage than in a private house, and the terrible jam at the supper-table is measurably avoided.

Balls thus given lack a certain social element, it is true, and it is also to be feared that the young men feel their obligations to a hostess even less, if that were possible, than they do under her own roof. Some party-givers compromise matters by giving a number of small dances at their own houses, — an excellent plan, but one which has also its own disadvantages. There is a saying that "nothing makes so many enemies as giving small parties;" you cannot ask every one to them, and somebody is sure to be offended because he is left out.

The safest way, for those who can afford it, is to give one large ball or reception in the beginning of the season, invite all their friends and acquaintances, and after that to give as many small parties as they choose.

Another objection to small dances at private houses is that the mothers are often not invited. This is certainly to be regretted, especially as it is usually the very young girls — the débutantes, those who most need the counsel and protection of their mothers — who are invited to these dances. In small cities, or in good, quiet, sober-going Boston, such a custom is less dangerous than in a place like New York, where the immense foreign population has necessarily had its effect on manners and customs.

When making out a list of those to be invited to a ball, one should be extremely careful to include the names of the living only. It is very painful to receive an invitation for some dear relative who has passed away from this earth ; yet such a thing often happens. The reason for a mistake of this sort is that the hostess when about to give a ball necessarily asks many people with whom she is but slightly acquainted ; perhaps she includes her entire visiting list, or even goes beyond it.

But there are to be found in most cities a few learned individuals who make it their pleasant business to know everything about everybody. The worth of these persons is not always fully appreciated by mankind at large ; but they are invaluable in their way, and should always be consulted by the givers of balls and other festivities.

The best floors for dancing are the parquet floors that are now so fashionable. Where a house does not boast of these, the next best thing is to take up the carpets and to have the floors smoothed and planed by a carpenter, so that there shall be no danger of splinters getting into the feet of the dancers. Formerly, carpets were covered with crash, which was nailed down over them smoothly, and made quite a pleasant surface to dance upon ; but the fine lint which arose from it was found to have a very bad effect on the lungs of dancers and musicians. A favorite player of dance music in New York died a few years ago of consumption, caused by constantly inhaling this lint ; and the use of crash has now been abandoned in a great measure because it has proved so unwholesome.

Plenty of good music is a great desideratum for a ball. Where a band of four or five or more players is employed, it is usual to place them in a small room adjoining those used for dancing, or at the end of the hall, a screen of vines and flowers concealing the usually prosaic forms of the hired musicians.

What a pity it is that we cannot hire Apollo to play for dancing-parties ! Then we should not mind looking at him ;

and he, being a god, would not get so desperately tired as do the poor human musicians, who begin to wail out the dance music in rather lugubrious fashion toward three or four in the morning. How utterly inconsiderate and thoughtless, not to say selfish, are very young people! To them the fatigue of a fat, elderly German musician is incomprehensible; indeed, they cannot understand that he should even want to stop playing long enough to eat his supper.

It is lucky for the rest of the world that we can only be young once. Youth is a glorious period, but how it makes every one else suffer! Rapt in delightful roseate visions, the young man treads on air, and yet at the same time he manages somehow to crush all the gouty toes that are anywhere near him!

For a ball, all the appointments must be very handsome; there must be a first-class supper as well as good music, good floors, and plenty of illumination. Usually a wealth of floral decoration is an important feature of a modern ball-room; people turn their city mansions into temporary greenhouses, and waving palms, with every variety of potted plants and choice flowers, make a veritable Eden for the time being.

Where a ball is given in a public hall or a theatre, rich hangings and handsome rugs, with pseudo-old furniture and bric-à-brac, are disposed in such a way as to give the effect of a house as far as possible; for if we don't worship the Lares and Penates of home in this age, we do worship the idol bric-à-brac.

In a private house most of the furniture is necessarily removed from the ball-rooms to make room for the dancers; but a fringe of chairs and sofas should be left for the dowagers, who cannot be expected to stand during a whole evening. In England, people hire "rout-seats with velvet or damask cushions" for so much a foot; but in this country we hire only chairs for the german or cotillon, true to our principle of looking out for the comfort of the young people, and letting the elders look out for themselves. Paterfamilias must not forget to provide these seats for the german, which play an important part in the evening's entertainment. Fifty years ago the cotillon was danced without seats in New York; but we have changed all that.

Supper may be served continuously during the evening, or it may take place at a stated hour, — twelve or one o'clock, for instance. If the latter plan is adopted, it is advisable to have punch, bouillon, and other light refreshments placed where they will be easily accessible throughout the evening. Bouillon and ices are sometimes handed among the company at intervals. Those who dance the german will need a second supper; or, if that is not provided, bouillon and ices should be passed to them.

Oysters, — fried, creamed, escaloped, and raw, — salads, croquettes, cold salmon served whole and handsomely ornamented, boned turkey, terrapin, birds, ices of the most expensive forms and varieties, — such as frozen pudding, bombe glacée, café mousse, etc., — wine jellies and charlotte russe, fresh and candied fruits, bonbons, tea and coffee, and endless quantities of cake, are found on the supper-tables. Champagne and other wines are usually provided; and alas! it is sometimes wiser for ladies not to visit the supper-table very late in the evening, unless they wish to run the risk of meeting there young men who have drunk more than is good for them.

The quantity of silver plate, gold spoons, etc., displayed by some rich families on these occasions is very great, and detectives in evening dress are sometimes employed to watch the supper-table. Other entertainers do not use all their best plate and china at a crowded ball, but hire their supplies from the confectioner, thus giving themselves greater ease of mind than they could possibly have, were so much of their worldly wealth exposed to loss or destruction.

It is the rule that a hostess shall not be more handsomely attired than her guests, because if any one happens to be simply dressed the hostess thus keeps her in countenance as it were. But for a ball this rule does not hold. Here it is expected that every one will be *en grande toilette*, and the hostess therefore wears her handsomest robes, her most beautiful jewelry. Fashions in dress of course vary constantly; but it is an invariable rule that débutantes and very young girls should wear jewelry sparingly. If a young girl owns, for instance, a pair of large and valuable diamond earrings, she does better not to wear them until she has been in society for several years.

Young girls should always choose white, or light, delicate colors for ball costumes, and as a rule, soft transparent materials, such as tulle, mull, India muslin, etc.; it will be time enough to wear rich heavy brocades, silks, and dark velvets, when they shall have attained more mature years. Some young girls prefer silken materials for ball dresses because they are less perishable. Rich laces should be reserved for elder or married ladies; Valenciennes and the thousand and one pretty, cheap laces now in vogue are suitable for girls, but deep flounces, aprons, etc., of point lace are not appropriate for them.

Débutantes are often ambitious of wearing costumes that are altogether unsuited to their years. They do not understand that it is "better form" for them to dress youthfully; indeed, they are often ashamed of being so young, and try to hide their greatest charms, — youth and freshness! With such girls, mothers should exercise a proper degree of firmness on the subject of clothes, and in two or three years their daughters will thank them for it.

In this country dressing-rooms are always provided for balls, parties, etc., — one for ladies and one for gentlemen. It seems to us quite extraordinary that in London such a provision is often omitted, and a lady must put the last touches to her toilette before leaving her carriage.

In the lady's dressing-room, attendants should be in waiting to help the guests take off their cloaks, remove their overshoes for them, etc.; and one attendant at least should stay there all the evening, since young ladies are liable at any moment to need a ruffle mended or to have some other damage to their dresses repaired. The foot of man makes wondrous havoc with the light draperies of a ball-dress; and the Countess * * * gravely informs her readers that gentlemen should not wear spurs in a ball-room!

Where there are a great number of people present, it is well to have the cloak bundles numbered, each lady having a duplicate number in her pocket. At a public ball this should always be done. There have been some dreadful times at the White House through carelessness in this particular; and after General Grant's Inauguration Ball, people grew so desperate with long and vain hunting for their wraps, that many went home hatless and coatless in the night air like so many Cinderellas.

In the street, an awning overhead and a carpet on the steps and sidewalk should be provided for the comfort of the guests, and a policeman hired for the occasion; or a private servant should open the doors of the carriages and help the ladies out. This functionary should also number the carriages, giving one number to the driver and the duplicate to the occupants of the carriage, so as to simplify as far as possible the tedious process of finding one's carriage when the party is over. A servant should also be stationed at the door, so that the guests may be admitted without delay.

CHAPTER XV.

ETIQUETTE OF THE BALL-ROOM.

A LADY does not now enter a *salon* leaning on the arm of her husband or other escort. With the growing independence of women, this old custom is falling into desuetude. The lady enters first, the gentleman following her; if there are several ladies, the eldest goes first, mothers taking precedence of their daughters in this country, according to the Puritanical notion of respect for parents which we still believe in — in a few instances. In Europe the daughter who has married a man of higher rank than her mother has, takes precedence of her parent on all occasions, the latter following meekly in the rear.

The hostess at a ball does not usually shake hands with her guests, but makes them a sweeping courtesy instead. Where she is supported by several daughters or friends who receive with her, it is rather a severe ordeal for a bashful guest to go up and receive a perfect broadside of courtesies; nevertheless it must be done as soon as one enters the ball-room. Even if one comes late and the hostess has left her post, the first duty is to hunt her up, and the next, for a gentleman, is to shake hands with his host. If he has been invited through some friend and is unacquainted with his hosts, he should get his friend to present him; he should also ask to be presented to the young ladies of the house, and if he is a polite young man, he will ask to have the pleasure of dancing with them.

For the cotillon it is now usual to engage a partner before the day of the ball, and to send her a bouquet. This is a very expensive custom for young men, and one that many of them would be glad to dispense with, because they cannot afford it. What a boon it would be to society if some leading belle should take a hint from the present fashions in funeral arrangements, and announce to her adorers that "no flowers" would be received! Her popularity would increase fifty per cent, not only with the young men but with their fond parents, who groan in spirit over the immense florist's bills they are called upon to pay.

When asking a young lady to dance, be sure to dò so in a polite way. "May I have the pleasure of dancing the cotillon with you?" Never say, "Are you engaged for such and such a dance?" This is extremely rude, as it may oblige the lady to confess that she has not been asked for that dance. Yet some young men use this formula who ought to know better; they wish to save themselves the mortification of a refusal, and thrust upon a lady the position they do not wish to assume themselves.

That young ladies should never ask gentlemen to dance with them, is a self-evident proposition; nevertheless they sometimes do it, or young men say that they do. When a dance and the promenade which usually succeeds it are over, a gentleman should always ask his partner with whom he shall leave her, unless he already knows where her mother or other chaperone is sitting. No one should feel obliged to go on dancing or talking forever with the same person, and a young lady should be very careful not to detain a partner so that he will feel any awkwardness in excusing himself.

Mr. Howells has drawn a vivid picture, in his "Indian

Summer," of the dreadful consequences which ensue when a man endeavors to dance the Lancers' quadrille without knowing how; but infinitely more terrible are the results when any one endeavors to trifle with waltzing, — a most deadly and dangerous science, with which the unskilled should no more think of meddling than they would of handling dynamite.

In the first place, the waltz step is changed every few years; therefore even a person who could dance very well according to the old method should not venture upon the new one until he has tried it in private. Some of the very best dancers, however, are those who were wretchedly awkward in the beginning; and as we read about Demosthenes and the pebbles he carried in his mouth, so ball-room stories are whispered about the prowess of certain carpet-knights, — how this one practised with a chair till he mastered the Boston, how that one's pretty cousin drilled him until he acquired his present style, etc.

There are professional people whose special business it is to teach young men the current ball-room step; and even better than these, where their assistance can be secured, are graceful feminine friends who can dance with the neophyte and instruct him at the same time.

A gentleman should always make a bow to a lady when asking her to dance, and both of them should bow and say "Thank you" when the dance is over.

Despite the intricacies of the german, any one who is tolerably clear-headed and observant is safe in undertaking to dance it, provided he is a good waltzer. Those who are not familiar with the figures, however, should take their places near the foot, where they will have a good opportunity of watching others go through the various evolutions of the dance, before their own turn comes. The part of leader of the german is a very responsible one, and like all other positions of eminence, it involves arduous duties as well as honor and glory. No one should undertake it who is not thoroughly familiar with the dance.

One of its rules is that people shall not dance save in their turn; and although this rule is occasionally violated, still, where the leader goes around and requests the gentlemen "not to take turns," it is only polite to refrain from doing so. For a ball, a hostess needs to provide several sets of german favors, including a bouquet for each lady in the bouquet figure.

According to European customs any gentleman in the room may ask a lady to dance whether he has been introduced to her or not; and it is customary for her to accept the invitation, unless she is already engaged for the dance. After it is over, her partner leaves her at her place, with a bow, and their acquaintance, if such it can be called, ends with the dance.

In this country a gentleman does not ask a lady to dance unless he has first been presented to her. He should get the hostess or some mutual acquaintance to ask the lady if she is willing to have Mr. —— introduced to her. Mr. —— should in the mean time not stand so near that he will hear the lady's answer, for she may have her own reasons for not desiring to make his acquaintance.

Our young men have an odious and selfish habit of not dancing if they cannot secure just the partners they want, and of standing, a black-coated and dismal group, like so many crows, around the doorway. This is extremely impolite to their hostess as well as to such ladies as are not dancing. A well-bred young man should ask his hostess to present him to a partner, and should be polite in every way toward her guests.

Young ladies should not be too much troubled if they are not asked to dance as often as they would like, and above all they should never look hurt or vexed. A good-natured, happy-looking wall-flower often turns into a butterfly and finds her wings. Girls who are bright and amiable sometimes begin with receiving very little attention at parties, and end with being favorites after their agreeable qualities become known, "especially if they dance well." Some young ladies never are willing to be seen in a ball-room after the cotillon has begun, unless they have a partner. They either go home or sit in the dressing-room. Others remain in the ball-room looking very discontented, and refuse to go out in the german if they are invited to do so, which is obviously very foolish.

A young lady is much more apt to have dancing partners throughout the season if a ball has been given for her. Gratitude or some kindred emotion induces the young men to dance with her rather than with the daughters of a mother who never entertains.

In the german it is quite permissible for a lady to take out a gentleman whom she does not know, — because she must take out some one, according to the laws of the dance ; and if she knows very few of the gentlemen who are dancing, she must either take out a stranger or else call upon her friends or acquaintances over and over again. It is polite for a young man who has thus been favored, to ask for an introduction to the young lady with whom he has danced ; but in our Eastern cities, young men are in such a *powerful minority* that they do pretty much as they please.

Young ladies should be very careful not to forget their dancing engagements, and should never refuse one gentleman and then dance with another. A young lady may refuse on the plea that she is not going to dance that particular dance, but she must then be careful to sit through it. Where a young man has engaged himself to two young ladies for the same dance, he is in an awkward predicament indeed, from his own carelessness. He can only confess his fault, procure another partner for one or both of the ladies, and by subsequent attentions show that he is sorry for his blunder.

A hostess should endeavor to see that all her guests are provided with partners for dancing, especially for the cotillon. She usually has one or two young men who are friends of the family to help her in this matter, or she has ladies who receive with her, and thus enable her to slip away occasionally and attend to her guests. But where young men flatly refuse to dance, what can the hostess do? It seems incredible that they should be so rude; the fact remains that they are.

To strangers from another city special attention should always be paid. It has been said that strangers in Boston society always have either a very delightful or a very dull time. When supper is announced the host leads the way, taking in with him the most distinguished lady present; the hostess follows last, in order to see that all her guests are properly attended to. A gentleman takes the lady in to supper with whom he is talking when it is announced, unless he has made a previous engagement to take in some one else. In this last case he must be on the alert, and excuse himself to the lady he is with, as soon as the first movement toward the supper-table begins; otherwise he plays the part of dog in the manger, and prevents other gentlemen from escorting her to the supper-room. If a young man happens to be talking to a young lady and her chaperone when supper is announced, he should offer his arm to the latter, who should accept it, the young lady following close behind them or walking beside her mother.

A gentleman may always ask a lady if he can bring her some refreshment, even where she is a stranger to him. In fact, it would be very ill-bred for a gentleman not to do so, where he noticed in the ball-room or in the supper-room ladies to whose wants no one was attending. But he cannot with propriety enter into conversation with a stranger whom he has thus obliged. He merely bows and withdraws. Some young men attend to their own wants at the supper-table more faithfully than to their partner's, returning at long intervals to see if the ladies want anything more. But if greediness is unpleasant in a man, it is much less pardonable in a woman, and a young lady should be careful not to make too many demands at the supper-table lest she earn the reputation of caring too much about what she eats. It is wiser as well as more economical for the hostess to have hired waiters attend to helping her guests unless she has a large corps of servants of her own. Men whose business it is to wait are much more efficient and much more careful than young gentlemen; the latter are often very heedless, upsetting dishes and plates, and very wasteful, helping people to more than they can possibly eat.

It is not necessary to take leave of a hostess at a ball, especially if one leaves early and before the affair begins to break up.

Young ladies should have a little mercy on their unfortunate mothers and partners, and not stay too late at balls. The mammas find it dreary work indeed sitting up into the small hours ; and the young men, many of whom are obliged to go to business next day, of course cannot leave until their fair partners are ready to go. Thus the young girls are really the arbiters of the ball-room, and through thoughtlessness rather than selfishness they often make other people endure extreme fatigue. Indeed, the late hours and the wretched feeling of weariness incident to rising early after dancing nearly all night, are responsible for many of the dissipated habits that young men fall into.

CHAPTER XVI.

MUSICAL PARTIES.

It is very much the fashion now, both in England and in this country, to provide some more or less intellectual feast for the entertainment of guests; and music, readings, recitations, are all in great demand. Of these, music is the chief favorite, and the easiest to procure, since almost every young lady who goes into society has some vocal or instrumental accomplishment.

A little music, even if it is not very well rendered, makes a pleasant break in the monotony of a talking party; it gives those present an opportunity to change their places, to make an end of tiresome conversations, and to begin fresh ones. So if a young lady does not sing like Patti or Nilsson, we forgive her, as long as her voice is fresh and sweet, and provided her efforts are not too ambitious. An entertainment where a little music is given, however, is a very different affair from a regular *musicale*, whether it be *matinée* or *soirée*. Where this name is used, it must not be taken in vain; and the guests will have a right to be both discontented and satirical if they hear no music worthy of the name.

It is needless to enter here into a discussion of the merits of the different schools of music. Some very delightful musicals are given where the programme consists entirely of selections from the Italian operas; though most of us would prefer a sprinkling at least of the more intellectual harmonies of the German composers. Be that as it may, the most important point is that the music should be good of its kind, and interpreted by adequate performers, amateur or professional. No one should attempt to give a *musicale* unless he has a real acquaintance with the art of music, or unless he puts the whole matter in the hands of some thoroughly competent person. A man who should make a collection of pictures without having any knowledge of the art of painting, and invite all his friends to look at his gallery, would be voted an intolerable bore. The man who inflicts on you two or three hours of musical (?) torture, through his own ignorance and ambition, is even a greater bore; because you can turn your back on the pictures, but you *can't* get away from the music unless you stop your ears, which would not be considered polite.

Where the host's purse is sufficiently long, it is much better to employ some professional musicians, or what are called "semi-professionals;" that is to say, people who sing in church-choirs, etc., and are paid for what they do, although very often they have some other business or occupation.

The amateur is sometimes a brilliant performer or a finished vocalist, but he belongs to a most uncertain species, — uncertain in more respects than one. In the first place, you can seldom count on an amateur for any special occasion, particularly if he is a singer. Great are the disappointments caused by amateurs, as any one can testify who has had much to do with them. They are not paid for their efforts, — they simply sing or play to oblige other people, — hence they do not feel themselves bound to appear if they happen to feel a little unwell, or if they hear that some superior performer is going to eclipse them. Those who sing have more to excuse them than those who play, the voice being a delicate and unreliable organ, in the care of which an amateur rarely equals a professional.

10

The second point of uncertainty about an amateur musician is as to his talents and capabilities. A man's friends will say, "Oh, So-and-so sings *delightfully*, you must have him at your concert!" when So-and-so has only a mediocre voice, with very little cultivation. There is no uniform standard by which people judge musical performance, because so many know nothing at all about the art, and praise anything that happens to please them.

But if one employs professionals the case is very different. It is comparatively easy to find out what their musical standing is, and they are much less capricious than their half-brothers the *virtuosi*. Probably they have as much vanity and ambition as the latter; but the chariot of regular work has an amazing tendency to quiet Pegasus. When he is once hitched between its shafts, business habits become second nature, and the prospect of bread and butter is even more stimulating as a daily incentive than that of fame.

If a professional musician is asked to sing or play he must always be paid for his services. Some people, who ought to know better, invite well-known singers to their houses and then request these guests to sing for the amusement of the company. This is in contravention of all the laws of etiquette, and often produces much ill-feeling. The guest does not like to refuse, because that would seem a churlish return for the hospitality he is enjoying; at the same time he feels that it is treating him shabbily to invite him in his character of a private gentleman, and then expect him to display himself in his public and professional character as an artist. He feels also that it is a mean way of forcing him to part — for nothing — with what is in reality a part of his stock in trade. We don't invite merchants to our houses and then ask them for a chest of tea or a firkin of butter; nor do we take advantage of the presence of a doctor at a festive gathering to get him to prescribe for some ailing member of the family. An artist deserves quite as much or more consideration at our hands than do these others; for he is often a stranger, and feels himself in a delicate position. Often, too, he is of a sensitive nature and easily offended.

If you wish him, then, to sing or play at your party, he should be invited to do so beforehand in a careful and delicate way. You cannot command his services as you would order a ton of coal, — that is, not if you expect to get them. Artists are "kittle folk" to deal with, and when one remembers how badly they have often been treated it is small wonder. They feel, and rightly, that the profession they have chosen is not a degrading, but an elevating one. They are not the less gentlemen for being artists, but their social position is often disputed by those who should know better.

When Dickens was asked to read before the Queen of England, he replied that if he was invited as a gentleman he would do so, but not otherwise. In an interview which he once had with the same exalted personage he showed somewhat of the spirit of a lackey, however, for he stood during their long conversation — of an hour's length or more — and then complained about it afterward. How much more dignified was the conduct of Carlyle! When he visited the royal Guelph, he calmly sat down, not out of bravado, but because it was fatiguing to stand. Her Majesty gracefully accepted the situation, sat down herself, and waved her hand to those about her as a token that they also should be seated. She felt instinctively that she had met not only her superior, but one to whom the artificial divisions of mankind into classes made absolutely no difference. He saw so keenly the real and actual divisions made by the Almighty, — the superior qualities of some men, the inferior qualities of others, — that the little petty difference in outward appearance between a puppet prince and a peasant was to him of no real importance. Dickens and Thackeray cried out constantly about snobbish-

ness, because its yoke was around their own necks. The
man of greater soul did not complain of it, because his
thoughts were ever on higher subjects.

In our own country instances are not wanting of snobbish
conduct toward artists. A Boston Anglo-maniac said to the
artist who was painting his portrait, " Why don't you marry,
Mr. ——— ? It would be an excellent plan, if you should
marry some young woman of *your own class.*"

Where a musician is new in his profession, and wishes to
be made known and advertised, he may sometimes be glad
to give his services without compensation — to those who are
disposed to help him in his life effort, to those who are in
truth his friends and patrons. But one must have an actual
claim upon an artist, or know that he is a person really
obliging, and willing to give his services to please and amuse
others, before it will be safe to call upon him to do so. A
young pianist in Boston was seriously displeased because he
was asked to play, without previous notification, before half
a dozen people after dinner.

The host at a musical party has not only many snares to
avoid in the selection of his musicians, but he must also look
out for dangers ahead when he chooses his audience. A
musicale cannot be a success unless most of the hearers are
fond of music, and of the kind which has been chosen for
the evening's entertainment. Thus, it is best not to make a
general party of such an occasion, but to invite those only
who will really enjoy your programme. If the audience is
large and mixed, it will be safer not to have a strictly classi-
cal one.

It is very rude to interrupt a musical performance by talking or laughing. Those to whom music is a bore ought
either to stay at home or to keep quiet and allow others to
enjoy it. I think it was Liszt about whom a good story
was told *apropos* of interrupting music. He had been asked

to play before Queen Victoria, and had just struck the first few chords, when her Majesty turned and spoke to some one. The Maestro was much offended, but of course could not make any remonstrance; so he vented all his wrath on the piano, and played the scales with such violence that the Queen was obliged to get up and leave the room. As soon as she had gone, Liszt quieted down and went on with the performance with perfect calmness.

In arranging a programme *ceteris paribus*, the best performer should be given the last and not the first place. The simple pieces also should come before the more elaborate and florid ones. The reasons for these rules are obvious. No ordinary artist would wish to follow one of marked superiority, as the contrast would be disadvantageous to him. The interest of an entertainment, moreover, ought to grow and culminate, instead of declining.

Mrs. Caleb Perkins

At Home

Saturday afternoon, March twenty-eighth,

from three to five o'clock.

347 Beacon Street.

Music.

is a proper form for an invitation to a musical party. Camp-chairs should be provided for the accommodation of guests, and a good piano for that of the musicians. It is unfair to ask a pianist to play on a second or third rate instrument, especially as one can always hire a Chickering or Steinway anywhere within the boundaries of civilization. The manufacturers will send a piano to any reasonable distance. If the hostess has a good piano of her own it must be put in tune just before the *musicale,* and must not be tuned too high where it is to accompany the voice, unless the lady of the house wishes to receive the maledictions of tenor and soprano on her devoted head.

A great deal of wit has been expended in making fun of people who will not sing or play without an enormous amount of urging. No doubt young ladies — and gentlemen too — do sometimes behave in a foolish and affected way, and protest they cannot sing a note, when all the time they fully mean to warble as long and as loud as the company will let them. But there are other people whose natural shyness makes it positively painful to them to perform in public. Still another class of persons hesitate to sing or play when asked to do so, because they are not accomplished musicians and can only cause disappointment by their efforts. How true to nature is the absurd story in " Happy Thoughts," where the luckless hero is fairly forced to sing a comic song which he has half forgotten, to the disgust of himself and everybody present !

Miss A., let us say, is fond of music, has a sweet voice, and sings pleasantly enough at home, where she gathers her little brothers around her at that best of all times for music, the twilight hour. But her voice is entirely uncultivated, and she does not pretend to be a musician. At Mrs. D.'s *soirée* some injudicious person says, "Miss A., I hear that you sing so charmingly; won't you let us have the pleasure of hearing you ?" Others take up the chorus, and Miss A. is much troubled, because she is placed in a false position. If the occasion is a very small and informal one she will perhaps yield to the general entreaty rather than seem disobliging; but she will certainly refuse in the first instance, giving the real reason, namely, that her voice is not cultivated, and that she never sings except at home. If the party is a large one, Miss A., if she is wise, will not allow herself to be inveigled into displaying her home talent.

A hostess should have tact enough to see whether the guest who is asked to sing or play is really unwilling to do so, or whether he is only "shamming." It is both impolite and unkind to urge people to do what they evidently prefer not to do. *Per contra*, the "second person of the second part," if he means to sing, should certainly not wait till he is asked to do so many times, but should respond to the first or second appeal. It is more polite for a hostess to repeat her invitation only once. A person may naturally hesitate at the first asking, thinking it to be only complimentary, or not wishing to appear too eager to display his accomplishments; but with the second request he should comply, or else "forever hold his peace." Generally speaking, it is better quietly to do your best, and if you have any skill at all to give the company the benefit of it. A short piece should be selected for the first one, and if the audience like it they can easily ask for more. It goes without saying that no one should sing or play, unless at the invitation of the host or hostess.

An eminent musician said to his pupil (who was an amateur), "Do not attempt to play your most difficult pieces of music in public. Play something which you have thoroughly mastered and which is comparatively simple. . . . If you have made a false note by accident, do not go back to correct it." This gentleman knew something of the fluster and excitement which so often hamper the efforts of young people unaccustomed to play before even a private public, — if one may be allowed to use such an expression.

Children should be taught to play or sing before other people almost from the beginning. They will thus acquire a habit which may be invaluable to them in later years, and will probably never experience that *mauvaise honte* which is such a torment to those who are subject to it. It goes without saying that only children with musical talent should be brought up in this way. Neither should these be allowed to play before a large number of people until they are old enough and fitted to do so. A child who is put forward as an infant prodigy becomes conceited and odious. It is easy to observe a happy medium by confining the young lady's audience to a small circle of judicious friends, who will praise the music rather than the performer, and who will encourage her without over-stimulating her vanity.

People who have large houses and who really love music often have a room specially built and adapted for it. The first requirement for a music-room is that its acoustic properties shall be good; hence all draperies are strictly banished from it, — carpet, curtains, upholstered furniture. Indeed, one well-known pianist used to insist that all ladies should come to his chamber concerts without their bonnets, — because the bonnets absorbed so much sound!

There is a beautiful music-room in one of those exquisite houses which are the glory of new Boston. The colors are quiet and subdued, the decorations all harmonious but unobtrusive, since the ornamentation in a music-room must be of secondary consideration, and must not distract the attention of the hearers from the main pleasure, — that of listening. The walls are crowned by a white frieze composed of casts from the "singing boys" of Lucca della Robbia. The floor is of polished wood, guiltless of rug or carpet. Dainty and graceful cane-chairs, imported from Italy, take the place of prosaic camp-stools; the rest of the furniture is of gilt wood, with two empire sofarettes. The inevitable grand piano stands in one corner, while near by, its graceful ancestor the harp calls up the spirit of ancient times, looking like a gentle ghost of the past when compared with its prosperous and portly grandchild the Chickering grand. A quaint old mandolin completes the trio of musical instruments. No upholstery, no drapery of any sort is to be found in this classic apartment, severe but beautiful, like the harmonious sounds which echo within its walls. But when it is filled with richly-dressed women and gay cavaliers, then our severe room is like a marble Psyche which has come to life, and the cold white frame suits to perfection the beautiful warm picture which it clasps in its setting.

CHAPTER XVII.

THE ETIQUETTE OF WEDDINGS.

THERE is no social event which is of greater or more universal interest than a wedding. The mere mention of one makes everybody feel happy and good-natured; and when the great day itself comes off, it finds all concerned in the best possible spirits, even if a few inconsiderate people will persist in crying during the ceremony.

The betrothed — afterward the married — couple are for a time hero and heroine. Every one smiles and showers favors upon them; they are the great and central attractions of the hour. Their every movement is watched with an intense interest which ordinarily attaches to those of very distinguished persons alone. The world — even the fashionable cynical world — shows its approval of the step they are about to take by smiles and nods and figurative pats upon the back.

Marriage is evidently still looked upon as a beneficent institution, notwithstanding the foolish talk of some newspapers and people, — a sort of fashionable cant of the day, — and notwithstanding all the unhappy details of Divorce Court proceedings. It is a great thing, this Anglo-Saxon respect for and admiration of marriage; but some of the results of this feeling, the domestic commotion, undue parade and expense that grow out of it, are seriously deprecated by thoughtful people.

In the first place the bride elect, feeling the importance of her position, and the serious responsibility of making arrangements which shall be in keeping with the coming great occasion and important change in her life, often wearies herself out with extensive preparations for her *trousseau* and her wedding. If her parents are rich, or in comfortable circumstances, she spends endless days in shops and in conference with the mantua-maker and milliner. Not very great fatigues these, a man may say; but they are, when carried to excess, a very great drain on a woman's nervous energy. If the bride's parents are of limited means, her ambition, I am sorry to say, will be likely to be the greater rather than the less for that circumstance. She will toil incessantly over the sewing-machine, making her own outfit, until she is worn and haggard when the wedding-day arrives; whereas it ought to find her plump, rosy, serene, and happy. This is no imaginary picture; would that it were!

Then the expense which is so often thought necessary in order to have a wedding go off in good style is very objectionable where it induces people to spend more than they can afford, as, alas! they too often do. A gentleman in New York recently committed suicide a few weeks after his daughter's marriage. His wife, who was an ambitious woman, and who had succeeded in "marrying her daughter well," made such demands upon her husband's purse for the wedding expenses, etc., that he was led to forge checks in order to give her what she asked for, and took his own life rather than meet the disgrace which he knew must soon come upon him.

Let a wedding by all means be celebrated worthily, and with all due honor of ceremony and observance, but not with too much parade nor with excessive expenditure. One bride at a fashionable church wedding not a hundred miles from Boston was so intent on the success of her wedding procession, and so angry with the street urchins who thronged about the porch for interfering with it, that she scolded them roundly then and there, to the great amusement of the lookers-on.

But what would you? Where a procession has been carefully rehearsed, it is hard to have it interfered with; though some of us are old-fashioned enough to think that such rehearsals border on the profane.

It goes without saying that the bride names the day — after the bridegroom has asked her to do so. June is the favorite month for weddings, because in our climate it is one of the most beautiful months of the whole year. May is considered unlucky, and has been ever since the time of the ancient Romans. Ovid says, "That time too was not auspicious for the marriage torches of the widow or of the virgin. She who married *then* did not long remain *a wife.*" Where Easter falls late in the spring, it is usually succeeded by many fashionable marriages, and our beautiful autumn season is also a favorite time for them. At Newport there are usually several brilliant weddings in the beginning of September, when the gay season is near its end but still in full activity. Thus the prudent bride enjoys all the summer gayety and has plenty of time for a quiet honeymoon and rest before the winter festivities begin. With these advantages is combined that of a pretty summer wedding, and one that takes place with more *éclat* than weddings in large cities, where no single event can produce any very great effect.

Society has now extended its round of amusements so widely that no time of the year — save possibly Lent — is free from gayeties of one sort or another. Lenox and Tuxedo Park fill in the gap between watering-place festivities and those of the winter season. The gay world amuses itself, in the city and in the country alternately, with a vigor and constancy that would have very much surprised our quiet ancestors. Under these circumstances it would be mere cruelty to expect a fashionable bride to waste a month in a honeymoon of tiresome quiet at some dull spot. The retirement of the honeymoon is no longer, therefore, *de rigueur*. The wedding tour is also going out of fashion, or at least is no longer considered an indispensable adjunct to the marriage ceremony. This is a move in the right direction, as it has always seemed a senseless proceeding for a bride tired with the preparations for her marriage, and worn out with the excitement attendant on the great event, to start immediately on a long and fatiguing journey.

A proper formula for invitations to a church wedding is given below. For such an occasion it is usual to send out

Mr. and Mrs. James Sinclair
request the honor of your presence
at the marriage of their daughter,
Mary Clementina,

to

Mr. Paul Winterton Adams,
at St. Paul's Church,
on Thursday morning, October eighteenth,
at one o'clock.

cards to all the friends of the families of both bride and groom. These invitations are issued in the name of the bride's father and mother, the bridegroom, of course, furnishing a carefully prepared list of those persons whom he wishes to have invited. It is now the fashion to engrave wedding invitations in plain script on plain heavy white note-paper. No device is used, unless possibly the family coat-of-arms, or crest, embossed in plain white on the paper. The envelope is entirely plain.

The cards of the bride and groom elect may also be enclosed. Where people invite their whole circle of acquaintance to the wedding, it is not necessary to send out supplementary cards afterward, announcing the event. The formula of announcement has been very much changed within a few years. Formerly one often received a card simply inscribed with the

Mr. and Mrs. James Sinclair
announce the marriage of their daughter,
Mary Spofford,
to
Mr. Paul Winterton Adams,
on Thursday morning, October eighteenth,
Trinity Church,
New York.

names, " Mr. and Mrs. Alfred Townsend." To friends of the
bride living at a distance, who perhaps had never heard of
the bridegroom, these sphinx-like announcements remained
unsolved riddles for years, unless they were, by good fortune,
accompanied by cards bearing the bride's maiden name and
that of her mother. In these days the much more sensible
and convenient custom has arisen of "telling the whole
story." (See page 158 for formula.) These announcements,
like wedding invitations, are engraved on note-paper.

All wedding cards are paid for by the bride's family, as are
all the other expenses of a wedding, with the following exceptions. The bridegroom pays the clergyman's fee, and of
course provides the wedding ring and the bride's bouquet;
he also makes the bride a present, — in accordance with his
means, — and sometimes gives the bridesmaids some article
of jewelry not of an expensive nature, or a bouquet. To the
ushers he gives scarf-pins, or some similar gift, unless the
bride should make these presents, which she sometimes does,
occasionally providing also gifts for the bridesmaids. Wedding invitations do not require any answer unless one is requested, — as in the case of a sit-down breakfast, or of a
small home wedding. Friends living at a distance acknowledge a wedding invitation by sending their visiting cards
enclosed in an envelope addressed to the bride's father and
mother, or to the person in whose name the invitations
are issued. This is the proper course to pursue, even for
those to whom the bride's family are total strangers, their
only acquaintance being with the bridegroom or his parents.
Punctilious people consider it necessary to call within ten
days after a wedding; one should certainly call as soon
after as is convenient.

Where there is to be a reception after a church wedding,
additional cards are enclosed in the same envelope with the
cards for the church.

At Home
after the ceremony,
347 Beacon Street.

The above is a proper formula to use. These are often sent only to the relatives and intimate friends of the two families, as few people are so fortunate as to have houses large enough to accommodate their whole circle of acquaintance. The bride's family, too, may not wish to incur the trouble and expense of entertaining so large a company.

No one should feel hurt at not being invited to a wedding reception unless it be a general one. Where cards are issued for a church wedding, however, they are usually sent to all the acquaintance of the bride and groom, and those who do not receive cards have a right to feel themselves slighted. Still, it must always be remembered that such a slight may be the result of an oversight and not of intention, especially where the invitations are directed, as they often are, by a hired amanuensis.

Where there is reason to believe that the church will be overcrowded, cards of admission to it are sometimes issued. They are often worded thus : —

St. Mary's Church,
Ceremony at twelve o'clock.

It seems opposed to the spirit of Christianity, to treat a church as if it were a private house and to refuse admission to all but a favored few.   But of two evils, one must choose the least ; and it would hardly be fair that the general public should so crowd the sacred building as to leave little and insufficient room for the real wedding guests.

An English authority says " the bridesmaids may be from two to twelve in number ; " but in this country they rarely if ever exceed six or eight.   They should be chosen from among the sisters and other near relatives of the bride and groom, and from the bride's intimate friends.   According to the present fashion they are often dressed in picturesque, even quaint costumes, sometimes wearing bonnets or hats, sometimes with short veils, etc.   They should always wear very light colors, or white.   It would seem superfluous to say that a bridesmaid should never be a married woman, were it not a fact that married women *have* acted in this capacity in our own far West, and perhaps elsewhere where single women are "scarcer" than they are in Massachusetts.

Groomsmen are never seen at modern weddings.   Their place is usurped by " the best man," who " supports " the bridegroom much after the fashion of a second in a peaceful duel.   He is usually an intimate friend or near relative of the groom.   His duties are to accompany the latter to church, to stand by him before and during the ceremony, to hold his hat, fee the clergyman, and to assist the ushers in presenting guests at the wedding reception.   In short, his part is exactly the opposite of that played by Captain Cuttle at the celebrated Bunsby wedding ; for he, to all outward appearance, uses his best efforts to keep up the sinking courage of the groom, and never urges the latter to run away, so far as is known.

The bridegroom wears morning dress, as do all the gentlemen at a wedding in the daytime.   Fashion now decrees

11

that a dress-suit must be worn under no circumstances before evening, — or rather before late dinner, — but it leaves the bride quite free to wear full evening dress if she pleases, which is certainly very illogical. The groom wears a frock-coat, light trousers, and gloves if he prefers to do so. But he must not wear either white gloves or a white necktie, since these belong with evening dress only. He drives to church with his best man, and waits for the bride at the altar. If he is wise in his generation, however, he will remain in the vestry until the bride's arrival, since it is an awkward and trying position for him, — that of long waiting at the chancel rail, — and brides are sometimes late.

The ushers should be at the church in good season, to see that everything is in order, and to conduct the wedding guests to their seats as fast as they arrive. They are chosen from the relatives and friends of the bride and groom. The chief usher places a ribbon or arch of flowers across the church at a distance from the altar which will include space enough for all the invited guests. The relatives of the groom are placed on the right of the altar, that is, next the bridegroom ; and the bride's relatives sit on the left of the church, that is, on the bride's left. It is important that the ushers, or at all events the chief usher, should be acquainted with most of the relatives and guests, so that they may all be seated in their right places, the near relatives sitting nearest to the altar. It is perfectly proper for an usher to ask whether a lady is a relative of the bride or groom, as he cannot be expected to know every one of the relations by sight.

The mother of the bride comes in shortly before the bridal cortége, of which she usually does not form a part. It is better, if possible, to arrange this in the vestry rather than keep the bridesmaids waiting in the vestibule for the bride, who arrives last, accompanied by her father. When all is in readiness the organ peals forth a wedding march, and the ushers advance up the aisle in pairs, followed by the brides-maids, also in pairs. Sometimes additional bridesmaids in the shape of little children picturesquely dressed, strewing flowers perhaps, follow or precede the others. Little boys dressed as pages following the bride and holding her train are one of the modern innovations. Last of all comes the bride leaning on her father's arm.

When the procession reaches the altar the ushers divide, half of them turning to the right and half to the left; the bridesmaids do the same. The bridegroom then advances, the bride being close to the altar, and taking her right hand, leads her to her position before it. Here they both kneel, — that is, if the wedding takes place in the Episcopal Church. In churches of other denominations they often do not kneel. The clergyman then proceeds to read the marriage service. When he asks the question, " Who giveth this woman to be married to this man ? " the father, who stands a little behind the bride, usually gives his consent by bowing, instead of com-ing forward and placing his daughter's hand in that of the clergyman, as was formerly the custom. Having now ful-filled his part of the ceremony, the father takes his place beside the bride's mother in the front pew.

After the clergyman has pronounced the benediction he may congratulate the newly-married pair; but he does not kiss the bride, as it was formerly the custom for him to do. At the present day a wedding ring is used in almost all mar-riage services. It should not be so large as to seem vulgar or exaggerated, and is still the plain gold circlet, which seems to befit the solemn ceremony better than the richest jewel. The bride usually has the ring finger of her left-hand glove cut so that it can be readily removed, much to the relief of the first bridesmaid, who was expected in other days to pull off the whole glove, and whose efforts to do so were often embarrass-ing to all parties.

Soft music may be discoursed if the bride desires it during the marriage ceremony ; but to our thinking it sounds too much like what Artemus Ward called "dying to slow fiddling."

The organ breaks out with a triumphal peal, and the bridal pair go down the aisle arm in arm, and leave the church as quickly as possible, to escape the curious throng always so eager to catch a glimpse of them, or rather of " her." They are driven at once to the residence of the bride's parents. The rest of the bridal procession leave the church in the inverse order from that in which they entered it.

It will be seen from what has preceded that the bride stands on the bridegroom's left. She takes also his left arm when about to walk down the aisle. It is considered very "bad form" for a bride to bow or smile to any one either while entering or leaving the church ; but she is not obliged to keep her eyes upon the ground if she prefers to "look forward" instead.

The fashion of a bride's dress is so well known, and yet changes so often in its details, that it would be useless to speak of it save in general terms. The extravagance of to-day robes brides in the most costly fabrics, with veils or point lace and diamond ornaments, instead of the white silk dress, simply trimmed, and the tulle veil, that were formerly the fashion. White is so appropriate to a bride, as well as so becoming to almost all complexions, that it seems a pity every bride should not wear it, even if her dress be of simple white muslin. A tulle veil is softer and more becoming than a lace one, as well as infinitely cheaper. The lace veil is better suited, however, to certain people, especially to girls who are somewhat stout, or who have rather large heads. The extreme fulness of the tulle veil, and its dim outlines, make the wearer look larger than she really is.

Orange-blossoms are always beautiful and appropriate for a

bride, but they are often difficult to procure; hence other natural flowers often take their place in the bridal costume. Myrtle-leaves are emblematic of marriage, and are sometimes worn by brides. Garlands of artificial flowers frequently adorn a bridal robe.

In the days of good Queen Bess, brides wore their hair flowing over their shoulders. Ben Jonson says: —

> "See how she paceth forth in virgin white,
>   Like what she was, the daughter of a duke,
> And sister, darting forth a dazzling light,
>   On all that came her simplesse to rebuke !
>   Her tresses trim her back,
>   As she did lack
>   Nought of a maiden queen,
> With modesty so crowned and adoration seen."

In the Roman Catholic Church a bride is not allowed to wear a décolleté costume if the wedding takes place in church.

After the ceremony at church is over, the best man, or two of the ushers, hurry to the residence of the bride's parents, to be in readiness to receive the bride and groom.

At the wedding reception half of the bridesmaids stand near the bride and half near the groom. The ushers stay near the door of the drawing-room and escort the guests, as fast as they arrive, to the bridal party, presenting them by name, first to the bride and groom and then to the parents. It is also the ushers' duty to see that ladies who have no gentlemen with them are provided with refreshments. It is now fashionable to hold morning receptions by gas or candle light instead of by daylight.

After an hour and a half or more, the bride retires to put on her travelling-dress; usually only the intimate friends remain to see the bridal couple drive off and to wish them Godspeed. Rice and old shoes are thrown after the retreating carriage; but these missiles should not be aimed with too great accuracy, as accidents have sometimes occurred from breaking the windows or frightening the horses.

A bride does not usually dance at her own wedding, but she may join in a square dance if she wishes.

It is not usual now to show the wedding presents on the day of the marriage, as this custom was found, a few years since, to lead to a parade and display which were of very questionable taste. Sometimes the presents are privately shown to the intimate friends a few days beforehand. Wedding gifts themselves have changed in character, and the bride is no longer overwhelmed with articles of silver some of which are useful and others decidedly superfluous. There are now so many beautiful things in glass, china, bronze, etc.; so many *objets d'art* and delightful *bric-à-brac* for the buyer to choose from, that the wedding guest need be at no loss to select some suitable and charming gift, even if his means should be quite limited. Pictures, fine engravings, rare or handsomely illustrated books, mantel clocks and ornaments, lamps of artistic design, jewelry of *course*, handsome articles of furniture, such as chairs or writing-desks, — all these and many more are suitable for wedding gifts. Intimate friends and relatives often give money or silverware, or, if they like, some articles for the *trousseau*. If gifts are marked at all, it should always be with the bride's maiden name or initials.

Wedding-cake is not sent out as it used to be. It is piled up in boxes on a table at the reception, and each guest takes, let us hope, not more than one box.

Some brides prefer to be married in a travelling-dress and bonnet (usually of dark handsome silk or velvet material), and to leave at once without any reception. For a wedding of this sort cards may be issued to all the friends for the ceremony at the church, or the marriage may be celebrated very quietly, with only a few witnesses.

A wedding at home is usually more informal than a church wedding. The clergyman enters and faces the company, then the bridal pair enter together and stand facing him. An altar of flowers is sometimes arranged, behind which the clergyman stands, with a cushion or stool in front for the bridal couple to kneel on. After the ceremony is over they turn round in their places and receive the congratulations of their friends, but only those who are very near and dear are permitted to kiss the bride. The old-fashioned custom which allowed every one to do so, is now abandoned, as it deserved to be.

There are usually neither bridesmaids nor groomsmen at a home wedding. Sometimes all the guests are invited to the ceremony and sometimes relatives only are bidden to it, other friends being invited to attend the reception, which takes place half an hour later. A disadvantage of the latter plan is that in case the marriage is delayed through any circumstance, the reception guests will begin to arrive before the ceremony is over.

A widow should never wear at her second marriage either bridal veil, orange-blossoms, or white attire. She usually wears either a light-colored silk or a travelling-dress and bonnet. Unless she should be very young, it would seem in better taste that her wedding should be rather a quiet one.

A bride may drop her middle name and retain her family name if she prefers to do so. Fashion now favors this course, and a widow marrying again often retains the name of the first husband as a middle name where there are children of the first marriage living, as serving to show her relationship to them.

Where cards are sent out after a wedding they should give the residence of the newly-married couple, so that their friends may know where to call upon them.

Very often they hold one or two receptions soon after the marriage, or the bride issues cards for one or more of the afternoon occasions now so much in vogue. The refreshments for these may be very simple and inexpensive, — tea and coffee or chocolate, cake, and sandwiches, being amply sufficient. Bouillon or punch makes a good addition in cold weather.

It is especially important, where a bride goes to live in a new city, that she should, where it is possible and her husband's means allow, thus introduce herself to his friends. Newly-married people are not, however, expected to entertain extensively. On the contrary, entertainments are made for them, and every one who has been asked to the wedding should if possible invite the bridal pair in the course of the ensuing season. As has been said elsewhere, brides should be careful to return promptly the calls made upon them, especially if they go to reside in another city; otherwise they often give deep offence to people who have perhaps made a special effort to call upon them, from motives of kindness and hospitality, because they were strangers in the land.

CHAPTER XVIII.

MARRIAGE engagements, as all the world knows, are made in this country by the young people themselves, and very seldom by their parents. Managing mammas or match-making friends may contrive ways and means to bring à young couple together; but these outside influences are exerted indirectly, and the main actors in the drama are almost without exception the two parties directly interested.

A certain inconvenience sometimes results from this "American plan;" as, for instance, where two families who differ much from each other in their tastes, views, and habits suddenly find themselves on the verge of an unlooked-for and undesired connection through the threatened union of two of their members. We do not in these days "have it out" like the Capulets and Montagues ; but we sometimes *feel* very much as they did, and look daggers if we don't draw them.

Under these circumstances, much depends upon our Romeos and Juliets ; and if they are wise they will endeavor to smooth out matters (without resorting to the apothecary), and to soften the hearts of the obdurate parents. Juliet should remember that Romeo's parents may have had other and more ambitious views for their only son. Instead of feeling anger at their disappointment, she should try to change it to a pleasant one by making herself as agreeable to them as she can. Unless they are very obdurate or worldly people she will be apt to succeed, because she has a powerful ally under their own roof in the person of their son.

The elder Montagues and Capulets also should endeavor to modify their transports of wrath, unless in cases where they feel very sure that the proposed marriage would not be a happy one, or where there is some very serious objection to Romeo or Juliet. A little time ought to be given them to recover from their surprise, to make inquiries perhaps, and to determine what course they will pursue. But let it not be a half-way course. The *fiancée* of a son ought to be cordially received by her future father-in-law and mother-in-law, and a young girl's intended should be treated with kindness and courtesy by her relatives. Otherwise ill feeling is engendered which often will not be wiped out for two or three generations. To be treated with coldness or half-concealed contempt, especially under such circumstances, is a blow to their pride which most people do not readily forgive. A parent may be pardoned if he hesitates to give his consent to the marriage of a favorite child with a person about whom he knows little or feels uncertain. But his consent once given should be given freely and cordially.

A new and pleasant custom has arisen by which a young lady writes to all her intimate friends and tells them that her engagement will be announced on such and such a day, — of course a very near one. On that day accordingly her friends all call upon her and she holds a pleasant and informal reception.

Many of her friends send her flowers; and all who have heard from her should call, or send her a congratulatory note. If she is popular in society she will be invited to dinners, evening parties, etc., given in honor of her *fiancé* and herself.

A solitaire diamond is still the most fashionable engagement ring, though no young lady should expect or even wish to receive such an one where she knows that her lover's means are too limited to justify his making such an expensive present.

Very strict people say that a young man should make an offer of marriage to a young lady nowhere but under her father's roof. To most of us this seems overstrained; but he should certainly never make such an offer when the young lady is a guest in his own house.

Many fathers and mothers allow young people who are engaged to do pretty much as they please; but the world is so censorious, that a young girl will do well to observe the strict rules of etiquette on the subject. The parents of her *fiancé* may be very punctilious people, and she ought not to do anything to give them cause of offence.

According to the rules of etiquette a young lady cannot travel alone with the young man to whom she is engaged, nor stay at the same hotel with him, nor go to theatres, concerts, and parties alone with him. Fifty years ago brides did not leave the house — except after dark — after the invitations to the marriage were sent out. But public opinion no longer demands this unhealthy and absurd seclusion. Many young ladies, however, do not accept any invitations after their wedding cards have been issued.

A young lady at the sea-shore greatly shocked public opinion by going down to the surf beach and bathing on the morning of her wedding day.

The arrival of the wedding presents is always a signal for great interest and excitement in the household; but, strange to say, brides often forget or neglect to write and thank the donors. This is a very grave oversight, and makes the young lady appear very ungrateful. She should always write and thank each person who has sent her a present, either before the wedding or as soon after as possible.

Wedding breakfasts after the English fashion are sometimes given in this country, but are not very common.
They may be either "sit-down" or "stand-up" affairs. The
latter are less formal, and do not so severely limit the number
of guests as the former necessarily must. At a stand-up
breakfast small tables are arranged on one side of the room
for the bridal party, while a long table occupies the centre.
The gentlemen help the ladies and themselves, and the menu
is much the same as at a sit-down breakfast, save that hot
entrées are not provided.

Those who are invited to a wedding breakfast answer
promptly, just as they would in the case of a dinner invitation.
Ladies do not remove their bonnets. When breakfast is
announced, the bride and bridegroom lead the way to the
dining-room or other apartment where the collation is served.
They are followed by the bride's father with the bridegroom's mother, the bridegroom's father with the bride's
mother, the best man with the first bridesmaid, and the
other bridesmaids with the gentlemen who are appointed to
take them down.

At a "sit-down" breakfast the host or hostess informs each
gentleman which lady he is to take down, and presents him
to her, where they are not already acquainted. The bride
and bridegroom sit at the head of the table or at the centre
of one of the sides. Next to the bride sits her father with
the bridegroom's mother, and next to the bridegroom comes
the bride's mother with the bridegroom's father. The bridesmaids with the gentlemen who have taken them down
divide themselves into two groups, one group sitting on
each side of the table next the parents. This is the rule
where the bridal couple occupy the head of the table; when
they are seated at the side, the bridesmaids sit opposite
to them, each sitting at the right hand of her attendant
cavalier.

The menu usually comprises soup, hot and cold entrées chickens, game, salads, *pâté de foie gras*, jellies, creams, etc. Tea and coffee are not served, champagne and other wines taking their places. The sweets and fruit are placed on the table. The servants hand all the dishes in due course, and all the wines. Finger-glasses and doilies are not used at an English wedding breakfast, but dinner napkins always are.

After the more substantial courses have been partaken of, the bride cuts the cake ; though she is not expected to do more than make the first incision, and the real cutting up is done by a servant at the side table. The cake is then handed to all the guests, and every one eats at least a fragment. English wedding-cake is covered with a very delicious frosting strongly flavored with almonds and of a rather soft consistency.

The health of the bride and bridegroom is proposed by the oldest friend of the family.

The bridegroom responds in behalf of his wife and himself, and proposes the health of the bridesmaids. The best man returns thanks for the bridesmaids.

The health of the bride's father and mother is usually proposed by the bridegroom's father. The bride's father returns thanks and proposes the health of the bridegroom's parents. The bridegroom's father acknowledges the compliment. The speeches are usually made as short as possible ; but even with this precaution they are apt to be tedious and stiff, and the fashion of making them is not likely to take root in America. The bride leaves the dining-room to put on her travelling-dress as soon as the healths have been drunk. Gentlemen accompany the ladies to the drawing-room, and do not stay behind to take wine.

At an English wedding the bridegroom always provides the carriage in which he and the bride drive from church and again drive away after the wedding breakfast. White favors and bouquets deck the horses, coachman, and footman. There are neither ushers nor groomsmen at an English wedding. The sexton of the church and the pew-opener officiate instead.

CHAPTER XIX.

THE CHAPERONE.

"Young people think that old people are fools, but old people *know* that young people are fools," says the rather sour old adage.

When we are in the heyday of youth, full of spirits and gayety, and believing implicitly in the virtue and good intentions of every one around us, the institution of chaperonage seems to us a very odious and unnecessary restraint on our liberty. Alas, how different does the whole subject look when viewed through the spectacles of a more mature age! The belief in universal virtue has long since vanished, with other early illusions. Not only do we feel that mankind in general will bear watching, but most of us have grown a shade more worldly as well as a shade less hopeful with advancing years. We believe that chaperones are very necessary to guard young girls from bad and designing people, and from penniless young men and rash romantic marriages as well. Hence arises, as usual, a hopeless discrepancy between the views of youth and those of age.

Many American mothers, it is true, do not believe in a very strict chaperonage; at least, no such belief can be inferred from their actions. They allow their daughters to do very much as they please, to go about where and as they like, and in short "to hold the whip hand" generally. Sometimes this is the result of indolence or good-nature on the mother's part, and sometimes it comes from a conscientious belief that it is best for young people to have their own sweet will.

And so it was, perhaps, in the days when we were a young and simple people, living principally in small communities where every one knew every one else. What may be quite permissible in a village is out of place in a large city; the Joneses and the Browns, who have lived next door to one another all their lives, and who know each other intimately, may safely allow their young people more freedom of intercourse than the mother of a city belle could grant to her daughter, surrounded by a host of admirers about whom she knows little or nothing beyond the fact that they appear like gentlemen.

The old American way of putting young people on their honor, and taking it for granted that they would do everything that was right, certainly implied a much nobler view of human nature than the French system, for instance, which must have a very curious effect on the minds of the young. What a terribly wicked place the world must seem to a young French girl, since her relatives consider it necessary to shut her up from its evil influences behind the bars of a convent! How she must weary at times of the dull, monotonous life prescribed for her by the good nuns, and long for the arrangement of the marriage which will set her free from durance vile, and give her a chance to become part and parcel of that dreadful world, — to make up by plenty of gayety for the long, tiresome years of dreary routine! Her freedom begins where that of the American girl ends.

George Sand was brought up in a convent, and longed at one time to become a *réligieuse*. If she had been reared in a more healthy and natural manner, and allowed to choose her own helpmeet, might not these early and noble aspirations have borne their proper fruit in life and character?

Might not the stormy and disastrous career of this woman of genius have been mercifully averted?

It would be very unjust to charge Frenchwomen in general with possessing either the faults or the talents of their famous sister; but does she not furnish an extreme instance of the folly and wickedness of the French system, — a system which culminates in "le mariage de convenance"? Of the two extremes, surely the American system, which grants young people liberty to do just as they please in almost every instance, is the better one, at any rate for our people.

But we are not obliged to choose extremes, and the English method offers a safe middle course, which our people are gradually adopting. Americans now spend so much of their time in Europe, and foreigners do us the honor of coming to the United States in such large numbers, that our views on social subjects cannot but be influenced in some degree by theirs.

The chaperone may be said, therefore, to be slowly but surely extending her sway in this country, and it is to be hoped that she will make a good and unselfish use of her power. From a chaperone who is one in name only, — some young married woman who utterly neglects her charge and devotes herself to her own amusement solely, — from such may Heaven deliver us! A stationary chaperone is highly desirable for a young lady; not one devoid of the power of motion, that is to say, but one who at balls and dances remains always in the same place, or informs her charge when she is about to change it, so that the latter may be able to return to her without difficulty after every dance.

But a model chaperone needs many qualifications besides the one just mentioned. Indeed, the woman who can faithfully and efficiently perform all the duties involved in matronizing young ladies, must be very nearly an angel. Night after night she is obliged to sit up till the small hours, watch-

12

ing the same everlasting round of the german, eating the same indigestible supper, and talking the same wearisome small-talk to other tired dowagers or elderly beaux, all longing to be at home in their own comfortable beds.

She must not show fatigue nor look cross, no matter what her feelings may be. It is a part of her duty to be entertaining and agreeable, and thus form an attractive background, as it were, to her young charge. A brilliant woman who is also an amiable and unselfish one has great opportunities for helping her young people to "have a good time." Young men like to talk to her, and she takes care to introduce them to her daughters when they come up. If she has good spirits, they are contagious to all around her, and her cleverness and ready answers inspire and amuse the young people and put them at their ease.

She must not, however, endeavor to shine too brightly, lest she put out the lesser lights which it is her duty to tend and brighten. Neither must she say sharp things nor encourage her daughters to do so. Young men are very much afraid of clever girls who say sharp things; the mother's knowledge of the world has taught her this, and she should teach it to her children. If her daughters are neglected and are not asked to dance, she must bear it like a Spartan; nor must she ever say disagreeable things about other girls who are receiving more attention. She must endeavor to find out what are the habits and character of the young men with whom her daughters become acquainted, and she must as far as possible nip any undesirable friendships in the bud. At the same time she must not be harsh, severe, nor unjust, lest she lose the confidence and affection of those under her charge.

Even a model chaperone need not endure martyrdom until every ball breaks up. It is "better form" — as well as infinitely better for the health of all concerned — to leave in good season, and not to have the reputation of being always among the very last to go away. A chaperone accompanies those who are under her charge not only to balls and parties, but to the theatre, the opera, to dinner-parties and all evening occasions, and to all matinées, receptions, and other entertainments given in the daytime, unless they are of a very informal character. To the races, coaching-parties, yachting-parties, tennis-tournaments, etc., must the long-suffering matron go if her daughter does; and she must also go with the latter to pay visits. Even at home her watch and ward must still be kept up, for according to strict etiquette the chaperone must make a disagreeable third party whenever the young ladies under her charge receive calls from gentlemen.

Against this last restraint, however, American girls rebel vigorously, and with some justice. Mamma does well to sit in the other parlor with her book or work and give the young people a little freedom. Whether she remains in the parlor or not, however, she must never go to bed until all callers have left the house.

These very strict rules are modified somewhat after a young lady has been in society for a year or two, and as her youth and inexperience pass away, the added years give her an additional right to take care of herself. Still, even for a girl who is no longer very young, it is not desirable to go much into society alone, especially if she is handsome and attractive. Let her join forces with some young woman of her own age if she has no chaperone to accompany her. An elder sister sometimes matronizes one who is a good deal younger, where the mother is either dead or unable to go into society.

Where a family of daughters are left without either father or mother, it is very desirable, indeed almost necessary, that they should have an elderly cousin or some other woman of mature years come to live with them, that she may give a certain dignity to the household, and help them receive and entertain their guests, even if she cannot accompany them into society.

Young ladies who are engaged to be married need chaperones quite as much as do other girls; this subject has been already treated in the chapter on engagements.

For travelling, — especially for travelling in Europe, — a chaperone is highly desirable and indeed necessary, as the international novel has made Americans understand very clearly. In cities where it is considered highly improper for young ladies to walk abroad, or indeed to go anywhere, alone, what comfort can there be for a girl who has no accompanying matron to guard her from impertinence and even from insult? If she is at all sensitive she will stay in the house pining for want of fresh air, and losing the opportunity to see half the sights she longs to see, rather than be stared at or spoken to in a disrespectful manner.

In America it is quite permissible for a young lady to ride or drive with a young man in the day-time, provided a groom or footman accompanies them. In other words, the groom is the substitute on the road for the weary and long-suffering matron. In driving, this is not so much of a boon, as no matter how fast you drive you cannot shake him off; but in the saddle, a brisk trot or a sharp canter will leave James at a judicious distance in the rear, especially if he has been provided with a good, slow nag.

It is not according to etiquette that a young lady should go to a party or return from one under the sole escort of a young man, especially if she goes in a carriage. Where she has no mother or other "resident matron" who can accompany her to and from the evening's entertainment, she should endeavor to make an arrangement with one or two other young girls, so that they may hire the same carriage and go together. This is — or was — considered allowable in Boston, where there are a number of old and well-known livery-stable keepers who employ hack-drivers of the highest respectability. But it is not allowable — indeed, it would hardly be safe — to follow this custom in New York. A young girl in New York should never drive alone in a hack; if she arrives at the depot alone and is unfortunate enough to have no one to meet her (a most undesirable thing), she must take the cars and express her trunk, as it would be very unsafe for her to take a hack at the station.

It seems hardly necessary to say that a young lady must never go to a restaurant with a young man unless a chaperone accompanies them; neither must she go on "excursions" of any sort. Especially should she avoid the fascinations and uncertainties of a sail-boat. If the boat be becalmed, it may be hours before a landing can be effected; indeed, a sailing-party is sometimes obliged to stay out all night. Hence much unfavorable comment arises; and perhaps a single careless act of this sort may be remembered spitefully against a girl for many years. Especially will this be the case if she is pretty and attractive, and if she has frank and cordial manners. The plain woman and the woman of cold heart and severe demeanor run little risk of censure; but the beautiful and charming girl is too often surrounded by a host of detractors, — envious people who are delighted to catch up and magnify her every thoughtless word or act.

The woman who possesses beauty, possesses what most of her sex desire above all else; but often she pays dearly for this much-coveted gift of Nature. Slander and envy place a thousand thorns in her path; her own sex can seldom forgive "the most beautiful." Wise Minerva and queenly Juno could not forgive Venus; and after three thousand years the fair sex have still a root of envy lurking in their hearts.

Let us all remember, therefore, to guard against this fatal weakness from which even goddesses were not exempt, and to believe only a small fraction of the slander hovering in the air, especially the slander directed against beautiful and attractive women.

A woman of business, an artist or a physician, is not usually thought to need a chaperone in our country. But if she is at all young or pretty, it is very advisable for her to take at least a companion of her own age with her, especially if she is obliged to call upon shop-keepers, men of business, etc. It would certainly seem as if her vocation should afford perfect protection to such a woman; but practically it does not always do so. There are some people of mean and base spirit who will treat with profound respect the young lady of wealth, since her patronage will increase their store of dollars and cents, but whose civility is scanty toward the woman who has her own way to make in the world.

To do the tradesman justice, it is not the degree of the wealth of the person with whom he has to do that alone influences him. No; he instinctively recognizes a rival, a competitor, in the woman of business. There may be apparently no possible danger that their interests will ever clash; but he is prepared for all possibilities, and he at once places himself on the defensive.

Perhaps, too, he has been imposed upon by adventurers and swindlers, and the remembrance thereof makes him cautious, makes him bristle at the recollection of past wrongs to his pocket. For all these reasons the business woman must not expect to be treated with the same courtesy that ever follows the footsteps of her more fortunate sister. And she must above all things avoid the pretty little airs and graces, the charming ways which are so delightful in a parlor, but which are utterly out of place, nay, even dangerous, in the arena of daily struggle for bread and butter.

She must remember that it is the fact that her calling
obliges her to make these visits which alone justifies her in
doing so, and her manner should be serious, quiet, business-
like, — in fact "impersonal" as far as it is possible to make
it so.   While her dress may very properly be of handsome
materials, it should be quiet, plain, and severely lady-like.
It is never in good taste to wear showy, gaudy raiment when
walking in the public streets, and especially when on an
errand of business.

CHAPTER XX.

CONVERSATION IN SOCIETY. — HINTS ON HOW TO AVOID SOME OF ITS BESETTING DANGERS.

In order to be an agreeable person in society, it is by no means necessary to be a burning and a shining light therein. On the contrary, the average man and woman (under one or other of which heads most of us belong) are a thousand times more agreeable if they don't try to shine. The art of effacing one's self, as the French say, — that is, of being quiet, of not asserting one's own importance, — is an art for whose cultivation (in others) people are always profoundly thankful. Beware, then, of talking too much; do not talk to show how clever you are or how much you know, but rather to amuse and entertain the person with whom your lot is cast for the moment; or, better still, carry on your conversation with him in such a way that you may be mutually benefited and instructed, remembering always that your topic should not be too serious for the occasion. A sermon would be out of place in a ball-room.

In one of Balzac's stories a lady advises the hero not to be too brilliant, and never to amuse the company too palpably. "Que votre supériorité soit léonine," she says.

A good listener is better appreciated by nine people out of ten, in this world of ours, than the most brilliant talker.

But in order to be a good listener, one must listen. Alas, how hard that is sometimes when one is detained in the clutches of those Ancient Mariners of society, the long-winded bores! For the bore is usually long-winded, although the existence of silent bores, especially among the very young, cannot be denied. The silent bore is but half a bore, however; he is a sort of albino of the species, and the world calmly treads on his corns and his prejudices, ignores him, and usually tolerates and forgives him.

Some people acquire the art of appearing to pay strict attention to what is said to them, when their thoughts are in reality a long way off; but this is a very dangerous game to play at. Your interlocutor is always liable suddenly to put some question, your answer to which will be pretty sure to betray that your mind has wandered to other pastures. A gentleman who was a great favorite in society said lately that when he wanted to have his mind free to hear what the couple next to him were saying, he would observe to the lady with whom he was conversing, "What did you do to-day?" Her naturally prolix answer gave him the needed time to hear what his next-door neighbors were saying. Such a ruse is only safe, however, for an accomplished *habitué* of society.

If you wish to be agreeable, avoid personal anecdotes about yourself, your family, and friends, unless in talking to those with whom you are really intimate. Remember that to most people a story about yourself may be interesting, if it is interesting *per se;* otherwise it will not be.

"Mortify your own vanity if you don't want other people to mortify it for you," would be an excellent social maxim. Avoid vain repetitions in conversation as well as in more serious matters. If you are in the habit of repeating the same stories and relating the same experiences, you will run great danger of repeating them to the same persons to whom you have told them once before, — nay, perhaps twice or even three times before. I have known people who were in other respects conscientious and reputable members of society, but whose guilt on this dreadful question of repeating themselves was too black to be in any way palliated or denied. When Jones tells me for the fifteenth time how he rescued his uncle from a watery grave in the Public Garden pond by means of the head gardener's hay-rake, what are my feelings? They are too tumultuous to be put on paper, or rather they were. From the third to the tenth time that he related that fearsome tale, I used actually to wish his uncle had drowned then and there. What are the lives of a whole generation of Jones's uncles compared with my peace of mind? But now I have become quite hardened; I even help him out with the story sometimes when he forgets a detail. Would *I* could forget one single item of that wretched anecdote!

All this misery which vain repetition insures to weary listeners might be avoided, however, — certainly a great deal of it, — if the story-teller or the relater of his personal experiences (the last-named is usually the most difficult to cure of his bad habit) would observe a few simple rules. First, confine your reminiscences to accounts of events that have recently occurred; in this way you will not be apt to forget to whom you have or have not told them, although when in doubt it is always a good plan to say, "Did I tell you about so and so?"

A young man said not long ago that he thought he should shoot the next person who asked him if he had seen the A. T. Stewart collection; that young man had my profound sympathy. The rule spoken of above was suggested to me by the conversation of a very brilliant woman, but a woman who liked better to be agreeable than to talk about herself. As she saw a great deal of people and things, she naturally spoke of what she had seen and heard, — of interesting and quaint individuals whom she had met. But the events thus related were almost invariably of recent occurrence, or else they were stories about people whose names had already occurred in the conversation, and stories that were not generally known, — perhaps about those old times that are so old as to be new to the present generation.

Howells, in his "Indian Summer," makes his hero so economical of topics that one would be spread out so as to cover a number of different conversations — in the course of the day or evening. This is safe enough to do if you only obey the second rule ; and that is, after airing your topic or your story, or whatever it is, well and thoroughly, put it in the bottom of a barrel, like the minister's sermons. After five years, or certainly after ten years, you can safely bring it out again. Even the newspapers tell us the same things every ten years. They calculate that it takes about that length of time for a new generation to grow up, and a new generation needs to be told the old truths and the old stories. Strict originality, of course, we cannot expect. Emerson says that no thought is entirely original, but can be traced back through generations of thinkers, ending with the archangels perhaps.

We all know to our cost that jokes are immortal; or at least that most of them date back to those champion wits and thinkers, the ancient Greeks. But every now and then society rises in its might and says it will have no more of a certain joke, so it is temporarily buried, — *not* cremated. A joke cannot, in the nature of things, be cremated, since its resurrection is only a matter of time.

It is of course a very nice question just how much or how little to talk, and just what to say, on social occasions of various sorts and sizes ; but it is a question in which a regard for the feelings of others, a desire not only to enjoy one's self but to have others enjoy themselves also, will be of the greatest assistance. It is said by thorough horsemen that no matter how skilful one may be in the saddle or on the box, a man should *never cease to watch his horse.* No one can tell at what moment the animal may play him a trick, — become suddenly frightened, or in some way call for the instant tightening of the reins, with words of reassurance or command, as the case may be. Now that unruly member the tongue needs to be held under just such close surveillance. Conversation has been aptly likened to fencing. But in a society that is truly polite, the guard which keeps the foil from making any deadly thrust is never removed, even though the combatants, if at all wary, are sure to be protected by fencing-masks. In the face of the accomplished man of the world it is not easy to read his thoughts. He does not " wear his heart upon his sleeve, for daws to peck at."

Having spoken of the cruelty of those who tell always the same tale, like the hand-organ, a word should be added as to how their hearers should bear themselves under the torture. This can best be done by citing the behavior under such circumstances of a lady who is, and justly, a general favorite wherever she goes. She listens quietly to the "same old story," betraying neither by word nor deed that she has ever heard it before. Above all, she does not interrupt the story-teller, and set him right if he makes some mistake in telling his beloved anecdote. There is sometimes a great temptation to interrupt a speaker where he makes a mistake; but it is never polite to do so. If he is making a statement of fact that is calculated to do injustice to somebody, or that will be prejudicial to the truth, one may say politely, after the other speaker has finished what he has to say, that one differs from him, or that one has heard the story otherwise; but where no question of principle is involved, what does it matter whether Jones plays his tune straight or with variations?

Remember that it is never polite, in general conversation, to talk long upon a subject about which some of those present know nothing. This is just as true whether your subject be an elevated one, or merely society small-talk and gossip. Young people who belong to the same set and have a great deal in common to talk about, will sometimes do this thing thoughtlessly when one or two strangers are present. They forget that, interesting as it may be to themselves to hear about Tom's new dog-cart, or who danced the german, and with whom, at the Snifkinses' the night before, such details cannot have the same charm to a young lady from another city who has never seen Tom, and possibly never even heard of the Snifkinses! It is better even to talk about the weather (blessed topic!) than to leave some one present permanently out of the circle of conversation. What people do to eke out dreadful gaps in conversation in California, where the weather changes only two or three times a year, no one has yet told us. It is to be presumed that they fall back upon the game of Brag, and praise their ever-smiling skies.

It goes without saying, that people should "sink the shop" — that is, not talk of their business or profession — in public. Yet any careful observer must have noticed that as it is with morals so it is with manners. We may know perfectly well that to do such and such a thing is a breach of the social code; but if we wish to very much, we are very apt to do it. A young surgeon, not long since, very much disgusted some ladies of his acquaintance by his bloodthirsty (it seemed to them) encomiums upon surgery. "The knife, the knife is the only thing!" he vehemently exclaimed. And yet this young fellow belonged in what is technically termed Good Society, — belonged to a "good old family," had had a college education, and was in general extremely polite!

It is well to avoid riding one's favorite hobby too much in general society, though that would be a cruel rule which denied all hobbies an entrance into the drawing-room. If it were put at the foot of invitations, "No hobby-horses allowed," probably many more refusals would be sent in for "talking-parties" than is now the case. If you cannot be happy without your hobby, bring it with you, but keep it concealed as much as possible, remembering that that is a poor mind which can entertain only one subject.

Although it is often interesting and agreeable to hear people talk about the books they have read, one should never "cram" for any particular occasion, unless *bien-entendu* that one is going to make a speech. A person who "crams" for a dinner-party, or for a visit to the country, is pretty sure to be found out. For in order to introduce the subject he wishes into conversation, he has either got to "drag it in by the head and ears," or else adopt some circuitous route, — some leading-up to the subject which will be apt to betray the purpose of its bringing-in.

Curiously enough, this habit of cramming is sometimes indulged in by those who least need its aid, — by men of literary attainment and good conversational powers. They seem to forget that this special preparation destroys all the sparkle, all the spontaneity of conversation which should bubble up from the meeting of active minds just as the contact with the air makes the champagne foam. Society always finds this trait hard to forgive. Not only are the rest of the company taken at an unfair advantage, but the little game itself is a sort of deceit, and shows an undue desire to shine on the part of the person who makes use of it. Another habit to which society strongly objects is that of punning. Of course an occasional pun can be forgiven; but constant punning, in these days, is frowned upon by general consent. It is true that the custom is a very ancient one, — as old as the times of the Greeks. It is true also that the great Shakspeare indulged very lavishly in plays upon words, according to the fashion of his day. I believe it was Foote who said that no one objected to a pun but the man who could n't make one. He was naturally biassed in his views, however, from the fact of his being personally an incorrigible punster.

The great objections to punning are that it breaks up the thread of conversation, and wearies the mind by turning it constantly into some new and unexpected channel. It is necessarily an interruption; and even agreeable interruptions become tedious if repeated too often.

A few additional hints as to what should be avoided in conversation will not perhaps be out of place here.

Beware of making jokes in general society. To the man of literal mind a joke is entirely incomprehensible. An elderly lady, who was completely destitute of all sense of the ludicrous, remarked recently, apropos of Frank Stockton and his delightful nonsense, " He will be sorry, when he grows older, that he spent his time in writing such stuff!"

Never make personal remarks or jokes. The latter are very liable to be misunderstood, even when made with perfect good-nature. Especially is this the case with personal jokes made in letters, where voice and gesture are lacking to convey adequately the intention of jesting. One must never ask a person's age, or call attention to his dress and personal belongings. ·

Avoid stormy discussion in a mixed company, and, consequently, avoid those subjects on which people are apt to feel most strongly, and differ most widely, namely, politics and religion. The anecdote of the Englishman who discussed politics with a stranger in a stage, and who became so excited that he knocked the head of his antagonist through the stage window, is only a slight exaggeration of the scenes of excitement which most of us have witnessed when politics were under discussion.

A truly well-bred person will endeavor to change the theme of conversation when he perceives that those with whom he is conversing are becoming unduly excited.

An essential part of the art of conversation consists in the ability to "draw out" others, and to make them talk on the topics with which they themselves are well acquainted, and in which they are interested. This was a rule with Emerson, as well as with other truly wise men and women. The wise man is continually searching for more light; and he knows that from comparatively humble people, even from the mechanic or artisan, there is much that he can learn. Therefore while he is quite willing to give light to others if they desire it, and to impart information, he despises, as unworthy of a great mind, that sort of conversation which is indulged in merely to show off what a man knows, in order that he may excite the admiration of those about him.

It is surprising, therefore, to see the fatal mistake which many persons of superficial accomplishments make, in endeavoring to display their little learning, when talking to a man or woman of superior intelligence and solid acquirements. They cannot resist the temptation to show what they know, and are so blinded by their own vanity that they do not see what folly they are guilty of; nor do they perceive that "out of their own mouths they are judged," their loquacity betraying the narrow limits and the superficial character of their attainments.

If such people would be content to talk about some subject with which they were thoroughly conversant, — even if it were a *shop* subject, — they would find in the learned man an interested listener. For though one should not as a rule talk shop, it is permissible to do so to a person who is evidently interested in the subject.

The pygmy who rashly tries his strength against the giant, is guilty of a more noble fault, however, than the giant who, without provocation, crushes the pygmy. The man who takes pains constantly to make a display of what he knows to other persons of decidedly inferior education and accomplishments, is sadly wanting in magnanimity.

It is not in accordance with the spirit of our age to pay empty and unmeaning compliments. In our self-assertive day men do not praise their neighbors, and the old-fashioned elaborate and flowery language of compliment has fallen into disuse. This is scarcely to be regretted, for sincerity is always good, even the sincerity of selfishness. Besides, the moment that selfishness ceases to masquerade under the garb of hypocrisy, its true character is at once made known, and being made known, will ere long be corrected.

That young men still say pretty things to young and charming women is not to be denied; but our belles will not tolerate compliments unless they are well turned, and, in appearance at least, sincere; nor will they allow a fond youth to repeat the same pretty speech to half a dozen girls. In the delightful moments of confidence and retrospection with which young ladies indulge themselves after a ball, the youth who has said the same thing to all of them is severely condemned by the fair conclave, amid peals of silvery laughter.

It is not polite to express doubts of a story, even if many large fishes are introduced into the tale; neither is it polite to criticise or find fault with pictures, bric-à-brac, etc., which are displayed for your admiration. "I wish," said a clever woman, "that I could borrow that sweet smile of ——'s. He never praises what he does not admire, but he smiles so benignly, that he satisfies people just as well as if he broke out into the most extravagant encomiums."

The man or woman who can say sharp and witty things is usually unpopular; the world fears more than it likes such a person. Where a man possesses the delightful faculty of being witty and amusing, and of saying bright things that are neither unkind nor satirical, he is, of course, the prince of good fellows, as he deserves to be.

13

Of gossip and slander it is, let us hope, needless to speak. It is as ill-bred as it is unchristian to indulge in them; and the present renaissance of learning (I refer to the epidemic of reading-classes, literary clubs, etc., now so prevalent in our cities, towns, and villages), if it accomplishes no other good, at least vastly diminishes the tendency to gossip about one's neighbors.

CHAPTER XXI.

ON VOICE, LANGUAGE, AND ACCENT.

"THY speech bewrayeth thee," said the Jewish damsel to Simon Peter. How often do we see people who have with painful effort acquired all the social graces and even a certain elegance of manner, but who still betray — by the misuse of a single letter it may be — the defects of their early education! It is in vain for the woman who says "kep" instead of "kept" to have armorial bearings emblazoned all over her plate, and a whole gallery filled with the portraits of her ancestors. That one little letter *t*, with which all her wealth cannot supply her, settles her former social status in spite of her many protestations.

The wisdom of all ages has recognized this traitor-quality of voice and language. Æsop sets it forth in his fable of the Ass in the Lion's skin; and the old fairy story tells us how the good girl was known by the roses and pearls that fell from her lips, while vipers and toads betrayed the vixenish heart of her unkind sister. The modern saying has it that a fool may pass for a wise man if he only knows enough to keep his mouth shut.

People are not on their guard as to their manner of speech; their own ears are so accustomed to it that it makes little impression on them. If phonographs were as common as looking-glasses, we might be as watchful of how we talk as we now are of how we look. A keen observer can judge of

a man's age, character, manners, and morals, by the sound of
his voice alone.

The proper cultivation of the voice is of very great importance, especially for Americans. "Whether it is the climate
or the 'abits," we undoubtedly have a tendency to speak in
harsh nasal tones as the candid foreigner takes sincere pleasure in informing us. Proper cultivation and use of the voice
not only increase its beauty, but prevent its becoming thin
and cracked with age, and add greatly to a person's health
and strength. You will hear women of forty speak, whose
voices are thin and worn because they have never used them
properly ; while other women of threescore and ten or even
more years speak with round, full, strong tones that are
delightful and refreshing to hear.

Public speaking, singing, acting, are all healthful pursuits
in spite of the late hours they involve. Even reading aloud
is said to be an excellent preservative of the voice. Probably
nothing is worse for it than scolding in a high key, or than
the deplorable habit, so prevalent in some houses, of "yelling"
up and down stairs.

Children should be trained not to pitch their voices too
high; indeed, every one should speak in chest tones, and not
from the head and throat. A successful school-teacher said
to the writer, "If children are inclined to be unruly and
troublesome, don't raise your voice and scream at them, but
drop it ; speak lower and not higher." If you speak loud
and high, it shows that you yourself are excited ; but if you
speak in a low, firm tone, you show that you command yourself and mean to command others. In "Daniel Deronda,"
Gwendolen's hateful husband speaks in a low voice of repressed power whenever he means to be especially disagreeable, and the high-strung, spirited woman feels obliged to
submit to his tyrannical mandates, soft-spoken though
they be.

A clever man who was very attentive to a beautiful but not very intellectual woman, was once asked what great charm he found in Miss ———, and whether her conversation was not very dull. "Oh, no!" he replied; "she does n't say anything that is very startling, but I like so much to hear her talk. When she tells me that she had bread and butter for luncheon, she pronounces 'bread' and 'butter' in such a charming way that it is truly delightful!"

There are certain words which seem predestined to martyrdom, so persistently are they mispronounced and abused. Take for instance the word "gentleman;" certainly it does not seem very difficult to pronounce in the right way, that is, just as it is spelled. But many people make a curious mumble in the middle of it, so that it sounds much like "gempman" or "gehempman" or "genelman." The man who aspires to be a gentleman should be very careful to pronounce his own title distinctly. The abbreviation "gents" is never used by people of education. Another very common but less damning error is to omit the *n* sound in government, and to pronounce it "goverment." Even well-educated people make this mistake through carelessness.

A distinct utterance and the careful enunciation of every letter when pronouncing a word are of the greatest importance. One should not be slovenly in speech any more than in dress, handwriting, or any other detail of the conduct of life. It is not necessary to speak loud in order to speak clearly. A soft, low, and gentle voice we hold to be "an excellent thing in woman," as much as Shakspeare did. But beware of a woman with a voice that is *ever* soft! Often she is very sweet-tempered, but you will find her to be of no soft will, and as hard to move as adamant, from any determination she has once formed.

Some women who speak with soft and pleasant voices mar what would otherwise be the perfect whole of their speech, by a peculiar indistinctness of utterance, which conveys to the by-stander the impression that their mouths are full of pudding. This is a more agreeable extreme than the sharp, hard, nasal tones of many Yankees; but it savors of affectation, and makes conversation difficult and one-sided. Such an enunciation — pretty, but hard to understand — is like the much-abused English hand-writing popular with many ladies. A letter written in the extremity of this style is very pretty and interesting, unless you happen to wish to read it!

The general tendency of Americans is toward distinct, although it may be unmusical utterance. We do not slur and abbreviate names as much as the English do, and our tendency to pronounce all there is of a proper name is sometimes carried too far. When a brakeman screams out "Green—wich, Nor—wich, Bruns—wick," the polite ears of the passengers are deeply offended. "Grinnidge, Norridge, Bruns'ick," have become the standard and recognized mispronunciations originated by our British brethren, who seem to have a special dislike to the letter *w* as well as to the letter *h*. Berwick, they pronounce *Bĕrrick;* St. John (used as a proper name), *Sinjun;* Gower, *Gore;* Salisbury, *Salzbury;* Cockburn, *Cŏburn;* Cowper, *Couper,* the *w* taking the sound of *u;* Brougham, *Broum;* Pontefract, *Pomfret;* Geoghegan, *Gaygan;* Belvoir, *Bever;* Beauchamp, *Beacham,* etc.

Other instances of names whose spelling and pronunciation are at deadly feud with each other are too well known, perhaps, to need mention, — "Cholmondeley" and "Marjoribanks," which look so stately in print, but whose owners must be addressed as plain "Chumley" and "Marchbanks;" "Cavendish," which is pronounced "Candish," etc. Less known than these, and more singular than any, is the name of a certain family in Virginia who spell their name "Enroughty" and pronounce it "Darby."

While Americans are justly proud of the comparative freedom from dialects which distinguishes our great country,
they still love to poke a little fun at one another on account
of slight local differences in accent and speech.   The New
Englander smiles at the "spŏŏn," "av'noo," "chick'n," etc.
of "N'Yawk," and thinks it is utterly foolish to flatten the
a in bath, last, dance, etc.

The New Yorker responds by pointing out the evident
absurdity of calling coat "coăt" (wherein he is right) and
the great advantage of saying "dawg" as he does, rather than
"dŏg," as we do (wherein he is wrong).   And the inhabitants of both sections of country agree in wondering at the
folly of Westerners, with their wonderfully rolled *r's*, and
of Southerners, with their "paws" and "maws" and various
negroidal peculiarities of dialect.

Now that the English accent has become so fashionable,
the New Yorker is endeavoring rapidly to broaden his *a's*,
while the Bostonian strives to shake off the nasal quality of
his tone, and to *dwell* a little longer on his words.   Thus
are two hostile factions peacefully united in their loving imitations of a third party !

"English as she is spoke" by well-bred Englishmen themselves is certainly a very charming tongue, and much more
poetical than our American version ; but the imitations of
English speech that are becoming so current here have the
pinchbeck quality of all counterfeits.   In the first place,
they seem affected ; and affectation is a form of insincerity
which may be very innocent, but is almost universally dis-
liked.   In the second place, imitation is a sign of weakness
in nations and in individuals.

Emerson says that nations are great and vigorous while
they are occupied with their own affairs.   The following
passage from one of his essays might be read with advantage
by the dudish youth of to-day.   "The young men in America

at this moment take little thought of what men in England are thinking or doing. That is the point which decides the welfare of a people; *which way does it look?* If to any other people, it is not well with them. If occupied in its own affairs and thoughts and men, with a heat which excludes almost the notice of any other people, — as the Jews, the Greeks, the Persians, the Romans, the Arabians, the French, the English, at their best times have done, — they are sublime; and we know that in this abstraction they are executing excellent work."

Herodotus says : "The Persians are of all nations most ready to adopt foreign customs; for they wear the Medic costume, thinking it handsomer than their own; and in war they use the Egyptian cuirass. And they practise all kinds of indulgences with which they become acquainted." How little these imitative and rather foppish Persians were able to withstand the Greeks, every schoolboy knows.

All of which is respectfully submitted for the consideration of the grand army of returned Anglo-Americans who have with so much difficulty learned the trick of a new speech, and very imperfectly, after all their trouble. It is not possible for us, with our nervous organization and quickness of thought and action, to speak with the graceful slowness (sometimes called drawl) which distinguishes the elder, slower, more mature branch of our race. A kitten might as well attempt to imitate the gait of an old and very respectable tortoise.

Englishmen have a way of dwelling lovingly upon their words, which is very pretty to hear. Even ugly words become attractive from the caress of their speech. I once heard an Englishman of some literary note pronounce "vulture" in such soft lingering accents, with so long a dwelling upon the first syllable, and such a soft liquid sound of the *l*, that the odious bird of prey seemed for the moment transfigured into

an amiable and poetic animal.   Even the curt monosyllables
"yes" and "no" the Briton contrives to make of a respectable length by judiciously hissing the *s* and adding a *w* sound
to the *no*.

That dreadful vulgarism perpetrated by some Americans of
saying "yeah" for yes, cannot be too severely condemned.
Not only is the mispronunciation hateful, but it creates confusion by making "yes" sound too much like "no."   The
negative and affirmative in our modern languages are of very
different sound — in order to avoid any possible mistake.
We could not now tolerate "yea" and "nay," because they
sound too much alike.

Another unpleasant abbreviation is that of "gen'ally" for
generally.   Some people find it very difficult to pronounce
th before *s*, and say "clo'es" and "mon's" instead of "clothes"
and "months."   Others drop the *h* after *w*, saying "w'ite"
and "w'en" for "white" and "when."   This suppression
of the letter *h* is also characteristic of the speech of a certain
class of Englishmen, as all the world knows.   Why Americans do not also add the *h* in the wrong place, like their
cockney brethren, is a puzzle to the learned, and students of
language have brought forth various theories to account for
this curious fact.

The elision of the *g* final in such words as "going, saying,
doing," etc., is not often heard now in the speech of educated
people ; but twenty years ago there were still a number of
elderly persons who never thought of saying aught but "goin',
doin', sayin'," etc.   The shortening of the *o* in "stōne" is an
ugly but common mistake ; still worse is the childish error
of adding *r* to words ending in a vowel sound, as "idea*r*,
saw*r*," etc.

When it comes to the pronunciation of foreign words, one
is treading on dangerous ground ; it is better not to quote
from other languages unless one is familiar with them, and

knows them by sound as well as by sight.   Even then, quotations should be sparingly used, as it is in very bad taste to interlard one's discourse constantly with French or German words; neither is it now the fashion to do so.

To quote Latin, and get the quantities, genders, and cases wrong, seems a needless barbarity toward a poor language that is already dead.   And with anglicized Greek and Latin words it is a poor plan to venture on a plural unless you have sufficient grounds for supposing it to be the right one. Thus people who wish to be especially correct will carefully say "memorandas," every time, in a way calculated to make Harkness, Allen, Greenough, and the rest writhe with torture and surprise.   *Memorandum* is now an English word; and though educated people generally use the Latin plural, memoran*da*, it is quite allowable simply to make the plural like that of any other English word.   A woman who wished to be extremely exact in her conversation said lately to a friend, "You can telegra*m* if you wish to!"

It is a safe rule not to follow every new wind of doctrine in pronunciation, as in other matters.   Often it is raised by some one who has a very imperfect knowledge of the subject, and by following his lead a person often appears ridiculous, and reveals, perhaps, the defects of early education as well as an over-ambition to speak "in the newest manner and the politest fashion."   Whereas if one pronounces a word in the ordinary or old-fashioned manner, attention is not specially drawn to it.

Thus it is rather amusing to hear a country dressmaker speak of a "polon*ay*" in a mildly corrective tone, which rebukes the ignorance of her customer for calling the garment a "polonaise."

While nothing is quite as bad as coarseness and rudeness of speech and language, there is still a sort of affectation, of over-delicacy, and would-be precision, that is almost as bad.

You will find these neither in the works of the best writers nor in the mouths of the most refined and cultivated men and women.   They are the characteristics of people who either have not had a liberal education or who have not enjoyed the best social advantages.

The perpetual use of the word "limb" for "leg," and "retire" for "go to bed," are familiar instances of this over-delicacy.   "He fell and sustained a fracture of the limb" is an absurd and needlessly vague way of intimating that a man broke his leg; and while it is perfectly proper and correct to use the form "retire" occasionally, yet the constant eschewing of the plain old English phrase seems both affected and prudish.

The over-precision of which I have spoken can perhaps best be defined by calling it grammar-school precision; since it is of a kind found often among grammar-school teachers and graduates, and suggestive of this degree of education rather than of a higher.   A seamstress of peculiar "refinement," of whom a lady had ordered a set of nightgowns, sent in her bill for the making of so many "bed-dresses."   The expressions "lady friend" and "gentleman friend" have been so persistently held up to deserved scorn by the "New York World," that we may hope their fate is sealed.   The use of the word "female" for woman is rapidly going out of fashion, as it deserves.   It is inelegant, and very derogatory to one half of mankind.

"Newspaper English" often amazes us with its persistent affectations, and with its constant and absurd use of certain pet phrases which are evidently deemed by the writer to be extremely elegant.   Thus, according to some newspapers, no events of moment ever take place or happen; they always "transpire."   Neither does any citizen live or dwell anywhere; he always "resides."   It goes without saying that these remarks do not apply to the editorial pages of first-class papers. "A little knowledge is a dangerous thing," here as elsewhere. As a remedy for over-formality, I would suggest copious doses of "our best writers" and strict attention to the language of our best speakers.

A lady was reading a manuscript production aloud to a friend, when the latter exclaimed in horror, "You must alter that — and that !" "If you had seen the manuscript, you would have known that both those expressions were quoted," was the reply. "One was from Carlyle and one from Emerson."

Where people of imperfect early education have supplemented it later in life by a course of reading, the effect on their pronunciation is sometimes very curious. They know the words by sight but not by sound, and will call them "out of their names" in a very funny way. Children who have not been well trained in reading aloud fall into the same errors. Hence it is very important for pronunciation, as well as for the voice, to drill young people thoroughly and long in reading and speaking. A bright boy of thirteen, who was very fond of books and could spell more than ordinarily well, ceased to attend the reading-class at his school because his parents thought it needless for him to do so any longer. But when they heard that boy say "hummid" for "humid," "delic'acy" for "del'icacy," they sent him back to his class in very short order. A course of Webster's Unabridged will undoubtedly cure these defects, if the patient has the courage to take it.

Only the State and its rulers have the right to coin money; and only the kings of language have the right to coin new words. They, the great writers and thinkers, may do it, for they do it intelligently, and will not abuse their privilege by debasing the coinage or overcrowding it; but that every newspaper writer should be allowed to make new words and scatter them broadcast over the country is simply barbarous.

Allusion is not here made to slang (which is the necessary concomitant of a living language, and not altogether a bad thing in homœopathic doses), but to such dreadful evolutions of speech as "donate," "orate," "walkist," "residential," "disconcertion," etc. Occasionally these new words, though barbarous, have the merit of filling a gap in the language; but oftener they are invented for the sake of greater (?) elegance, or for their novelty. But when you have the good Saxon words "give" and "speak," why change them for such weak words of Latin derivation as "donate" and "orate"?

It is a well-known rule, with few exceptions, that one should choose words of Saxon rather than of Latin origin; but the grammar-school or affected style always takes the Latin word. The person who uses it may perhaps be quite innocent of knowing its derivation; he likes it because it is long, and has a learned sound.

It is well known that the greatest writers use the largest number of different words, just as the uneducated man uses the fewest. Sophocles, the Greek professor at Harvard, once gave the writer a very interesting account of the different number of words used by persons of different grades of education; of all which I can only recall the fact that the smallest vocabulary was limited to a few hundred words, and that of a college graduate to a few thousand.

Shakspeare used more words than any one writer in the English language, — about fifteen thousand. Milton comes next, but with a much smaller vocabulary.

One of the exceptions to the rule of using the Saxon word in preference to the Latin is found in the word "folks." It is now considered inelegant to use this word as applied to a family or number of people; indeed, those who are careful in their speech do not use it save in the singular number and in an historical connection, as in "folk-lore."

" How are all your folks ?" certainly has a very barbarous sound to ears polite. And yet it is hardly safe, in greeting a friend whom one has not seen for some time, to ask for each member of his family separately ; some one may have died or gone crazy in the interim. But one can always say " How are all your family ?" because it is a safe, noncommittal sort of inquiry, and still it covers the ground.

In the words " waistcoat" and " trousers" we find the world polite eschewing once more the French and Latin equivalent expressions. " Pants" and " vest" are not used by people who are careful in their speech, though they sanction the rather outlandish word " knickerbockers," as applied to short " trousers" for little boys.

While it seems unnecessary to speak of slang as if those who used it were monsters of iniquity, and guilty of the seven deadly sins, still its habitual use is much to be deprecated both as inelegant and unmeaning. People use a slang expression to save themselves the trouble of defining precisely what they mean ; hence they become inexact and slovenly in thought and speech. " Awfully jolly," for instance, when applied to everything, from a new style of bonnet to a surly far-from-jolly-looking bull-terrier, ceases to have any meaning at all, beyond the vague general commendation that it implies. Another great objection to slang is, that it often has a secondary meaning, and people innocently use expressions of this sort which they have picked up, without being at all aware of the *double-entendre* implied in what they say.

CHAPTER XXII.

GESTURES AND CARRIAGE.

THERE are no more crucial tests of good breeding than a man's carriage, his way of moving, and the gestures which he makes. The heroine in Julian Hawthorne's "Bressant" says of a gentleman: "He was dressed like one; not *bandboxy*, but nicely and easily, and he stands and moves well." You can tell a race-horse by his gait, and a gentleman by his walk. Virgil uttered this same sentiment nearly two thousand years ago, when he said of Juno, *Incedo regina,* —— "I walk (or move) a queen."

After the lapse of all this time we have not found a better phrase to express true queenly dignity. King Lear's "Ay, every inch a king" voices much the same thought; namely, that majesty and high breeding are not shown by the face alone, but by the carriage and attitude of the whole body. It is said that Queen Victoria's bearing is very majestic and imposing, despite her short stout figure.

From this it would appear that a commanding stature or even a commanding figure is not essential to a dignified and high-bred carriage. What then are the necessary elements that go to its composition? Are they not — first, a proper self-respect, second, the habit of good society, and third, a perfect command over all the muscles?

The second element is not always at command; but the first and third — self-respect and a perfect control of one's muscles — ought to be within reach of most people.

It has been said that it is very difficult to stand erect in the presence of a great man; in other words, people are too much inclined to truckle to those who hold power of one sort or another, and in the effort to do homage to the great, men barter their self-respect, and with it the upright bearing of the body which ought to accompany an upright mind.

The awkwardness of movement and carriage that is simply physical and muscular can be removed wholly or in part by physical exercise; those exercises are certainly best which use all the muscles and develop them symmetrically. Dancing, fencing, riding on horseback, skating, playing tennis, calisthenics, — all are excellent for this purpose. Rowing or using rowing-weights develops the muscles of the upper part of the body and so tends to make a man top-heavy, unless he supplements it with running or some other exercise which calls into play the muscles of the lower limbs. Dio Lewis's system of calisthenics, which is a modification, I believe, of a German system, is very good for the purpose of which we are speaking; and as the calisthenics are not violent, they are well adapted for girls and women.

Riding on horseback is said to be one of the most perfect forms of exercise, calling into use all the muscles of the body. And yet Punch — that excellent authority on manners and morals — speaks of a dismounted dragoon as bearing a strong resemblance to a swan on a turnpike road! Which only proves that if one takes *all* his exercise on a horse's back, one may forget how to walk well.

The sort of awkwardness that torments many people in the society of others arises from an unhappy self-consciousness which cramps the body as well as the mind. They take too much thought as to how they are looking and how they are moving; hence all the ease of nature is lost, and they have no adequate art with which to replace it. Emerson says: "Nature is the best posture-master. An awkward man is graceful when asleep, or when hard at work or agreeably amused. The attitudes of children are gentle, persuasive, royal, in their games and in their house-talk and in the street, before they have learned to cringe."

If you can get one of these awkward, ungainly youths, to whom society means utter constraint and misery, to forget himself, and to think and talk about something that interests him, you will find that he ceases to be all arms and legs, elbows and knees, and becomes a reasonable, properly articulated human being. Talk to him about his base-ball nine, or his studies, or some subject for which he has an enthusiasm, and if you can but succeed in drawing him out and in making him think you too care for his hobby — presto! what a change will take place! Instead of the ugly duckling you have a cygnet.

I think this power of transformation, which belongs to the accomplished society woman, one of her most delightful and enviable possessions. What can be pleasanter than to be a Circe of this kind? To be able to bring life and animation into the trembling heart of the shy, to drive away the nightmare of *mauvaise honte*, and to change an awkward hobble-de-hoy into an Adonis, is a most desirable faculty. For a young unmarried woman it may be a dangerous one. If she is too sympathetic, she may make a deeper impression than she intends, and one that the unhappy youth may retain in his heart for many a day.

It is a bold saying of Emerson, that it is the want of thought that makes people awkward. "Give me a thought, and my hands and legs and voice and face will all go right. And we are awkward for want of thought. The inspiration is scanty, and does not arrive at the extremities." This seems at first a startling hypothesis, and one calculated to makes the famous Lord Chesterfield shiver in his genteel grave. But the more one looks at it the more rational does

14

it appear. As the seer of Concord goes on to demonstrate, men of thought sometimes appear awkward in society because they are out of their usual element, and the conversation probably turns on subjects unfamiliar and uninteresting to them. If the company consists, however, of men and women who are intellectual as well as elegant, behold, your timid sage becomes an inspired lawgiver, and his gestures adapt themselves to his new and natural mood.

If another argument were necessary to prove this saying, would it not be found in the noble attitudes, commanding and graceful, with which sculptors and painters in all times have clothed their inspired figures, their men and women who are filled with high thought and purpose? Do not we ourselves, in our minds, always invest high thinkers with a noble bearing?

What people were ever such thinkers as the ancient Greeks, and yet what people were ever so graceful in all their motions? The well-known case of Demosthenes shows that they would tolerate no inelegance of voice or gesture; while the perfection of their statues still gives the civilized world its highest ideal of the poise and attitude of the human form divine.

Let the shy man, therefore, endeavor to have thoughts that are worth something, and above all things let him keep his thoughts, if possible, from dwelling on himself. Let him remember that people are not thinking about him nearly as much as he supposes, — they are all too busy thinking about themselves. Let him especially avoid nervous awkward tricks — playing with his cane or his hat or his watch-guard. If he can once learn to sit perfectly still, he has done a great thing, although he must beware of a repose that is too stiff, and he must not look as if he had been frozen into one special attitude. We Americans are too nervous and too energetic to care to sit entirely quiet for more than a very short time; and yet the ability to do so in company and *malice prepense* shows one has reached the high-water mark of good breeding.

To move well, to be graceful and easy in manner while speaking,—either of these is far easier than to sit perfectly still and yet to be free from all awkwardness. The grace of repose is far harder of attainment than the grace of motion. Talleyrand said of a great statesman, "He is imposing in his own repose." Lord Bacon said, "Men's behavior should be like their apparel, not too straight or *point device*, but free for exercise or motion."

Goethe, in his "Wilhelm Meister," thus admirably defines the carriage of a person of good breeding :—

"A well-bred carriage is difficult to imitate, for in strictness it is negative; and it implies a long-continued previous training. You are not required to exhibit in your manner anything that specially betokens dignity; for by this means you are like to run into formality and haughtiness; you are rather to avoid whatever is undignified and vulgar. You are never to forget yourself; are to keep a constant watch upon yourself and others; to forgive nothing that is faulty in your own conduct, in that of others neither to forgive too little nor too much. Nothing must appear to touch you, nothing to agitate; you must never overhaste yourself, must ever keep yourself composed, retaining still an outward calmness whatever storms may rage within. The noble character at certain moments may resign himself to his emotions; the well-bred never. The latter is like a man dressed out in fair and spotless clothes; he will not lean on anything; every person will beware of rubbing on him. He distinguishes himself from others, yet he may not stand apart; for as in all arts, so in this, the hardest must at length be done with ease; the well-bred man of rank, in spite of every separation, always seems united with the people round him; he is never to be stiff or uncomplying; he is always to appear the first, and never to insist on so appearing.

"It is clear, then, that to seem well-bred a man must actually be so. It is also clear why women generally are more expert at taking up the air of breeding than the other sex ; why courtiers and soldiers catch it more easily than other men."

These remarks Goethe puts into the mouth of one actor who is advising another as to how best to play the courtier.

In our own day we see some very good counterfeit presentments of gentlemen on the stage, made by actors who in many instances have had few advantages of early training. And is it not by thought and study that they succeed in these representations? Nevertheless, the imitation is not quite perfect. I know a middle-aged gentleman in New York — an aristocrat by birth and breeding — who dislikes very much going to the theatre to see "society plays," because, he says, the actors and actresses so travesty the parts of ladies and gentlemen ! This critic is a person of little imagination, as one might guess. It is said that Lester Wallack wanted his actors to attend a performance given by amateurs at the Union League Theatre, that they might get some hints for their own carriage and demeanor upon the stage.

Affectations of carriage should be very carefully avoided by those who wish to attain elegance of poise and motion. True, they are sometimes used by well-bred people, but it is a dangerous matter to try to counterfeit them. Like flourishes in handwriting, they are always doubtful ornaments, and intolerable unless supremely well done. The Grecian bend and Alexandra limp seem very absurd as we look back upon them, but there are affectations in vogue at the present day that are quite as ridiculous. One of these is the custom — for men — of carrying the elbows raised and slightly projected. No doubt this curious fashion arises from the worship of the groom and the stable, now so prevalent among young men of fashion. It reminds one of the "elbows square, wrist

pliant," of the stage-driving hero of "The Road to Ruin."
But besides that it is horsey, it is truculent as well, and
imparts a sort of defiant, arms-akimbo, fishwife expression,
that often contrasts widely and curiously with the mild
look on the countenance of the gentle dude who adopts
it. "Suit the action to the word, the word to the action,"
said Hamlet in his famous directions to the players; and
the meaning, the language of gesture is a thing we do
not study half enough. The famous Frenchman Delsartes,
who, from a ragged street-boy, grew to be a great singer and
actor, crowned his life-work by a long and arduous study of
gesture, — of the language of the body. He studied in the
streets, the hospitals, the theatres, and even the battlefields,
and founded a system which has now many followers among
actors, artists, and others. Whatever one may think of the
Delsartian exercises, — and they are said to impart flexibility
and grace, a symmetrical development to the body, — the subject is one that is full of interest. One would hardly wish to
make a study of every motion; but it is both agreeable and
useful to learn what construction such a careful thinker as
Delsartes has put upon different gestures; nay more, to
learn what were the results of his long and laborious observation.

The bow of many fashionable youths is strongly objected
to by Delsartians, and with good reason. A short, sharp
bending at the hips, with no movement of the feet or knees,
the elbows curved outward, the chin poked forward, — what
grace is there in a bow of this sort, or what respect does it
show? It is a mere mockery of a bow, and full of self-assertion. The bow should be made first by inclining the head;
if you wish to show more respect (and certainly a movement
of the head alone can be but a nod, quick or slow), the inclination must extend to the shoulders, to the waist, even to
the whole body where you wish to show deep respect. But

to square back the shoulders like a prize-fighter, and suddenly double yourself up as if you had received a blow in the stomach, or as if you were made of two pieces of wood hinged in the centre, — surely this ought to be an abomination to gods and men!

No woman could be guilty of doing a thing in such shockingly bad taste; her intuitions would warn her against it. It is only the reflecting male animal that makes such gross mistakes of "deportment." Howells, in his "Indian Summer," thus describes the modern bow: "The officer whom Imogene had danced with brought her to Mrs. Bowen and resigned her with the regulation bow, hanging his head down before him as if submitting his neck to the axe."

To make a reverence! How little that old expression has in common with our modern bow! True, it denoted a feudal condition of things that would ill suit our times. We do not "bow down" to idols in the shape of people of high rank, as the world used to do; at least, we say we don't.

According to the observations of Delsarte, the greater the emotion, the more will it extend over the muscles, until at last supreme emotion affects the whole body. Hence the artist who painted a picture of despairing Hagar with square shoulders, painted an artistic anomaly. In moments of despair the whole body droops.

There is a way of moving the body from side to side in walking, which some women use who ought to know better. It is rather pretty, even though it savors of affectation, in a brisk French nurse-maid; but in the walk of a lady it is wholly out of place. Sometimes this swinging motion is made very slightly and very slowly. In this case it is less objectionable only because there is less of it. Another ugly trick is that of allowing the whole body to rise and fall with every step, so that a man seems to be walking with his shoulders quite as much as with his legs. This slouching or jerky gait is to be seen in some children, and should certainly be corrected while their muscles are still young and easy to bring under control.

Indeed, most people need to be trained to walk well just as much as they do to ride, drive, or dance well. A mincing gait is extremely disagreeable in a man, and will always make him appear effeminate. In the same way women should avoid a long striding walk, which makes them look ungraceful and masculine. Very high-heeled shoes, especially where the heel is placed very far forward on the sole, give the wearer a tottering ugly gait that reminds the beholder of the Chinese women, and their absurdly small feet. These shoes are also said to be extremely injurious to health, because they throw the body into an unnatural position.

A satirical writer thus commented on the fashionable gait of the young men of his day : " In receiving the attentions of a male acquaintance, remember to proportion your civility to the depth of his neckcloth, the cleanness of his top-boots, or the number of his seals. Take especial care likewise that his toes are significantly turned inward in walking, as it is meant to betray great skill in riding."

The comments of the Baron de Mortemart Boisse, on the postures assumed by Americans thirty years ago, are both shrewd and naïve : "A French dandy desiring to see the beauties of New York, arrives and walks up Broadway on a bright Sunday morning, looking at the windows of that thoroughfare of which he has heard so much said. He sees nothing but the boot-heels of the citizens of Broadway; proving that the fashion in this country is to occupy the windows with the feet and not with the head. These gentlemen smoke their cigars and sit with their legs in the air and their feet on the window-sash."

Tennis and other athletic exercises, now so much in favor with young girls, no doubt assist greatly in producing a good muscular development, although tennis is such violent exercise that one cannot recommend women to make use of it, except with a good deal of caution.   It is said that the habit of carrying burdens on the head produces the finest carriage of the body, and gives also great freedom and elasticity of movement.   Certainly the free graceful walk of the Italian peasant girls contrasts very favorably with the constrained gait of many American women tottering uncertainly on their high heels.

CHAPTER XXIII.

INTRODUCTIONS.

When shall we introduce our friends and acquaintances to one another, and when shall we refrain from doing so? This is a difficult question to answer, especially at the present moment, when the social world in our own country is divided against itself with regard to this important subject. It may be said that we are in a transition stage between the old theory of general and frequent introductions and the new one of non-introduction.

Old-fashioned people, and people who are of a cordial disposition, and dislike excessive formality and ceremony, favor the old-school doctrine; while those who hold more rigid views on the subject of making new acquaintances incline strongly toward the new theories.

The tendency of the present time is certainly toward lessening the frequency of introductions, — a tendency which many people lament as lessening the cordiality and good-fellowship of social gatherings. The modern doctrine is that no formal introduction is necessary for those who meet under a friend's roof; that it is entirely proper for people to speak to one another under such circumstances, thus avoiding the stiffness of sitting silent, and also avoiding the serious drawback of making any undesirable acquaintances.

All this sounds very fair; and then it is English, and that is sufficient recommendation to many people. But in reality it is a far from democratic doctrine, and has its origin, not only in a desire to imitate British customs, but in a feeling of exclusiveness that is rapidly increasing among a certain class of people in our country.   This class "views with alarm" the great and growing army of *nouveaux riches* who are springing up all around us.   To the question, " Why have not these new people as good a right in society so-called as you have ?" they have no adequate answer to give, save that the "ins " always want to keep out the " outs."   So they are very glad to avail themselves of the polite fiction that it is just as pleasant to talk to some one whose name you don't know, and who does n't know yours, and whom you will meet to-morrow as a perfect stranger, as it is to converse with a person to whom you have been duly presented, and with whom you may, if agreeable to both parties, form a pleasant acquaintanceship or perhaps a lasting friendship !

Just here some one will say, " The writer is full of old-fashioned prejudice ; " and, however little we may like the new plan, certainly none of us would wish to force our acquaintance on those who did not desire it.

An American who was travelling in England with his wife received an unpleasant but amusing lesson on the subject of which we are speaking.   Happening to find themselves in the same railway carriage with an English gentleman and his wife, our American couple gradually fell into conversation with the Britons, whom they found to be agreeable and polite people.   Both parties chanced to leave the train at the same station, the English couple getting into a coronetted carriage which was waiting for them, and the others contenting themselves with a plebeian cab.   The American, a man remarkable for his good-breeding and politeness, thought it only civil to bow a farewell to the lady with whom he had been conversing but a moment before.   To his astonishment and indignation the lady responded with a well-bred but

stony stare! She no doubt regarded the salute as an over-
ture on the part of the American toward making her
acquaintance; whereas he, in the simplicity of his republican
good manners, merely intended to bid her a courteous and
eternal farewell!

But let us here take up the subject of introductions in
greater detail. According to the new fashion, if two or three
or more visitors are all calling upon a lady at the same time,
she does not introduce them to one another, but endeavors to
divide her time and attention equally among them, and expects that they will assist her by talking together. It goes
without saying that many people do not pay any attention
to this rule, but adhere to the more cordial and older custom of introducing the different visitors to one another,
where their number is not too large. Of course where a
great many callers are present at the same time, — at an afternoon tea, for instance, or on a lady's regular reception-day, —
the hostess would not then introduce all her visitors to one
another, because this would be awkward, as are all general
introductions.

At afternoon teas, kettledrums, etc., many hostesses do not
introduce at all, especially if no gentlemen are present; where
there are, more introductions take place, since it is a less
formal and less solemn matter to present a gentleman to a
lady than to present two ladies to each other.

At houses where the hostess is more anxious that her
guests should have a good time than she is to preserve great
state and ceremony, she will make some introductions both on
afternoon and evening occasions. Of course she will exercise
this prerogative with tact and caution, taking care not to make
people acquainted where one or both parties might object to
the introduction, or where they would be mutually unsym-
pathetic, and would have no interests in common. She will
be especially careful about introducing two ladies who live in

the same city; since there may be some special reason which prevents their forming each other's acquaintance, and also because such an acquaintance between dwellers in the same city would not be a mere temporary affair, as it might be in the case of people who lived at a great distance from one another.

With strangers, a hostess will feel much more at liberty to do as she pleases. The ancient traditions of hospitality towards them are not yet forgotten; and these dictate that not only the lady of the house, but her friends also, shall welcome the stranger that is within her gates. Neither need she stand so much on ceremony with young girls and men as with married ladies and older gentlemen, although, to tell the truth, it is in young men that she will be most apt to meet with a want of breeding and courtesy, especially if she wishes to introduce them to dancing partners. But where a man is a dancing man and nothing more, where his sole capital lies in his heels, perhaps he has a right to economize the use of them.

However, it is clearly the duty of a hostess, at a ball or dancing-party, to endeavor to provide her guests with partners, and for that purpose she must either make introductions herself or through the help of others. She must always ask permission before presenting a gentleman to a lady, — permission which should never be refused unless the lady has very good and strong reasons for declining to make the gentleman's acquaintance. Young men often present each other to young ladies, and it is entirely proper that they should do so if they have first asked leave. A gentleman may also ask a lady, if he know her well, to introduce him to another lady when a proper opportunity shall occur. Of course he could neither wish nor expect his friend to cross a crowded room with him to make the introduction; because she would then be left to make a bad third, or else to retrace her way alone. The situation would be awkward, except for one of the ladies of the house.

Gentlemen do not ask for introductions to one another, because they do not generally wish to become acquainted, or if one wishes to do so he very properly hesitates to force himself on the attention of another person, who may be unwilling to know him. Ladies do not, under ordinary circumstances, ask for introductions to one another, for reasons which will be very readily understood from what has gone before. If one lady does ask, however, the person to whom she applies should find out before making the introduction whether it will be agreeable to the other lady.

An exception to this rule, both for ladies and gentlemen, is found in the case where they are invited especially to meet some person. One not only has a right to ask to be presented to the guest of the evening, but not to do so would often show a lack of courtesy. At a very large gathering, or where the honored guest is a person of distinction, one should not be too forward about pressing one's claims, especially if the guest be already talking with people of more importance, or with those who might be more agreeable to him. Modesty is usually a safe virtue to cultivate.

Another exception to the rule is found in cases where it is evident, from the circumstances, that the hostess has omitted the introduction, either from forgetfulness, or because she supposes that the ladies already know each other. In this case a lady might ask the hostess to make the introduction.

If a gentleman meets in the street two ladies, one of whom he knows, and if he joins them, he should be presented to the lady whom he does not know, in order to avoid awkwardness. But if he merely stopped a moment to speak to a lady, she would not then introduce him to her friend, unless she especially wished to do so, and had reason to suppose that the introduction would be agreeable to both parties. In all casual meetings in the street, in travelling, at the theatre, etc., — meetings, in short, on neutral ground, and where there is no hostess, the rule should be not to make undue haste to introduce people, but to do so whenever it is necessary to avoid awkwardness, or to avoid the appearance of neglect or rudeness to the friend in whose company one was at first.

Street introductions are much like what lawyers call street opinions; that is, they are easily given and do not amount to much. A lawyer does not expect to be bound by a "street opinion;" nor need any one who does not wish to, be bound by a casual introduction of this sort given as a matter of form, and where no real acquaintanceship has been made between the parties. As a lady, however, has the privilege of bowing or not bowing to a gentleman so introduced to her, he should, when he next meets her, give her an opportunity of recognizing him in case she may wish to do so.

The form of double presentation, as "Mrs. A. — Mrs. B., Mrs. B. — Mrs. A.," has now gone out of fashion, which is a pity on one account; and that is, because it gave the introducer neutral ground to stand upon, and neither party could complain because the other one's name had been spoken first. Where Mrs. B. is of about the same age as Mrs. A., it would be proper to avoid this difficulty as far as possible by saying, "Mrs. A., this is Mrs. B.," and at the same time pronouncing the two names with equal emphasis. Single ladies should be presented to married ones, and younger ladies to older ones. The formula, "Mrs. A., allow me to present Mrs. B.," is used in formal presentations only; but the name of the older or more important person should be spoken first.

A well-known society belle and a very charming woman was asked recently what her views were on the subject of introductions. "I never make them when I can avoid doing so," she replied. "What would be the use? People do not thank you for extending their circle of acquaintance ; of course in the case of strangers it is a different matter. I should introduce a stranger to any one whom I thought it would be agreeable for him to know ; and I should do it with as little formality as possible. For instance, I should perhaps say, 'Mr. Thompson, you know Mr. Great West, do you not?' or, 'Mr. Thompson, I want you to know Mr. Great West.' I should not take one up to the other if I could avoid doing so. If one gentleman joined me in the street while I was walking with another, I should certainly *not* introduce the former to the latter ; because he would have no business to join me unless he knew the gentleman with whom I was walking; and I would not allow myself to be made a pretext by one man who sought the acquaintance of another." In this little speech we have the key-note of the modern theory, — the avoidance of all formal presentations wherever it is possible to avoid them.

When one lady has asked for an introduction to another, of course it is proper to present the lady who has made the request, to the lady whom she has expressed a desire to know, if the latter consents to the introduction. Although we have neither rank nor titles in this country, still we accord the "pas" to men and women whose genius has won them distinction, military, political, literary or artistic ; and to such people those of lesser mark should be presented, as a rule, always remembering that a lady must never be presented to a gentleman, no matter how distinguished he may be, — the gentleman should always be presented to the lady.

Many years ago, when Paul Morphy the chess-player was at the height of his fame, an entertainment was given for him in Boston. The host, with more zeal than discretion, asked a lady who was well known in Boston society if she would not like to be presented to the lion of the evening. " I should be very happy," she replied, "to have Mr. Paul Morphy presented to *me*, but I do not wish to be presented to *him*." The distinction thus made was entirely correct, although it is one which Americans sometimes forget in the national passion for lion-hunting. In presenting a gentleman to a lady one may say, "Miss A., allow me to present [or to introduce] Mr. B.;" although, to tell the truth, little is usually heard of the ceremony of introduction beyond the names. Even these are sometimes ruthlessly massacred, or lost amid the surrounding noise and confusion. One should always try to pronounce names very distinctly in introducing people; and where one or both persons are well known on any account, it is perhaps well to point this out in some way, — by giving the person's full name and title, for instance, as, "Miss Jones, allow me to present Dr. Oliver Wendell Holmes to you;" or, "Miss Jones, this is Dr. Murfree, the inventor of —" etc.

Some celebrities who are of a modest turn of mind object decidedly, however, to hearing their deeds or qualities rehearsed; how much more do the brothers, sisters, wives, and daughters of distinguished people object to being placarded with such a title as, "Sister of the Member from Missouri," for instance. There is nothing more exasperating than to go through life as the brother of a great man; it condemns a man forever to a secondary place, and he feels, perhaps keenly, that whatever he can do to make an honorable name for himself, that name will always seem as nothing in the shadow of the greater one which eclipses it. How unpleasant it must be for the Marquis of Lorne to be known always as the brother-in-law of the Prince of Wales or the son-in-law of Queen Victoria, instead of as the heir to one of the oldest and most honorable titles of the British empire, — that of Duke of Argyle! With the son or daughter of a distinguished man the case is not as bad; but still it is not quite pleasant for either of them to have a person give a look that plainly says, " Well, I should have liked to see your father, but that does not make me glad to see you ! "

Should one shake hands with a person when introduced to him? It is our ordinary custom to do so in America, and the custom is a pleasant and cordial one.   Gentlemen always shake hands when they are introduced to one another ; ladies do so as a rule when they are introduced to other ladies ; when gentlemen are presented to them, many ladies offer their hands, especially if they are married, or no longer very young.   Young ladies often merely make a bow or a courtesy, particularly if they know that they do so gracefully.   Much depends, of course, on the time and place where the introduction is made.

In the ball-room the latest and most elegant fashion is simply for the lady to courtesy and the gentleman to bow ; on less ceremonious occasions a lady would usually shake hands.   Where informal introductions are made, or introductions merely to prevent awkwardness, as in the case of several callers meeting in a parlor, or in other chance rencontres, no hand-shaking is necessary.   Again, much will depend upon whether the people who are made acquainted with each other through an introduction are entire strangers, or whether they already know something of one another by report.   Thus a lady would shake hands with a gentleman who was a friend of her husband or brother, or of an intimate friend of her own.

It is the lady's privilege to offer her hand first, as it is to bow first ; but as in these matters, just as in duels, everything happens quickly if not simultaneously, a lady should accept a gentleman's hand if he offers it, to avoid awkwardness.

In her own house a lady should, in her capacity of hostess, shake hands with those who are introduced to her as well as with all her other guests, — except in case of a large ball or ceremonious reception, where, as has been said elsewhere,

15

she may merely receive them with a courtesy if she prefers to do so. The custom of making general introductions — of introducing a new-comer to a whole roomful of people — has quite gone out of fashion, lingering only in quiet country places. It is not to be regretted, since it subjected a stranger to a most trying ordeal, in which he almost invariably made a bow to the wrong person. It is now usual, at a lunch or dinner, to present a stranger shortly after his arrival to one or two persons, and afterward to others, as circumstances permit.

CHAPTER XXIV.

LETTERS OF INTRODUCTION.

In this age of universal travelling, letters of introduction fly about as freely as commercial paper, and sometimes with equally disastrous results. If one is going to England, the Continent, or even to our own Pacific Coast, it is as necessary to have these documents, in order to see anything of social life, as it is to have a letter of credit to pay one's hotel bills. Hence people importune their friends to give them letters, and the friends, in a moment of weakness or carelessness, write letters of introduction when they have really no right to do so.

There are two points which should be very carefully considered before giving letters, and these are — first, has one a right to do so ; and second, will the introduction be agreeable to both parties? To relatives, intimate friends, those whom one has received and entertained in one's own house or country, and to those who expressly give one leave to do so, one may certainly send letters introducing other friends. But because people have been polite and kind to us, because they have received and entertained us, — this gives us no right whatever to call for further favors from them. This ought to be as clear as day, one would think ; and yet our countrymen, misled probably by the cordiality of their English hosts, sometimes err in this respect.

Thus a distinguished American, Mr. ———, once met on his own doorsteps the Englishman to whom he (Mr. ———) was

bringing a letter of introduction. The latter read it, and
with true British rudeness tore it up before the face of the
bearer, saying, "This person has no right to send letters to
me!" He added, however, with true British hospitality, that
he was exceedingly glad to make the distinguished man's
acquaintance for his own sake, and treated him with just as
much courtesy and consideration — after that first dreadful
act — as if he had brought the most powerful letters of
recommendation. It is when one meets with such little
contretemps as this, that one realizes the value of knowing
and obeying the laws of etiquette. The silken strands of
their network are usually invisible, and are so loosely drawn
that we feel no pressure from them; but when they do come
to light, when they do become strained, we find they can cut
and gall very deeply.

Even where one has a right, however, to give letters of
introduction, one should use it very carefully, remembering
that their acceptance entails a hospitality that may be burdensome to one's friend, and also that two people will not necessarily be congenial to each other because they both happen
to be friends of a third person.

The most approved way to deliver a letter of introduction
is to leave it with one's card, not asking, however, to see the
person to whom it is addressed. This rule is not always
clearly understood in the United States. Two English
ladies who were staying in New York once came in their
carriage to leave a letter of introduction with their cards,
according to strict etiquette. The New York ladies to whom
the letter was addressed, responded very properly by calling
on the British dames and inviting them to lunch. What was
the horror of the latter, however, when their new acquaintances, meaning to be particularly polite, said that they were
so *very* sorry not to have seen the English ladies when they
called! Of course the English ladies had not intended mak-

ing any call beyond the formal card-leaving. On the Continent, where it is the custom for new-comers to call upon the residents of a place first, this rule need not be observed.

The reason of the rule is very obvious.   To deliver a letter of introduction in person, and wait below while it is read, like a tradesman with a bill or a servant with a recommendation, certainly does not put one in a very dignified position. It also in a measure compels the recipient of the letter to see you whether he wishes to do so or not.   Where you wish to see him on business, or when time presses, it is proper to wait and see whether he will be able to receive you.

If a gentleman brings a letter of introduction to a lady, he may also, if he pleases, send up his card and ask whether it will be convenient for her to receive him.   She will feel less constrained to do so than she would in the case of a feminine visitor; besides, there would here be no question of which should call first, as there would be between two ladies.

When one calls in acknowledgment of cards left with a letter of introduction, it is necessary to go in if the lady or gentleman, as the case may be, is at home.   Nor are all the duties of politeness incumbent on the person alone to whom the letter is addressed.   The person introduced should also take great pains to receive "letter-visitors," when they call upon him, with cordiality and politeness, instead of imitating the conduct of one distinguished Englishman in this country, who took out of his pocket a list of people to whom he had brought letters of introduction and ran it over in the presence of his visitor, saying, " Smith, Smith, Smith, — let me see where that name is on my list !"

While it is extremely desirable to be furnished with a number of letters of introduction when one is about to go to Europe, it is nevertheless highly indelicate to ask mere acquaintances for these social passports.   Not only would this be asking a favor where one had no right to do so, but it would also be putting the acquaintance in an awkward dilemma. If he were good-natured he would not wish to disoblige the person who had made the request; neither would he wish to introduce to his friends some one about whom he knew very little, and who might be extremely uncongenial to them. It is rash to give letters unless to people whom one knows well, or at least knows all about; and it is especially rash to give letters to foreigners, unless they can "read their title clear" beyond any doubt or peradventure.

Letters of introduction should always be left unsealed, as a token that the bearer is at liberty to read them. Hence, they should be brief, giving the full name and residence of the person introduced, but avoiding a multitude of complimentary phrases. A modest man will dislike to deliver a letter containing a high-sounding panegyric on himself.

It is usually sufficient to say that Mr. C. T. Brooks of Sheffield is a friend of the writer, that any attention which it may be convenient to show him will be a personal favor, and that one has no doubt the acquaintance thus begun will be mutually agreeable to both parties. On receiving such a letter one should call in a day, and the person introduced should return the call quite promptly, — say in a week. It is also necessary to show a new acquaintance whatever attentions are in one's power, — to invite him to dinner, enter his name at one's club, or at least take him to the theatre, or show him about the city or place in which one lives.

CHAPTER XXV.

LETTERS AND NOTES.

As the steel pen drove out its gentle brother the quill, so it in turn is being driven out by the telegraph wire, the type-writer, and the thousand other novel agencies which are constantly springing up in our midst as if by magic. People do not have time in this busy age to write letters, in the old-fashioned sense of the word. The telegraph wire is such a convenient medium for letting one's friends know of one's well-being, that people of means do not hesitate to use it daily, instead of writing to their families; while for business communications, the type-writer saves the busy man from the drudgery of handling the pen. Probably the most luxurious method is that of employing a stenographer to take down the golden utterances of a merchant prince, whose words, however worthless to posterity, have a momentous market value altogether beyond the conception of a mere outsider. As these great men speak, stocks — nay, the fate of nations — rise and fall.

Steam is too slow a medium for conveying our thoughts in these days. We feel about it much as Charles Lamb did in regard to writing letters to his friend in Australia, — letters which would be many months old ere they could reach their destination. With playful wit he shows the folly of sending such communications, of exporting such stale news; and the modern world finds six days to be as long and tedious as he found six months!

Still, though we are too impatient either to write or read the long and courtly letters of our grandparents' days, we do write a great many notes of one sort and another, and in some respects we are more critical about those we receive than were our forefathers. We insist that our correspondents shall spell correctly, that they shall write handsome or at least fair hands, and that they shall write straight. In looking over old manuscripts, one is struck with the school-boy appearance of the chirography, and with the almost more than school-boy quaintness of spelling. People certainly write much better than they did fifty or a hundred years ago. We have improved in the manner, if not in the matter of our communications.

It has been said elsewhere in this volume that to use ruled paper for writing invitations is considered very "bad form." Ruled paper should be kept for business communications only. Those who have not learned to write straight must content themselves with using lines under their paper.

The forms and colors of note-paper are so constantly changing and shifting, that it is hard to lay down any lasting rules in regard to styles. But it is always safe to choose plain, substantial paper, either white or of some light tint, and to avoid bright or striking colors, eccentric shapes, etc. Perfectly plain thick white paper is preferred at the present moment. French water-lined paper is not much in favor now, but it is always allowable to use it for letters, especially if it is white. For notes of invitation it is hardly heavy enough, the thinness of the paper seeming to denote a want of formality, an absence of starch, which these missives require. Rather small note-paper of the best quality should be used for writing and answering invitations. Monograms are little used now, although some persons still fancy them. A lady's initials, copied from her own handwriting, are sometimes placed diagonally across the left-hand corner of the sheet; but the envelope must be perfectly plain. An excellent and popular fashion is to have one's address — in colored letters, usually blue — engraved at the head of one's note-paper. The address and date should always be put either at the beginning or at the end of a letter. For notes, the latter is usually preferred. It is better, in dating, to use both the day of the week and the day of the month, though for a note the day of the week is sufficient. In a letter, the date of the year is given; in a note, it is not. The new business method of dating, whereby the name of the month is omitted and its number substituted, is surely a most senseless innovation. "7—11—87" may mean either the seventh day of the eleventh month, or the eleventh day of the seventh month. At best, this mode gives people the trouble of calculating the number of the month; because they do not always remember, unless they stop to think, that October is the tenth month, and not the eighth, as its name implies.

A commercial or clerk-like hand is not a desirable one to cultivate; not only does it smack too much of the counting-room, but it is too precise and formal, too much lacking in all originality and spontaneity. While every one should be carefully trained to write a good hand — handsome, even, and legible — he should be trained to write his *own* hand, and not simply to imitate some one's else. It is sometimes amusing to read the advertisements of certain wonderful systems of instruction in writing, and to note the specimens written "before" and "after" instruction. To many of us it would seem that a deterioration had taken place in the latter, and a good honest individual handwriting, sometimes a handsome one, changed to a meaningless scroll-bedecked copperplate script.

Lord Chesterfield says in his letters to his son: "I do not desire you to write a stiff, formal hand, like that of a schoolmaster, but a genteel, legible, and liberal character." Flourishes in a signature, except for a writing-master or a really great man, seem pretentious and out of place.

The extremely pointed English or Italian character, so much in vogue a few years ago, is now less fashionable than it was, which is surely a subject for thankfulness, as this special variety of ladies' handwriting is exceedingly illegible.

Great care should always be taken to fold and direct a letter neatly, and to put on the stamp evenly, in the proper corner. Would that we could use stamped envelopes! But Dame Fashion excludes these from genteel correspondence, because they are cheap, and perhaps seem careless. Fashion is a very exacting task-mistress, and usually expects us to choose the more difficult path, where two lie open. In folding a letter, care should always be taken to fold it right side up ; that is, so that the person who receives it shall not have to turn it, after taking it out of the envelope, in order to read it.

Sealing-wax, the use of which had almost died out in this country, has taken a new hold on public favor, and among the elegant appointments of a writing-desk, sealing-wax and taper are now to be reckoned. No one should use wax who cannot make an even, handsome, clearly-marked seal ; because a slovenly one looks much worse than none.

A new method of writing is to write on the first and fourth sides of a sheet, and then opening it, and turning it the other way, to write across the third and second sides continuously.

"My dear Mr. Lemprière," or "Dear Mr. Lemprière," —— which is the more formal? This is a question that is sometimes asked ; but whatever arguments may be used in favor of either form of address in the abstract, ordinary custom, in this country at least, has adopted "My dear Mr. ——" as the usual form for beginning a letter : hence when the "My"

is dropped, greater familiarity is implied, because less ceremony is used. If one wishes to be still more formal, it is
very easy to be so.

Mr. John Watkins, OR *John Watkins, Esq.*

My dear Sir, OR *Dear Sir,*

would be the proper way to begin a letter in such a case.

An excellent English authority says, "An unmarried lady
cannot address a gentleman as '*My* dear Sir,' unless she is
very old, and he too. It should be 'Dear Sir.'" It is rather
difficult to say which is the more familiar of these two forms,
and the question which of them should be used seems of very
little importance, since both are decidedly formal. Formal
letters to clergymen begin "Reverend and dear Sir."

The signature should always include the full name, or the
last name with the initials. Nicknames, such as "Carrie,"
"Bessie," should never be signed to any letters save those
written to relatives or very intimate friends. An older lady
writing to a younger one would not sign her Christian name,
but would sign herself "R. V. Bacon;" the same signature
should be used in writing business letters, letters to servants,
etc. It is not considered allowable to sign one's name as
"*Mrs.* R. V. Bacon," or "*Miss* A. B. Bacon." If it is desirable
to let one's correspondent know by what title he is to address
one, it is very easily done by inserting this formula: "Please
address Mrs. R. V. Bacon." A woman of business once
signed her name thus: "(Miss) Brooks of Sheffield," and her

correspondent, taking the " Miss " as a gentle hint, gallantly answered her with an offer of marriage ! The custom of signing circulars or business communications with Miss —— or Mrs. —— seems to be growing in public favor, nevertheless the form should be avoided wherever it is possible to do so.

The signature should correspond with the tone of a letter. " Yours with much regard," " With kind regards believe me yours cordially," are friendly, but still somewhat ceremonious. " Yours truly," " Yours very truly," " Sincerely yours," " Very sincerely yours," " Faithfully yours," " Cordially yours," " Aff'ly yours," " Affectionately yours," —— this list shows a sliding scale from most to least formal. " Yours respectfully " is only used for business letters, or in writing to a superior — either in age or position. " Yours truly," or " Very truly yours " are also reserved for business letters. " Your obedient servant " is much used in formal and business letters, and is always dignified and courteous.

The old custom was to write to servants or tradespeople in the third person. It is sometimes done now, but except for a very short communication it is an undesirable form, because awkward and indirect ; besides, it is undemocratic.

Abbreviations of words should not be used in writing : such as " & " for " and," " wh " for " which," etc. So much fun has been made of women's letters on account of their frequent underlinings and inevitable postscripts, that it is not necessary to dwell on these points. It certainly destroys all the force of italics to use them constantly, besides giving a letter a very school-girlish tone ; and while a postscript is very good for its proper purpose, that is, for adding something which has been forgotten, it is certainly not the right place to put the most important matter in the whole letter, as if one were afraid or ashamed to speak out until the last moment.

A letter should never be crossed. In these days when note-paper and postage are both cheap it is inexcusable for any one to write across the paper, thus trying to the uttermost both the eyesight and patience of a friend. Figures should not be used except in designating dates or giving the number of a house and street.

A note written in the third person must of course never be signed. Thus, to write

> *Mrs. ——— will call on Wednesday, at Mr. ———'s store, and select a carpet.*
>
> *Yours truly,*
>
> *Mrs. ———.*

would be simply barbarous. A note written in the third person must so continue all through. "Mr. Smith accepts with pleasure *your* kind invitation" is inadmissible. "Mr. Smith accepts with pleasure Mrs. Brown's kind invitation, etc.," would be a correct formula.

People who are in mourning generally use black-edged note-paper, although some persons dislike and never use it. All matters connected with mourning ought to be left to the judgment and feelings of the mourner. It is cruel to enhance sorrow by binding it around with the silken serpent of etiquette.

Where black-edged paper is used the border should vary in depth according to the length of time the writer has been in mourning, and the nearness of the relative mourned. *Very* broad mourning borders certainly seem affected as well as gloomy. The autograph letter of condolence which Queen Victoria sent to Mrs. Lincoln when the President was assassinated was written on note-paper with a black border nearly an inch deep!

A letter to a married lady should always be directed with her husband's name or initials, and not her own : thus, "Mrs. James Nevins," or "Mrs. J. B. Nevins." One cannot write "Mrs. *Rev.* Thomas Brookes," or "Mrs. *Dr.* Simeon Thomas." It is proper, however, to write "Rev. and Mrs. Thomas Brookes," or "Dr. and Mrs. Simeon Thomas." Of course where the lady is a minister of the gospel *in propria persona*, or a Doctor of Medicine, it is quite right to give her her title, — "Rev. Olympia Brown," or "Dr. Emma News." In addressing a letter to a gentleman, custom prescribes that "Esq." shall be added after his name unless he has some other title, as "Dr.," "Rev.," etc. As "Esq." is a matter of courtesy and not of right in this country, it is better to omit it where one can without leaving the name standing baldly alone. Thus "R. V. Rich, M. D.," "C. B. Roe, Jr.," look better written without the "Esq. ;" some people add it, however, and write "R. V. Rich, M. D., Esq.," and "C. B. Roe, Jr., Esq." In directing notes of invitation "Mr." should be used, and not "Esq."

Although it has been mentioned elsewhere in this volume, it is proper to repeat here that great care should be taken to write numbers, dates, and proper names with distinctness. In the case of ordinary words, the context will often furnish some clew whereby they may be guessed ; but in the case of a proper name — perhaps one that is entirely unknown to the recipient of the letter — there is nothing to assist him in deciphering it.

While it would not be fitting, in writing "the letter of the period," to imitate the diffuseness of the classic letter-writers either of antiquity or of comparatively modern times, one might with advantage copy their graceful style, and take from them many hints as to what should and what should not find place in a letter that is meant to give pleasure. Letters that are intended to annoy or irritate the recipient — angry letters — would much better not be written, on every one's account. The minute descriptions of Madame de Sévigné, whereby she gave "airy nothings a local habitation and a name," are still charming reading after two centuries have elapsed; but not even to a friend in the country would one think now-a-days of elaborating trifles at such length, even if one possessed the grace and imagination of this celebrated letter-writer.

Terseness and that brevity which is the soul of wit are essential to the composition of a modern epistle; and if a picture is to be drawn it must be photographed by the instantaneous process, not slowly worked out with the graver's tools. And yet, no brusqueness must find place in a letter. One must be concise, but never curt. Few people can trust themselves to write anything longer than a short note when in great haste; one is so apt, if not to make a mistake, at least to say something carelessly, or to leave something unsaid which if said would very essentially modify the tone and meaning of the whole. Especially is this the case where one is writing anything personal; great care should be taken to express one's meaning clearly, and to remember that the written word is so much more formal than the spoken word, that what would be passed over as a jest in the latter seems like reproof in the former. In fact, it is a very dangerous matter to find fault with people on paper; misconceptions so easily arise which in conversation would be set right in two minutes; and the receiver of the letter is sure to imagine that the writer means twice as much he says, and the former therefore proportionately magnifies what is actually said.

Hence, if one *must* write a fault-finding letter, it is only safe to express about one fourth as much as one feels. Lawyers say that the fondness of mankind for writing letters, and getting themselves into no end of trouble by their folly in so doing, is perfectly extraordinary. A conscientious lawyer will beg and pray his client to do anything rather than write a letter. *Litera scripta manet*, as astute politicians and diplomats well know. Avoid the pen as you would the Devil, when you are angry; and if you must commit follies, don't put them down on paper.

If a letter is intended to give pleasure it must not be simply an echo of the letter to which it is an answer. While it is proper to make short comments on what has been written to you, these are generally not of special interest to your correspondent, who wants usually to hear about what is going on at your end of the line, for he knows already what is happening at his own. Thus one receives some charmingly written and gracefully expressed letters, which mean and say absolutely nothing! Egotism — the other extreme — is also to be avoided in a letter, especially complaining egotism. What a terrible warning are the letters of Jane Welsh Carlyle against "growling on paper"! And what a contrast to them are the letters of the Carlyle-Emerson correspondence, where the real nobility of thought and character of these two great men stand out in such plain relief! How little did Mrs. Carlyle imagine that the grumblings by which she occasionally relieved her heart and temper were, after her death, to prejudice many minds against the husband who truly and deeply loved her! How different might all have been if she had told him frankly of her discontents, instead of writing them to other people, for the world to gossip over in the years to come!

The letters of the younger Pliny show a cheerful, amiable disposition, giving us at the same time that innocent gossip in which the human mind ever delights, and many interesting pictures of the manners of his day. He is not a bad model for a correspondent, especially as his letters are not usually long.

A letter should be cheerful in tone, and it should not be written unless one has something to say. If a person is obliged to write and has nothing to say, he should not go on saying it for several pages.

A brief but courteous note is far pleasanter to receive than a long-drawn-out letter over which the writer has labored long and painfully. It is a good rule always to read over letters before sending them. Copying is to be deprecated, as it is apt to make letters stiff and formal.

One should be very careful not to write familiarly to people whom one does not know well, to those who are much older, or to people who hold a high position in the world. A letter may be entirely courteous and dignified, and yet not at all familiar. Indeed, it shows a want of self-respect to attempt familiarity where one has no right to do so, and where it may be resented. In writing to friends and intimates it is of course proper to adopt a very different tone, and not to offend them by what they would rightly consider stiffness; though the same form of words might be entirely proper and courteous if addressed to a comparative stranger.

Jesting in letters is rather a dangerous matter, since such jokes are often misunderstood, and being taken in earnest often cause much annoyance and even unhappiness. It is sometimes said of a person who is skilful in writing letters whereof the tone is easy and conversational, " He writes just as he speaks." A little observation, however, will generally bring out the fact that the writer is possessed of the *ars celare artem*, just as the realistic actor is; the skilful letter-writer has the art of making his letters appear as if they were

16

"frozen conversation," but the tinkling ice-crystals are not the result of simple congelation : say, rather, they are the work of a skilful confectioner, who can make his ice at any time of year.

There should always be more formality in the written than in the spoken word ; even the most familiar letter should be worded and expressed with greater care, with more grammatical exactness, and with greater rhetorical precision, than is called for in ordinary speech. It seems a much easier thing to write a good letter than it really is ; just as the flowing, easy, and graceful style of some authors impresses the reader with the feeling that he himself, or any one, could write like that ! But a brief trial will speedily convince him that he cannot.

Slang should not find a place save in the most familiar letters. Care also should be taken to avoid mixing up pronouns, and making " he," " she," " it," etc., refer first to one person or thing and then to another in the same sentence. We need several new pronouns in English, as our language is sadly deficient in them. The man who should successfully invent or derive from classic tongues some new pronouns would deserve the gratitude of the whole English-speaking race. As a matter of fact, he would be sent either to a lunatic asylum or a dungeon cell. We can invent " dudes " and discover planets, but the lost pronouns will never more be found ! And yet to what subterfuges and circumlocutions is the writer not driven for the want of an equivalent to " he;" " him," etc., and for a singular form of "they" which should be of common gender ! " John met Mr. J——— ; he asked him whether he would not go and take a drive in his new dog-cart." But instances of this painful nature need not be cited, as they are so common.

After making a visit at a friend's house one should always write a note or letter acknowledging the kindness and hospitality of host or hostess. When answering even a familiar note of invitation, one should be very careful to do so courteously as well as promptly, wording the answer as much like the invitation as possible. The day — and for a dinner or lunch the hour — should be repeated, so as to be sure that there is no mistake ; as for instance, —

My dear Mrs. Jones,

It will give me much pleasure

to lunch with you on Thursday

at half-past one o'clock.

With kind regards, believe me

Cordially yours,

Delia H. Jenckes.

13 Chestnut Street,

Monday.

A written invitation must never receive a verbal answer, but always a written one. To send an answer by word of mouth, except where one has been invited in the same way, is extremely impolite. One must never send a visiting card with "regrets" written on it. To do so would be very "bad form." Invitations must be answered on note-paper, and not on visiting cards. The custom of writing "Present" or

"Addressed" on a letter which is to be delivered by a private messenger is rapidly going out of fashion. The same is true of the superscriptions "Kindness of Mr. Smith," "Favored by Mr. Smith," etc. It suffices to direct such a letter to the street and number only, — omitting the name of the city or town, — or with the name of the gentleman's place, if he lives in the country. Thus: Mrs. James Meredith, Beaulieu.

CHAPTER XXVI.

ON DRESS.

THE wise physician does not take his own drugs, neither do the wise and witty Frenchwomen follow their own fashions, — that is to say, they do not follow them to extremes, nor adhere to them with the martyr-like fidelity which so strongly characterizes Americans. At last, however, our countrywomen are beginning to think for themselves a little in the matter of dress. Since it has grown to be fashionable to dress becomingly and with a certain amount of individuality, we have plucked up a little spirit, and have even signed a sort of moderate and feeble declaration of independence against our old enemies, French fashions and perfect uniformity in dress. How well I remember a certain spring season in my childhood when every woman between the ages of twelve and forty wore a yellow straw-bonnet trimmed with green ribbon on the outside and pink on the inside! And that autumn after Napoleon III.'s campaign in Italy, when no respectable person thought of having her bonnet trimmed with any other color than solferino or magenta! Now, if we come across a bit of one of these old and crude colors in looking over some ancient store of scraps and pieces, how we shudder! We can hardly believe that "gentlewomen wore such caps as these," or could have made themselves so supremely ugly.

The study of dress is in these days an approved branch of feminine education. It has never been wholly neglected, only women have too often pursued it with their eyes shut, and now they mean to keep them open, — a very great improvement.

The two chief points which a woman should always bear in mind in regard to dress are — first, is it appropriate ; second, is it becoming ? A lady should never be tempted to wear a costume which is unsuitable to the occasion, merely by the fact that she looks well in it ; because in so doing she violates that harmony which is one of the first laws of art and nature alike. Instead of pleasing other people she will jar on their sense of fitness, and she will be apt also to render herself conspicuous, and to appear to display unnecessary vanity.

Dress should always be subordinate to the wearer ; for if a human being is of any account at all, he is surely more important than his own clothes. Never dress in such a way, therefore, that your clothes shall attract every one's attention, as if you considered them of vastly more consequence than yourself. We all remember the old Roman joke about "the sword that was seen with a little man tied to it." We should "dress to live, not live to dress." And yet some women will spend their whole time and energy in devising and planning what they shall wear, and wherewithal they shall be clothed, as if they themselves, their own hearts and minds and bodies, were of comparatively small importance beside the vast, never-ending subject of clothing !

Lord Chesterfield says, " The difference in dress between a man and a fop is, that the fop values himself upon his dress ; and the man of sense laughs at it at the same time that he knows he must not neglect it."

What tremendous satire lies in Thackeray's caricature of Le Grand Monarque Louis XIV. ! First, we have the man and his clothes combined ; second, we have the little old king, looking small enough without his grand finery ; and third, there is the finery alone, — enormous wig, great wide-sleeved, long-skirted coat, and shoes with lofty heels. Really, it looks almost as well without any one in it. It can "stand alone" quite as well as some of the rich silk dresses that are supposed to be able to do so. And if Thackeray is powerful on this subject, what shall we say of the great master Carlyle and his wonderful "Sartor Resartus," in which not the folly alone of man's making a clothes-horse of himself, but the folly and unworthiness of so many pursuits that go to make up the sum of human life are portrayed with the author's inimitable satire, from which pathos is never far distant! Carlyle's laughter comes ever near to tears.

Whether Woman is behind Man in civilization because she pays an attention to dress which he has long ago disused, or whether her devotion to it is because man requires her to be robed in gay attire, is a question which I shall not here enter into. Suffice it to acknowledge that women are expected in this age to pay more attention to dress than men do, and that they are therefore justified in so doing — within limits.

In determining whether a lady's dress is or is not appropriate, we must take into consideration not only the occasion on which it is worn but the worldly means of the wearer. It is decidedly inappropriate, and in very bad taste, to dress more expensively than one can afford to do. No one thinks better of you for doing so. The spiteful will laugh at you, and the "judicious will grieve," to think that you have gone to an expense which you could not afford, and for which you may pay dearly in some way. Never ape the finery of those who are much richer in worldly goods than you are; of great statues we have plaster casts, it is true, but a cheap copy of a handsome dress is apt to be a wretched affair. There are certain styles which look well in all materials, but these are the exceptions. As a rule, what is appropriate in a silk dress is not suitable for a calico, and *vice versa*. A cheap material, especially if it be of woollen, and intended for every-day use, should be trimmed very plainly. How often do we see in the horse-cars (where enforced idleness gives one leisure for the study of sumptuary laws) garments made of cheap, flimsy dry-goods elaborately garnished with ruffles and "bias folds," poorly cut, and considerably the worse for wear, — some light color which shows every spot, adding to the general inappropriateness of the costume! A dress should be made very simply if it is expected to do service for a long time. Elaborate trimmings soon grow shabby.

Another fatal error which some women make is that of putting handsome, expensive trimming on cheap gowns. It fairly makes one shudder to see iridescent beads on an ill-fitting garment which cost twenty-five cents a yard! How much better would it have been to take the money spent for these inappropriate gewgaws and to pay therewith for the services of a good dressmaker! Or if a woman is obliged to do all her own sewing, let her save the time spent in making deforming ruffles and expend it in learning to make her dresses fit well. The result will be much more stylish and more satisfactory in every way.

All scholars know the difficulty of translating a poem from one language into another. To translate a Worth costume meant to be worn at receptions and kettledrums into a home-made gown intended for walking in muddy streets through all weathers is just about as easy. A wise woman will not attempt " to keep to the original metre " in such a case.

Oscar Wilde, who is a man of considerable parts, despite his numerous follies and affectations, has written a very interesting article, in which he points out how much thought Shakspeare gave to the subject of dress, and what an important part it has in the dramatic effect produced by his plays. Many of the characters describe their own costume, although the description is so skilfully interwoven with the rest of the text that one does not think of it as a stage direction "what to wear."

Of Juliet the article says, " A modern playwright would probably have laid her out in her shroud, and made the scene a scene of horror merely ; but Shakspeare arrays her in rich and gorgeous raiment, whose loveliness makes the vault 'a feasting presence full of light,' turns the tomb into a bridal chamber, and gives the cue and motive for Romeo's speech of the triumph of Love over Life, and of Beauty over Death." An inventory, still in existence, of the costume wardrobe of a London theatre in Shakspeare's time contains a most astonishing number and variety of garments of every sort, including a robe "for to go invisibell," — no doubt for the ghost in Hamlet.

The Greeks, — from whose school of taste and art what modern nation can hope to graduate ? — the Greeks finished their statues as perfectly behind as in front, even those which were placed so high in the friezes of the temples that no one could possibly see the reverse side. Women can well take a hint from this many-sided perfection, and remember that the effect of a costume should be studied in the rear and in profile quite as much as in front.

The side view of a woman's face framed in one of the very high bonnets of the present time is singular enough. A diagonal line drawn from the chin to the top of the topmost feather represents the greatest diameter —and what greatness ! Meanwhile the hair is absorbed and drawn up under this towering finery, leaving the shortest diameter — from the nape of the neck across to the mouth — wonderfully short.

Every woman who can possibly afford it should have a cheval-glass, or at any rate a glass long enough to reflect her whole figure from head to foot, otherwise she cannot know with any certainty the true appearance of her costume. This is specially necessary for people either much shorter or

much taller than the average height, since the result may
be very disastrous if they attempt to copy a style of dress
which looks well on some woman of medium height, without
stopping to think whether the same thing will be becoming
to a person of different figure. The same advice may be
given to very stout or very thin women, to very pale or very
florid ones; in short, to any one who differs decidedly in
any particular from "the average woman." The average woman only can copy with impunity or with anything resembling it. Garments are made to fit her, and fashions are
designed more or less to become her; but even she must not
revel in sheep-like imitation if she wishes to look her best.

It is only a very good figure which looks well when all its
outlines are shown distinctly; a woman with a poor figure
should seek rather to soften and disguise it, be she angular and
high-shouldered, or short and stout. What painful displays
of ugly forms we have all seen since the advent of the recent
fashions, which decree that a woman shall wear neither cloak
nor mantle in the street, but go abroad in a costume which
would have been considered rather a questionable one even
for the house twenty years ago! Questionable, because fitted
to the form with an exactness which was not then considered
allowable.

A very tall woman who wears a very long skirt should
have a good deal of trimming on it, because this breaks
the line of the skirt and makes it seem shorter. A short woman, *per contra*, should wear little trimming on her skirt, or
should have it near the bottom, so as to make the lines long.
She should, for the same reason, avoid basques, except very
short ones. One of the most fashionable women in Boston
wears a perfectly plain plaited skirt for a street dress, because
it is becoming to her and makes her look taller.

A very tall woman should never wear a broad flaring round
hat, unless she wishes to look like Mrs. Japheth or Mrs. Shem

just coming out of the ark. A short-waisted woman should never wear a belt. A very stout person should wear dark colors (which make one look smaller), and materials which are close and fine rather than loose and rough. The effect of a stout woman arrayed in gray furzy cloth covered with imitation snow-flakes is very like that of a polar bear. Another delusion of short stout elderly women is that very tight-fitting polonaises are becoming to them; and so they allow their mantua-makers to array them in clinging garments which make them look like closely-draped beer-barrels.

When the great Beau Brummell was asked why Englishmen were so much better dressed than Frenchmen, he replied laconically, " 'T is the hat." And some beaux in these days maintain with a good deal of reason that if a man's hat is new and in good style, it does not so much matter about the rest of his clothes. Good gloves, good shoes, and a fresh hat or bonnet are certainly very important items in a person's appearance. The great man quoted above said that a gentleman should use six pairs of gloves in a day! Gloves should be well fitting; it is seldom an economy to buy cheap ones.

According to the present fashion, ladies do not take off their gloves at a ball, reception, or other occasion where the collation is a stand-up affair. They keep their gloves on while eating, although to many of us it seems far from neat to do so, since one cannot hold cake, sandwiches, etc., in one's fingers without soiling the gloves.

A foolish newspaper rumor has gone abroad that the lady of the White House eats her dinner with her gloves on. But this story is a highly improbable one; and if it were true, the example thus set would not be followed by our best society, the members of which are too sensible to be governed by the fancies of any (native) leader of fashion. It is considered "bad form" to sit down at table with gloves on; and they are always removed at breakfast, luncheon, dinner, tea, and at a formal supper, where all the guests sit at table and the service is in courses.

Gloves appear to have been very ancient concomitants of civilization. In the Odyssey, Homer describes Laertes as working in his garden with leather gloves on to protect his hands from thorns. Gloves are also spoken of in the Bible, — in the book of Ruth and in that of Kings. Queen Elizabeth of England wore sweet-scented gloves, which were brought from Italy during her reign by Edward de Vere, Earl of Oxford.

Never allow one garment to be so expensive or showy that the rest of your costume will contrast badly with it. Do not wear a thirty-dollar bonnet with an old and shabby dress. Let all your garments have a certain accord with one another, so that they may seem to belong together. If the colors contrast, let it not be with too much violence.

One should be very careful to select materials and styles of dress that are suited to one's age, figure, height, and complexion. A great many women consider only the beauty or ugliness of a garment in itself, and quite forget that the same costume will make one woman look like a scarecrow and another like a goddess. They see in the street, perhaps, some "love of a bonnet" worn by a charming young girl with fresh bright complexion, and are filled with a desire and a determination to have one just exactly like it, never stopping to think whether it will be equally suitable to a person of a totally different coloring, age, and figure.

There is an old saying that a sheep does not look well dressed up in a lamb's clothing. Miss Maria Oakey, in her little book on "Beauty in Dress," points out to women that as their age increases, the tints of the complexion necessarily change, and that therefore the same colors will not be becoming to a woman of forty and to a girl of sixteen. It is the same old story that Dr. Holmes tells so charmingly in his

" Autocrat of the Breakfast-table."   Old Age (so the witty Doctor says) comes to us in the guise of a friend, and offers us now a cane and a pair of arctics to aid our steps in slippery weather, and now a muffler to keep out the winter's cold. And we are quite indignant at his first visit. We inform him that he has mistaken the house, and we go bravely out, scorning his proffered aid.   But a fall on the ice or an attack of sore-throat teaches us that Old Age was right, and the second time he calls upon us we receive the wraps and mufflers with a thankful and humble heart.

So it is, or so it should be, with dress; and both men and women should remember to modify the style and fashion of their raiment as they grow older.   But, alas ! many people are seized with a sudden desire for youth just as it is slipping away from them, and men of forty-five will shave off their beards and appear with the smooth face which looks well only on a young man or a very handsome one.   Women of mature years will wear round hats, or bonnets without strings, forgetting that age shows about the throat and neck as much as at the corners of the eyes.

Many people, however, go to the other extreme, and knowing that their youth is a thing of the past, they pay little attention to the question whether their dress is becoming or the reverse.   They fossilize into a certain style of costume and into a certain way of arranging the hair.   Every woman, if she lives long enough, reaches this state of fossilization of coiffure.and dress ; but some women reach it at an unduly early age.

While the affectation of youth is a thing to be strenuously avoided, it is still to be remembered that at every age the human form divine possesses some degree of beauty.   The beauty of middle-aged and elderly people is not usually perceptible to the very young, but it is to their contemporaries ; and it is patent to all the world that every one, even a plain or elderly person, looks better when becomingly dressed.

Therefore, when a middle-aged woman imagines that no one cares how she looks or dresses, she makes a great mistake. To her husband, her children, and her friends it is surely gratifying to see the mother of the family clad in becoming raiment; and while, like the pelican, she may strip off some of her fine feathers for the benefit of her nestlings, she should not imitate the conduct of fond and foolish Lear, and give her worldly all to her children.

American women wear much more showy and elaborate costumes when walking in the street than do their European sisters, who consider it unladylike to go abroad in gorgeous raiment except in a carriage. We are beginning to be of the same opinion in this country; witness the quiet tailor-made street costumes now so popular.

Diamonds and handsome jewels are never worn in the street nor in travelling by Englishwomen of quality, who consider that such ornaments should be reserved for the evening or for large and gay occasions. In this country the rules in regard to wearing jewelry are much more lax; but ladies of good taste seldom wear bracelets or much jewelry of any sort in the morning, or in the street at any hour. Many ladies wear diamond earrings in the daytime, especially if the stones are not very large. It certainly seems inappropriate to time and place to wear large and expensive diamonds when walking in the street. One incurs also no small risk of having them stolen.

The woman who walks abroad or goes in the cars very showily dressed and covered with jewelry, conveys to the beholder the idea that she does not belong to what is technically called society; that she has no legitimate opportunity to display her handsome clothes, and therefore is obliged to wear them in the street or not at all.

CHAPTER XXVII.

THE DRESS AND CUSTOMS APPROPRIATE TO MOURNING.

It seems a strange thing that we, who profess and call ourselves Christians, should yet think it right to assume the trappings of the deepest woe and gloom upon the death of a near and dear friend. According to our belief the loved one has gone to a happier world, free from all pain and care. Why, then, should we surround ourselves with the tokens of a woe that is in some sort a rebellion against the decrees of Divine Providence? Many people, reasoning thus, feel that it is not right to put on any outward show of mourning, and it must be confessed that their argument is a logical one. Others, again, object to wearing weeds because the custom is such an expensive one, and because poor people feel that they must comply with it, or seem wanting in respect for the dead ; whereas if the rich did not set them the example, the poor would not feel obliged to follow it.

On the other hand, there are many reasons to be urged in favor of allowing people to assume a mourning garb where they wish to do so. The voice of society is not cruel enough in these days to dictate a universal law on the subject, though it may once have done so ; nor does it hold up to scorn and obloquy those who from conscientious motives refuse to comply with its mandates. A mourning dress is a great protection against thoughtless and painful inquiries. It shows at once to all friends and acquaintances that the wearer has recently lost some near and dear friend, and warns them not to jar upon a sad mood with a merry one, nor to ask careless questions. Some people are so deficient in tact that they will ask a person in deep black for whom she is wearing mourning, but fortunately such people are not very common.

In the first prostration of a heavy sorrow it is a comfort to many persons to have something that is purely mechanical with which to fill up the time and to distract the mind, even if only in a very small measure, from the crushing grief which threatens to overwhelm it. Thus the necessary arrangements for mourning, etc., are really a painful blessing, though one does not always know that they are so at the time.

One of the most poignant regrets, secondary only to the sense of the loss itself, is caused by the feeling that the dead must, in the nature of things, soon be forgotten, and their names as well as their places be lost from among the living. Hence those who are in deep sorrow cling beyond all things to the memory of their dead, and to whatever tends to keep it alive. They feel, too, that garments of mourning are a fit outward sign of a true inward sorrow, and that in wearing them the last token of respect and affection is paid to the dead. Many of us have seen people who did not believe in the custom of wearing mourning, who thought it an empty show and formality, and yet when their own time of real trouble came, were very glad to take refuge in sable trappings.

Mourning is not now usually worn for so great a length of time as formerly; and although some people — at least some women — are very censorious and exacting on the subject, society in general allows more liberty of choice than it once did both in regard to wearing mourning at all, and to the length of time for wearing it. In New England, public sentiment has never required so much outward show in this and other matters as is found in the Middle States. Philadelphia, again, has the reputation of being more ceremonious than New York. But the old-fashioned and extreme tyranny of mourning, which forbade women to appear in the street unless they were covered by a suffocating and unhealthy crape veil, and which declared that windows giving on the street must be darkened for so many weeks or months after a death in the house, — all this has passed or is passing rapidly away.

Physicians have objected so much to the injurious habit of covering the face with crape, that veils of this material are now used much less than formerly. They are replaced by nun's veiling, — a fabric at once prettier, softer, cheaper, and more durable than crape. It must never be worn over the face, however, unless at a funeral, as it is very injurious to the eyes.

The length of time for wearing mourning varies greatly according to individual taste and feeling in this country, with a tendency, however, to shorter rather than longer periods, save with ultra-conservative people.

We are still inclined to be shocked at the brevity of French mourning; but it must be remembered that the longer people wear black, the harder it is for them to leave it off, so that in some cases daughters who have lost a parent can hardly persuade themselves to put on colors again after four or even five years. This is morbid and all wrong; it comes from a confusion of ideas, and a misinterpretation of the meaning of mourning. By resuming our ordinary garments we do not signify that our sorrow has become no sorrow, but rather that it has assumed a different phase, and has ceased to be the prominent, nay, the all-absorbing feature in our lives that it was at first.

According to French etiquette a widow wears mourning for her husband during one year and six weeks. This period is subdivided into three shorter ones; namely, six months of deep mourning, six months of ordinary, and six weeks of half

17

mourning. For a father, mother, or wife the French wear mourning for six months, divided into three of deep and three of half mourning; for a sister or brother two months, of which one is deep mourning; for a grandparent, two and a half months of slight mourning; for an aunt or uncle, three weeks of ordinary mourning; and for a cousin, two weeks.

Deep mourning consists of plain lustreless woollen stuffs and crape. The stuffs should be of handsome material and fine texture where the means of the wearer will allow, but should always be made up in a simple and unostentatious manner, and not overloaded with crape. Not only is the custom of wearing a great quantity of crape going out of vogue, but it is also a very objectionable fashion, because real sorrow should never be made to appear like a sort of dress-parade. Dull jet beads are now much worn in mourning, but a profusion of them is not appropriate to its earlier stages.

Silk trimmed with crape is not considered to be "deep black," but is worn in the secondary stages of mourning. Woollens trimmed with lustreless silk, and bonnets made of or trimmed with silk, also belong to what may be called ordinary mourning. Jet is not considered allowable save in slight mourning, in this country, although it is in England; neither is lace used. In half-mourning, black and white as well as gray are now worn, but not violet and lilac, as was formerly the fashion. Complimentary mourning is black silk without crape.

It is difficult to lay down exact rules, — where custom varies as it does in this country, — and the best that can be done is to approximate ordinary usage as nearly as may be in regard to the length of time during which mourning is worn in various cases. Widows usually wear deep mourning for two years, and in some cases retain it for life. It is in very questionable taste, however, for a young and pretty widow to wear her mourning after she has become " reconciled " to the death of her first husband and is quite willing to marry a second. A widow still wearing her weeds, and at the same time carrying on an animated flirtation with some new admirer, is a sight to make the gods weep. We do not wish that women should commit suttee in any form ; but to angle for a second husband with the weeds worn for the first, because they are becoming, is a thing that should be forbidden by law. Where a widow is leaving off her mourning, of course the case is quite different, because she has then already begun to signify her intention of wearing black no more. If a widow happens to become engaged to be married while still in mourning, many people think she should not discard her black robes until her marriage ; where a suitable length of time has elapsed, however, after the death of the first husband, it would seem more appropriate for her to leave off her mourning gradually.

For parents, mourning is usually worn during two years, and made lighter in the second year. Many people, however, continue to wear deep mourning, crape veil and all, for two years. For brothers and sisters, the usual period is one year of deep mourning and a year or less of lighter mourning. For uncles, aunts, or grandparents, three to six months of ordinary, not deep mourning are usually thought sufficient, unless where the tie has been an unusually near and dear one. Indeed, many people do not put on mourning at all, save for very near relatives. The custom of wearing deep black for long periods of time as a compliment to one's husband's relations is certainly a very objectionable one. It seems to take all the real meaning from mourning, and to make it a mere form and show. For in the very nature of things one cannot love another person's kindred like one's own.

Parents often wear mourning for grown-up sons or daughters during two years. For children, most people do not wear crape ; not because the grief is not of the deepest, but because very stiff formal mourning seems utterly unfitted to express the tender though poignant grief caused by the loss from this world of a child's pure innocent spirit. In the same way mourning for young children is not usually worn during more than a year ; this, in spite of the fact that the loss of a child often causes sorrow more enduring than any other. The idea of respect for the dead enters more or less into all our theories of mourning, and this respect seems specially due to older people.

When one is in deep mourning, one does not go into society, nor does one receive nor pay visits. Neither does one go to the theatre, or other public place of amusement, unless it be to a concert, until at least six months have elapsed after the death of a near relative. After three months it is considered allowable to attend concerts. Some people make this period of strict seclusion much longer ; but it must always be remembered that to many persons this isolation continued for months or years, this deprivation of all save the most limited society, and of every sort of relaxation or amusement that could take their minds from the one preoccupying thought, is not only very depressing but extremely injurious. We are not all alike, and to some minds it is fatal to be allowed to prey entirely upon themselves. Hence, while people in deep mourning should certainly avoid gay society, they ought not to be too strictly judged, if, after a decent period of time, they find it to be for their comfort and happiness to see their friends occasionally in a quiet way, or even to seek the consolation of music at concerts. The strictest and most formal mourning is not always the most sincere. In the charming story of " Edelweiss," the author describes a son, who crushed with grief

for the loss of his mother, finds his only consolation in resuming work at his trade as soon as the funeral is over;
the neighbors are of course deeply scandalized at his proceedings, as they listen to the *tap*, *tap* of his shoemaker's
hammer.

Older people should not expect younger ones to remain in
strict seclusion as long a time as they themselves do; the grief
of youth is often very intense, but it does not usually last as
long as that of persons of mature years. Moreover, it is a
cruel thing to shroud the natural gayety and bright spirits of
the young in long-continued mourning and depression. They
should of course be willing to pay a proper respect to the
memory of the relatives they have lost; but no young life
should be permanently shadowed by grief and sorrow.

Some gentlemen put on complete suits of black, weeds on
their hats, and black gloves, on the loss of any near relation.
Most men, however, confine their mourning to a band of
crape on the hat, except at the funeral, when they wear black
suits and black gloves. Custom varies on this point in
different cities. In New York, it is much more common to
see gentlemen dressed in mourning than it is in Boston.
Men are not expected to seclude themselves from society
for so long a period as women, though every one is shocked
to see a man appear in the gay world soon after the death
of a near relative. A widower often wears black for two
years; it is perhaps needless to state that many men cease to
be widowers long before that period is over. The feeling of
society, however, is in favor of a man's remaining faithful to
the memory of his wife for two years; longer than that no
one expects him to wait before consoling himself. A widow,
however, is never quite forgiven by the world at large if she
marries again, —this difference in our judgments of the conduct of the two sexes shows plainly a survival of savage ideas
in the midst of our boasted civilization.

Some formal people dress children in mourning after the loss of a near relative; but to most of us it seems positively wrong to depress the spirits of a little one by such solemn garb. Childhood comes but once. God endowed children with a bright and happy spirit; they cannot understand the meaning of death and sorrow, why need we try to teach it to them? The compromise of dressing children in white is a rather unpractical and expensive one.

The custom of putting coachmen and footmen into mourning livery seems a very empty and formal one; nevertheless among rich people in New York and elsewhere, it is quite customary to do so. It is usual to wear black or quiet colors when attending a funeral.

When there has been a death in a family, it is customary for friends and acquaintances to call within a month, not with the expectation that they will be received, but merely to show their sympathy. Intimate friends call much sooner, — before the funeral, if their intimacy warrants it, or shortly after. They of course ask to see the family; but no one should feel hurt if mourners, in the first prostration of grief, refuse to see anybody.

When people in mourning feel ready once more to receive visits, they announce the fact by sending out black-edged cards enclosed in envelopes to those who have called upon them. This is by no means, however, a universal custom, although a convenient one.

According to an old superstition, it is unlucky for any one to appear at a wedding dressed in black. It is usual, therefore, even for those in deep mourning, to lay it aside for that one occasion, and to appear in white, gray, or purple, or in other and brighter colors. Of course people who are in deep mourning attend only the weddings of relatives or intimate friends, and would not in any case be present at large or gay wedding receptions. In England, deep red would be worn at a wedding, as the alternative for mourning,— an idea perhaps derived from the Chinese, whose mourning color is red and not black. Indeed, an Englishwoman wearing crape will sometimes appear with an artificial red rose stuck in her bonnet. In this country, no one would think of wearing colored artificial flowers, and many people object even to natural flowers of bright colors when worn with mourning. In second mourning, however, it seems quite proper for a lady to wear natural flowers of any color that she pleases,— not, of course, in profusion.

Mourning dress should be left off gradually. It is startling to see a person one day in crapes and the next in bright colors.

Formal letters of condolence have now gone out of fashion; even intimate friends confine themselves to writing short notes, in which they strive to express their real sympathy, or to give utterance to some comforting thought, rather than to preach, or inculcate a lesson of resignation, in the old-fashioned cruel manner. Sympathy is grateful to almost every one, and we are all glad to hear words of hope and cheer from those who have a true and living faith in things immortal and invisible; but sorrow brings its own lesson, and seldom do we need additional ones from self-constituted mortal teachers, when we are already learning from a Higher Source. It must be added that to many people letters of condolence are only distressing, and serve merely to keep the wound open. If these letters are sent at all, it should be promptly, if possible within a week or two after a death. In that early time of grief, the mourners' hearts are so filled to overflowing that they cannot do anything but think and speak of their sorrow. Later on, after they have begun to take up again the business of life, while they may grieve as deeply as ever, a certain reserve comes over their feelings, which makes it very painful to many people either to read letters of condolence or to talk about those they have lost. Unless a strong feeling urges them to do so, persons who are not intimate friends should not write these letters; of course there are exceptions to this rule, notably in the case of public or other well-known characters, where their relatives feel that tributes to their worth and eminence are only right and proper, and to be expected.

Visits of condolence require much tact on the part of those who pay them, especially where they are made some time after a death has taken place. Unless the visitor is a very intimate friend, it is generally better not to intrude upon the other's sorrow by talking freely on the subject. Rather should one lead the conversation that way, and give the mourner an opportunity — if she wishes — to speak of her grief and its cause. People differ much in this respect; to some it is a relief to pour forth their sorrow, and to others it is so painful to do so, that friends must steer a middle course between seeming indifferent and appearing intrusive. Tact, sympathy, and knowledge of a friend's character must dictate what one shall do or say.

Some well-meaning but thoughtless people will meet an acquaintance who is in deep affliction, in the street, or in a railroad station, and will perhaps say, " I am so sorry to have heard of your trouble!" Anxious to express their sympathy, they forget how torturing it may be to the other person to have her wound so suddenly probed, and in such a public place, where it would be most unfitting to give way to grief. It is quite possible by look, tone, and manner to indicate the sympathy which time and place forbid one to express.

Where those who are in affliction have a large circle of relatives and friends, the latter should remember that it may be extremely painful for the mourners to be obliged to recount the circumstances of their loss, and give a detailed account of the last illness and death, over and over again.

CHAPTER XXVIII.

HOST AND GUEST.

THE bond between host and guest has in all times been held to be of a peculiar and even sacred character. In ancient Greece hospitality was a matter of religion, and violation of its duties was thought to provoke the wrath of the gods. A stranger was regarded as enjoying the protection of Zeus Xenios, and was received and guarded from harm during his stay. Indeed, the roads were all sacred, and whoever passed over them was the guest of the land. A free lunch even was provided for him, since he was at liberty to take the offerings of food, etc., which were to be found in front of the statues of the tutelary deity of the road, who was generally that prince of thieves, Hermes.

When the guest parted from his host, a sort of true-love token in the shape of a die was sometimes broken between them. Each took a part, and a family connection was thus established, the broken die serving as a symbol of recognition. The guest was often presented with valuable gifts, which must have been rather troublesome to carry away in those times when express companies had not been invented. The common statement that a stranger was considered as an enemy is said to be a groundless one.

The Italian races had customs similar to those of the Greeks. *Jupiter Hospitalis* watched over the *jus hospitii*, or law of hospitality, and the connection between host and guest often became hereditary. In ancient Rome the law recognized between them a tie almost as strong as that which connected patron and client, and a guest could appear in a court of justice only through his host.

The hospitality of the Hebrews is familiar to us all from the pages of the Bible. Indeed, Oriental hospitality is so sacred in its character, and so picturesque and striking in its details, that it has come to be the source of imagery, and the type of which we all involuntarily think whenever the relations of host and guest are under discussion. As customs in the East have varied so little during many ages, we may still behold and wonder at ceremonies hospitable and otherwise, which have been practised there for countless centuries. To our more emancipated minds, however, the long and ceremonious salutations, the oft-repeated hand-shakings or prostrations, the giving and receiving of endless presents, together with the profound gravity pervading all these and other ceremonies, seem more like child's play than the behavior suitable to full-grown and rational beings. The hospitality of a nation will always exhibit some of its special characteristics. Munificence and elaborate ceremony are the important elements of Oriental hospitality ; but of the real every-day life of his host, a guest travelling in the East necessarily learns very little.

The Englishman's views of the proper reception and treatment of a guest are of a very different sort. Love of liberty and a fondness for domestic life are the strongest — or certainly the best — traits of the Briton, and he therefore shares with the stranger within his gates what he himself values most ; namely, perfect freedom, and the pleasures of home life, also roast beef and beer in abundance.

We Americans are so peripatetic in our habits, and so active in our tastes and pursuits, that we sometimes over-weary our guests by the number of amusements provided for their delectation. We fairly kill them with kindness.

The French value inordinately the conversational powers with which they themselves are so abundantly gifted. Accordingly they amuse their guests with a vast and never-ending flow of talk, and consider the mere providing of food and drink as a very inferior branch of hospitality. It certainly is ; and the civilization of a nation which holds it necessary above all things to stuff a guest thoroughly and well, as if he were a pig, is on a much lower plane than that of a people whose cardinal social belief is in the necessity and delight of an interchange of thoughts and ideas.

That was a grave charge which Mr. Alcott brought against the Chelsea philosopher. "I accuse T. Carlyle of inhospitality to my thought," said the Concord sage — or so the story runs. But no one less optimistic than Mr. Alcott could have hoped that a man holding ideas and theories so widely different from his own as did Mr. Carlyle, could even momentarily sympathize with his peculiar views.

The host is necessarily a sort of temporary ruler; if his guests misbehave in any way he is considered responsible for them. Like all rulers, he is liable to be in some degree a tyrant, though perhaps with the best intentions in the world. The old-fashioned host would not think of allowing his guests to leave the house before the proper hour for their departure, and detained them almost by force, — all in the exercise of his duty. Nay, he did more than this ; for he often compelled them to drink much more wine than was good for them.

The modern host is but a shadow of his ancient prototype. Indeed, one of the most striking changes in our manners is to be found in the surrender of the sceptre of hospitality to the hands of women. The host has become of little importance, the hostess is the powerful factor ; and even the invitations — for almost all social occasions — stand in her name alone. In America our men are too busy to give their time to the consideration of social matters. Besides, the women wish to rule, and the men of our country, with the latter-day common-sense sort of chivalry that distinguishes them above all others, think it only fair to grant us this privilege. They bear in mind the French proverb, "Les hommes font les lois, les femmes font les mœurs," and for the most part submit to the petticoat government of society without a murmur. Here and there a gentleman of leisure, endowed with social talent, aspires to leadership in the world of fashion; but he finds it a thankless task. A few people recognize his services, but the many are inclined to make fun of and sneer at him. "A government of the women, by the women, for the women," is our social motto in America; and with the conservatism peculiar to a republic, we do not readily abandon our creed.

While hospitality is undoubtedly a duty, it loses half its charm the moment people cease to look upon it as a pleasure. A conscientious but unwilling host is like those virtuous and austere persons who make goodness hateful because they practise it in such a disagreeable way. Nor should a truly hospitable person keep too strict a debit and credit account with society, — inviting his guests in order to clear off his social debts, instead of for the pleasure of seeing and entertaining them. "I can always tell," said a witty Boston woman, "whether a party has been made to pay off social obligations, or merely for the fun of the thing. Where the people are all uncongenial spirits, and bore their hostess and each other half to death, it is very evident why they were asked together."

Such a company will be much like a meal that is planned for the sole purpose of "eating up" what is in the house, or like a costume gotten up to wear out various heterogeneous garments that have no real relation to each other. Economy is an excellent minor virtue; but it is not noble enough to stand in the first place, and should always be gracefully concealed beneath some loftier motive. The spirit which cannot brook being under obligations even to a friend is certainly a churlish one. It is better — at least it is more independent — than the spirit which permits a person to receive favors constantly without a thought of doing anything in return, but either is undesirable. It is just as noble to receive a kindness gracefully, though without servility, as to give generously, yet not in a patronizing spirit. Indeed, only a generous nature understands either how to give or to receive. The man who knows the blessedness of giving is willing that his friends shall know it also.

How much pleasure do we lose in this life by the persistent habit of regarding certain duties as disagreeable which often prove to be just the reverse! "I have sixty calls to make during this month; how I hate the thought!" says some lady with a large circle of acquaintance. She starts out to make her round of visits, in the stern spirit of a martyr, rejoices greatly because eleven of her friends are "not at home," but has a delightful time with the single friend who is *not* out!

One old friend called upon another, not a thousand miles from Boston, and was exceedingly amused by a memorandum which was placed in the lady's bedroom in a conspicuous position. It was written in a large hand, and read, "*Must go to see So-and-so.*" The visitor was Mrs. So-and-so herself!

Some hosts entertain their guests with so much energy, and are so extremely conscientious about providing amusements of various kinds, that they are completely worn out by the time their friends leave. They dread having company because it implies to their minds a vast amount of fatigue and exertion. Such people have but one idea in regard to hospitality; namely, that it consists in killing the fatted calf, —

which they proceed to do in every sense, and with great thoroughness. Indeed, they offer up as a sort of holocaust to the visitor the time, comfort, and convenience of the entire household, — as far, that is to say, as the individual members of it will permit themselves to be sacrificed.

All this is a very mistaken notion of hospitality, and often proves as burdensome to the guest as to the host. Unless a person is extremely unobservant or extremely selfish it will make him very uncomfortable to find that every one else is put about simply for his convenience; and the feeling of unrest which pervades the household will communicate itself to him also. The good old saying, "Make yourself at home," — how much it implies! But a guest cannot feel at home where no one else feels so, — where every one is uncomfortable, and all ordinary arrangements are turned topsy-turvy. If an atmosphere of self-sacrifice fills the air, the stranger within the gates will inhale it, and he too will be in the prevailing mood. What an artificial and "strained" state of affairs this will bring about, most of us know from sad experience.

In order to make the guest feel "at home," the host must feel so himself. No one would think of leaving his house, when he expected company, in order that the guests might have it all to themselves; it would not be hospitable to do so. Neither is it true hospitality to abandon all one's ordinary habits and ways of life. Your friend wants to see you in your own home and in your own home-life, — modified for his behoof and convenience, but not turned inside out and upside down. The family skeleton, if there is one, may as well be put in the closet, and family jars may be shelved for a time, with advantage.

How blessed is that household whose every-day life is so harmonious and well-regulated that no unsightly bones have to be hidden away on the sudden approach of guests! I know of one such home, where the sun always shines in hearts and faces, where the children behave well every day, and the parents never quarrel. The motto of this house is, to use the best every day. The best manners, the best tempers, the best silver, china, glass, and linen you will see there, not on holidays only, but on working-days as well; and all the visitors who are lucky enough to stay at that house regard it as *the* ideal home, and *the* most delightful place in the world to visit.

It is in the country, of course. We must go to the country to find our ideal of hospitality; in town, people are so hurried and busy, and have so many other pleasures, that they cannot enjoy the full measure of hospitality which is given and received in quiet country places. You must have a desert before you can have an oasis; and it has been cynically asserted that the far-famed hospitality of our own South was due largely to the isolated and lonely position of those who exercised it, — people who lived on great plantations forty or fifty miles from any possible society. This is not quite just to our Southern brethren, because people who live lonely lives in quiet places are not always hospitably inclined; if they are naturally fond of dwelling alone the tendency will grow with what it feeds on, until an almost churlish spirit or seclusion and great social indolence will be developed.

What a picture does Susan Coolidge give, in her "What Katy Did," of the miseries suffered by two little girls who go to visit a kind but fat and lazy old woman in the country! The poor little souls are given a hot attic-chamber, with a feather-bed to sleep on, and a window provided with a rattling paper shade, but without mosquito-bars, — all this in the middle of summer! They find the butter melting into oil, nothing on the table that they can eat, and flies, flies everywhere! The old woman beams kindly on them when she is not asleep; but age and adipose prevent

her ever ascending her own stairs to attend to her guests'
comfort.

A very important rule of hospitality is not to invite people
to visit you unless you can make them comfortable. It is
generally unwise to invite any one to stay under your roof,
who is accustomed to a much more elaborate and expensive
style of living than your own. Of course there are exceptions to this rule; where, for instance, you can offer other
attractions to your visitor which should more than compen-
sate for the plainer mode of life. If your summer cottage is
on the sea-shore, or in any very attractive locality, you will
find most of your friends very willing to endure a little inconvenience for the sake of enjoying a whiff of the salt air.
Young people are usually not very particular about their
accommodations, as long as they are offered " a *real* good
time," in school-girl parlance. There are some young girls
who are so pampered and luxurious, however, that they
cannot be happy in any surroundings save those to which
they are accustomed. Hence a wise hostess will carefully
consider the character as well as the age and social condition
of the guests whom she proposes to invite. She will also endeavor to give them, as far as is in her power, the comforts and
conveniences to which they have been accustomed at home.
The guests on their part should endeavor to give as little
trouble as possible, and should conform their habits to those
of the household of which they are temporarily members.
They should be especially careful to be punctual at all
meals, and not to treat their friends' servants as if the latter were their own, sending them on errands or calling upon
them for special services. To do so would be to commit an
unwarrantable breach of the laws ot etiquette.

Mrs. Kemble relates in her journal that Mademoiselle
D'Este (an unfortunate lady whose principal aim in life appears to have been the assertion of claims to royal dignity

which were never allowed) used regularly to come down late to dinner when visiting at the country-houses of the English nobility. She knew that if she entered the dining-room with the rest of the company, the precedence which she considered her due might not be awarded her, and she was determined that no mere duchess or countess should go into dinner before herself. Therefore she entered alone, after every one else was seated, making a graceful inclination to her host, and an apology for her perpetual tardiness!

In this country it is not considered polite to take a valet or maid when going to make a visit at a friend's house, unless one has received special permission to do so.

A visitor should be extremely careful not to overstay the time for which he was originally invited, unless under extraordinary circumstances. When the day fixed for the departure arrives, a hostess often makes some polite remarks, to the effect that she is sorry her guest must go so soon, etc. This is said merely by way of compliment; but some young people who are careless and thoughtless allow themselves to be very easily persuaded to prolong their stay, if urged by the daughters or sons of the house to do so, forgetting that their invitation should come from the hostess herself, and that it must be more than ordinarily pressing before they are justified in changing the limit originally set for their stay. In England, guests at a country-house are invited always for a definite length of time, and on the appointed day the carriage drives up and the guest departs without peradventure. In this country, we are not always so exact. Where guests are invited to visit friends at a distance, a visit is usually supposed to be of a week's duration, if no time has been fixed; but an invitation for a few days may mean anything from two days to a week. According to the old English rule, a first visit should never exceed a week.

If a hostess wishes her friends to call upon her guest, she

18

should let them know beforehand at what time her visitor is expected, so that they may have plenty of time to offer any social attention which they may be inclined to show. The best way to secure other invitations for a guest, is to invite friends to meet her in the early part of her visit, issuing the invitations before her arrival ; for, if she is to remain only a week, and people are not invited to meet her until the middle of the visit, they will have scant time to show her any hospitable attentions. "You are going day after to-morrow? I am so sorry! If you were only to stay longer, I should be so glad to see you at our house," etc. A hostess often hears remarks of this sort made, and laments her own tardiness, which has destroyed all these charming possibilities for her guest's entertainment.

It is always proper to write and ask if one may bring a friend who is staying in the house, if one is invited to a ball, reception, or any large general occasion where an indefinite number of people are to be present. One or two, more or less, will make no difference in the hostess' arrangements for such an event. But it is not proper, under ordinary circumstances, to ask leave to bring a guest to a dinner or formal luncheon party, for obvious reasons. A hostess should not go out to dine, or spend the evening, unless her guest is invited also, or has some other amusement provided. Where the guest is an intimate friend, or constantly receives and accepts separate invitations, this rule is often waived.

It is not polite to invite a guest to any general entertainment without also inviting the lady under whose roof the former is staying. Even for a luncheon or dinner-party it is more polite to invite the hosts also whenever it is possible to do so.

When calling upon a guest, a card must invariably be left for the lady of the house also, as has been said elsewhere. Where one card only is left, it is always held to be for the hostess.

While one should endeavor to procure invitations and provide pleasant amusements for a guest, it is a great mistake to attempt to lay out all his time, or to try to entertain him all day long. It is said that the English understand to perfection the art or want of art that is necessary to entertain guests at a country-house. Everything about the house and grounds is put at their disposal; they may walk, drive, read, play billiards, smoke, or shoot, to suit themselves. In short, they may employ their time as they please until the late dinner-hour brings all together. In the evening every one is expected to remain in the drawing-rooms, and to contribute, as far as in him lies, to the general amusement of the company.

There is one great drawback to the pleasure of visiting at English country-seats, and that is the great expense it entails on account of the vicious system of fees. At a first-class house, belonging to one of the nobility or gentry, a pound sterling is the smallest fee that it is allowable to give; and this sum must be given freely to every servant who has performed any service, even the slightest, for a guest, such as the porter who has barely laid hands on one's portemanteau. A game-keeper must be feed on a much higher scale; twenty-five dollars is the least amount of money some of these dignitaries will accept! It is said that the English nobility themselves regret the existence of this system of extortion, but have not the power to stop it. Jeemes, with all his airs of humility, is in reality more of a despot than his master, the hereditary ruler.

As I take my leave of host and guest, there rises before me the well-known figure of one who is an ideal hostess, and on whose face there is a look of reproach which seems to say, "Am not I too worthy of mention?" She is a woman of tall and commanding figure, of ancient family, and of ample worldly means. All these advantages she uses, not to awe or humble other people, but to minister to their pleasure, — to give them the best of all she has. To entertain her friends is her greatest delight, and the absence of any invited guest causes her a real and unfeigned regret. As the hour for the feast approaches, her face fairly beams with the anticipation of the pleasure which she is to afford others. " Goodwill to men" is written there in letters of light, and each guest says to himself, as he looks at the bright, happy countenance, " I am truly welcomed ; how can I help enjoying myself?"

It takes two or three real persons, however, to make an ideal, and since the task has been begun, I must mention one more very charming hostess who has the art of entertaining her guests so that all are pleased, whether she is holding a stately reception or an informal picnic in the woods. This lady enjoys society, — not perhaps with the fervor of youth, but with a more quiet and enduring satisfaction. Her spirits rise as her guests assemble; indeed no woman ever becomes a social leader unless she takes real pleasure in meeting with her kind.

This lady has the art of compounding into a harmonious whole heterogeneous elements which could not be fused save by a master hand. With an apparent madness which yet has its method she mingles artists, poets, and mere society people in her magic caldron. Over all plays the benevolent lightning of her scintillating wit, and literary men and fashionable women find an unsuspected charm in each other's society while galvanized by the electric current of her social sympathy and power. Do more figures loom before me on the social horizon? Alas ! it was a rash act to summon one spirit from the great army of charming women. But I will hold parley with no more ghosts to-day ; " ab uno disce omnes."

CHAPTER XXIX.

COUNTRY MANNERS AND HOSPITALITY.

PEOPLE who live in the country often make the mistake of endeavoring to entertain their guests in city fashion. They think that nothing else will suit their town-bred friends; or perhaps they themselves have an overweening admiration for city life and all that pertains to it. Hence country cousins indulge in an imitation which is of course the sincerest flattery, but is nevertheless apt to be disastrous.

We go to the country because we are tired of the town; and we hope to find there, not a second or third rate reproduction of ways of life with which we are wearily familiar, but something new and different, — change, rest, and quiet, refreshing communion with Nature, and a mode of life less artificial than a city existence must of necessity be. We wish, of course, to find refinement of life and manners wherever we go, but in the country the heart of man longs for simplicity; alas! the longing is usually a vain one. Few dwellers in the country have the common-sense of Shakspeare's Shepherd, who says: "Those that are good manners at the court are as ridiculous in the country as the behavior of the country is most mockable at the court."

Manners do not need to be radically changed under differing circumstances, but to be adapted properly to time and place. Happy is the man whose manners fit his situation in life, — who can take a lower room, if such be the change fate brings him, without loss of dignity, and who can take a higher station without any assumption of arrogance or pride.

Every change in our circumstances must bring some change in our manners; it depends on ourselves, very largely, whether the change is for the better or the worse. Emerson says : —

" Manners are the revealers of secrets, the betrayers of any disproportion or want of symmetry in mind and character. It is the law of our constitution that every change in our experience instantly indicates itself on our countenance and carriage, as the lapse of time tells itself on the face of a clock. We may be too obtuse to read it, but the record is there. Some men may be obtuse to read it, but some men are not obtuse and do read it."

In our own country, fortunes change hands so constantly, and with such startling rapidity, that many men and women have their characters, and consequently their manners, put to a severe test. Of the two extremes, a sudden rise in fortune is a greater test of good breeding, I think, than a sudden fall. It takes greater strength to ascend than to descend, and we demand greater things of a successful man than we do of a defeated one. We worship the rising sun ; but our sympathies are with the sunset, and we admire it more than we do its gaudy and boastful brother of the early morning.

A lady dined, not long ago, with some friends in the country who had shortly before received a large accession to their fortune and had built unto themselves a new house, — wider, more costly, more elegant in its appointments than their former residence. On her return home she was closely questioned about her hosts and their new abode ; and she said much in praise of all the new finery, but with a certain reserve in her encomiums. " Were n't they cordial — were they haughty ?" said the inquisitor of the home-circle. " Yes,

yes," was the answer, "they were everything that was kind and cordial — but — but — *they aren't big or grand enough for their new house!*" which was a homely way of saying that their manners had not grown yet to suit their altered circumstances.

Some people never do change their manners, whatever may happen to their outer circumstances. It is said that at least one bonanza millionnaire of California retains his early simplicity of demeanor, although living in a palace fit for a prince. His wife, recognizing her own inability to be or appear like a fine lady, remains just as she was in the old days of poverty, and seems more like a respectable upper servant than the mistress of untold millions. Of course there is a striking incongruity between the demeanor of this worthy couple and their palatial surroundings; nevertheless they are much more respected than they would be if they tried unsuccessfully to ape the manners of another class, and to bridge over the fatal gaps in their early training and education. There are some gaps so wide that no social engineer has skill enough to throw a span across them.

But we are wandering from our main theme, — the manners suitable to a country life. It goes without saying that Newport and other gay watering-places do not — and in the nature of things cannot — have much in common with the real country, either in manners or in the general way of life. Still, even here, there is a growing tendency toward the ultra imitation of city life, which many people deplore. Rugged Mount Desert itself is becoming too stereotyped to suit the taste of these latter. They say — and with good reason — that they do not wish to spend the summer in a round of visiting, and perpetual condition of dress parade, — in a mere repetition, in fact, of the doings of the winter's gay season. When Bishop Heber wrote, —

"Though every prospect pleases, and only man is vile,"

it is just possible that he had in his mind the environs of a fashionable watering-place, — the splendid equipages, gorgeous toilets, and bored expression of countenance of the gay dames and their cavaliers, contrasting incongruously with the quiet green fields and pastures, and the peaceful cattle taking their ease therein.

Thackeray describes in his own inimitable manner the pitiful humbug, and striving after effect of a foolish family who live in the country. These people endeavor to keep up a style of living far beyond their means, and to consort with persons much richer and more fashionable than themselves. Hence they are driven to all sorts of petty subterfuges, in order to conceal their real manner of life; and live poorly and meanly in private, that they may make an occasional grand display before half a dozen county families.

The mother and daughter are "caught" by some of their grand acquaintances when in the act of trimming their own vines and fig-trees, and rush into the house by the back door, vainly hoping that they have not been seen in their old clothes !

Furthermore, they disgust the guest of the household (an old friend from town) by constant and tedious would-be fashionable talk, as well as by giving him an endless succession of dinners made from the family pig, relieved by sour beer and poor wine.

Yes, all this humbug and sham we find in the city too; but contemptible as it is everywhere, it is nowhere so much so as in the presence of the woods and fields and hills, where Dame Nature's broad smile invites us constantly to be at one with her, and to abandon all shallow pretences.

If a lady likes to tend her own flower-beds and prune her own vines, by all means let her do so, and let her not be foolish enough to feel any shame if she is seen engaged in so sensible a pursuit. If she wears a neat garden-hat, and a pretty, becoming calico dress, it does n't matter who sees her at her work.   But just here lies another difficulty ; namely, that many persons think any dress is good enough to work in, no matter how old, shabby, and soiled it may be.   This is a most unsound theory, and one which has more than a little to do with making people feel ashamed of work.

No matter what one is doing or where one is going, it is a part of self-respect to be dressed neatly and in whole raiment ; and it is surprising to find how seldom it is necessary to wear soiled or shabby clothes if one only determines not to do so.   With a good big apron, gloves, and short skirts, one may even work in the garden, — set out flowers and water them, — and look little the worse for it.   A person who thinks any clothes are good enough to work in does not appreciate the dignity of labor.

The difficulty of procuring good butcher's meat is apt to be a serious stumbling-block in the real country ; and when Thackeray sounds a note of woe apropos of being obliged (in the person of his hero) to feed extensively on the family pig, he touches a chord to which many a heart will thrill responsively. Country hosts should remember that guests from the city are accustomed to plenty of fresh meat, and to meat that is not tough.   But if the host cannot procure tender meat, he can at least avoid frying beefsteaks, and roasting beef and mutton to death.   Beefsteak should always be broiled over a clear fire and always cooked rare, — as also in a lesser degree should mutton-chops.

A guest at a country-house should be somewhat forbearing, and not unmindful of the difficulties that encompass a rural purveyor.   It would not be polite, for instance, to copy the behavior of a certain lady who drove several miles into the country to visit some friends, and who accepted their invitation to stay and take " pot-luck " with them. Roast lamb made its appearance upon the dinner-table, and was duly offered to the guest of the occasion. What were the feelings of the hostess and her family when their guest said in an oracular tone, "My grandmother Jones never could eat lamb, and *I* never can!" Luckily a small side-dish of chicken saved the hosts from utter confusion and disgrace; but supposing that there had been no chicken, what then?

In that case they would have been obliged to fall back upon their fruit and vegetables, which, with plenty of fresh milk, cream, butter, and eggs, must always form the chief strongholds of a country table. People who eat vegetables and fruit fresh from their own gardens every day, do not realize what a treat they are constantly enjoying. If they did they certainly would not, like some unwise country house-keepers, take endless trouble to make elaborate desserts and an infinite variety of cake, neglecting the delicious fruit at their very doors, or perhaps (to the still greater vexation of their guests) putting it all into the preserving-kettle to coldly furnish forth next winter's tea-table. Cream, butter, milk, eggs, fruit, vegetables, chickens, — let the country house-keeper have these written on her heart of hearts; and whatever else she may add thereto, she must never take these away, but remember that they are her crowning glory, and should always be of the best quality.

Next, let her have her table — and indeed all her house — cheerful and fragrant with fresh flowers. Of course it is her sacred duty to have a flower as well as a vegetable garden, and she should not forget to have her children gather the wild flowers whose delicate beauty is sought for vainly in the dusty town.

Let her call in the aid of the sun, too, to make her house bright and cheerful. It is far better that carpets and curtains should fade a little than that human beings should droop and pine in dim, secluded chambers. Of course, in extremely hot weather blinds must be closed in the middle of the day; but there is a vast deal too much closing of shutters in our part of the world, notably in the Middle States.

Wherever and whenever mosquitoes congregate, it is very desirable that guests should have mosquito nets provided for their beds. These can be made quite inexpensively by taking the frame of an old umbrella and covering it with double netting; around the edge of this as a centre two or more breadths of netting should be sewn. They should be long enough to reach nearly to the floor. The whole fabric should be suspended from a hook in the ceiling, and may be drawn up in the daytime for the sake of convenience.

It is quite interesting to know that the ancient Egyptians not only were troubled with mosquitoes, but were sagacious enough to use mosquito nets! Herodotus says:—

"They have the following contrivance to protect themselves from the mosquitoes, which abound very much. The towers are of great service to those who inhabit the upper parts of the marshes, for the mosquitoes are prevented by the winds from flying high; but those who live round the marshes have contrived another expedient. . . . Every man has a net with which in the day he takes fish, and at night uses it in the following manner: in whatever bed he sleeps he throws the net around it, and then getting in sleeps under it; if he should wrap himself up in his clothes or in linen the mosquitoes would bite through them, but they never attempt to bite through the net."

After the country housekeeper has provided her city guest with a comfortable sleeping apartment, she should take care that the latter is not aroused "at the screech of dawn" with the crowing of roosters, the clatter of the maid-servants and children, and other noises that seem to begin at such a very early hour in the country. A guest who is truly polite will always come down at the family breakfast-hour, unless it be in luxurious houses where breakfast is a movable feast, and every one can have a cup of tea and a roll in his own room if he prefers to do so.

As it is now fashionable to begin breakfast with a course of fruit, the country hostess should surely follow this wholesome custom, placing before her guests melons, peaches, or whatever fruit is in season. For the rest she should remember that people's appetites are sharpened by the fresh air of the country, and that the dishes provided should therefore be rather more substantial in character than those that are prescribed for a city table by the present fashion.

Still, it must be admitted that here "doctors disagree." At the country-seats of some rich families, whose eyes are ever turned city-ward in admiration and longing, you will find the *menu* at every meal exactly what it would be in the most fashionable city dwelling, and you will be helped to an unlimited amount of china and genteel fragments of food during an hour or two, three times a day.

Almost every one prefers to dine early in the country in summer, for a late dinner is sure to interfere with the pleasures of the afternoon — riding, driving, etc. — unless the hour is set extremely late, at eight or nine o'clock. Tea, therefore, becomes a very important meal in out-of-town households; that is, "high" "or stout" tea. It is a pity that this cheerful meal has almost disappeared from city life, driven out both by fashion and necessity, since business men in our large cities can no longer come home to two o'clock dinner as they did five-and-twenty years ago.

For "high tea" a white table-cloth should be used. The tea and coffee equipages stand before the mistress of the house, or sometimes are placed one at each end of the table. It certainly looks more cheerful to have tea made on the table; the simmering of the tea-urn, the actual presence of the fire — even of an alcohol lamp — give to the occasion a home-like

air which otherwise would be wanting.   Tea also tastes better when made in this way; but the process entails additional trouble upon the hostess, who already has no light task
to perform.   To be able to talk to guests and pour out tea
and coffee, — perhaps to flavor them as well, — all at the
same time, demands great nimbleness of wits.   Most hostesses
are sincerely thankful to those guests who are so considerate
as " not to speak to the woman at the wheel" until she has
finished the dread libation.

The table should be ornamented with fruits and flowers,
but not in the formal fashion of a dinner-party.   Preserves,
honey, etc., in dishes of cut glass or handsome china may
stand about the table, and also plenty of fruit, in the season.
Hot biscuits, muffins, crumpets, waffles, etc., are in their
greatest glory at the hour of tea, and should succeed one
another in relays, so that they may be always " piping hot."
Confectioner's cake or nice home-made cake also stand upon
the table.   The more solid dishes — cold ham, escaloped
oysters, chickens cold, fricasseed, or fried, moulded tongue,
omelet, salads, and cold meats of various kinds — may either
be helped by the servants from the sideboard or placed on
the table and served by the master of the house, assisted by
other members of the family; the hostess during the earlier
part of the meal at least, will have her hands too full with
pouring out tea and coffee to do much else.

Vegetable salads of various kinds are always welcomed on
the tea-table, and are preferred by many housekeepers because they can be prepared beforehand.   But there must
be some hot dishes on the tea-table, otherwise the feast will
be an imperfect one.   It suffices, however, to have hot bread
or cakes of some sort, and to have the meats, etc., cold, where
this arrangement is the most convenient one.   In that delightfully primitive city, Philadelphia, tea-drinkings still occasionally take place, though even here their glory is departing;

they must be accompanied by at least two substantial dishes, — oysters and chickens, for instance, — or they are not considered to be *comme-il-faut* in the Quaker city.

At the seaside, fresh fish nicely broiled is excellent on the tea-table, as are also lobsters, crabs, clams, etc. Cream and cottage cheeses, curds and whey, and other preparations of milk are liked by many people. They certainly look cool, refreshing, and seasonable, and are usually considered very wholesome.

If one is invited out to take tea at Newport one will sit down to what is a dinner in all but the name. The floral decorations will be more simple, but otherwise the tea will be in reality a *diner à la Russe*, perhaps with seventeen courses.

Every house in the country must of course be provided with a wide piazza if the inmates intend to have either comfort or pleasure. In the hot summer evenings guests should be allowed to sit on the veranda, when they show a disposition to do so, and not be dragged into a hot parlor, will-they, nill-they, to take part in a game of cards.

Now that the guitar and mandolin have again come into fashion, they fill very pleasantly a "long-felt want" in the summer evenings. Many young ladies sing simple ballads and folk-songs under the moon to the tinkling of the guitar, and every one is pleased. The same music heard in the prosy atmosphere of the drawing-room under the glaring gas-light would perhaps sound tame ; but in the open air it takes very little to make us contented.

CHAPTER XXX.

AMERICAN women are so much accustomed to receiving the utmost courtesy and consideration at the hands of men, they are so well used to breathing the air of freedom from their very birth, that they sometimes forget how great are their actual privileges, and grumble because they have not others which would no doubt be pleasant to possess, could we have everything as we would like to have it in this transitory sphere.

American men are more truly chivalrous than any others upon earth; their respect for womankind is not only very deep, but entirely unaffected. It is a part of their education, almost of their nature, and to it we women owe among other things that priceless boon, — the freedom to go about where and in whatever way we please.

In no large European city is it safe or proper for a lady to walk abroad alone; yet in America our women not only enjoy this inestimable privilege, but many others of the same kind. How great would be the surprise of a foreigner of distinction if he should happen to catch a glimpse of the interior of a Boston horse-car, at that time in the evening when the continued performances at the theatres and concert halls have just come to an end! If you should tell him that those groups of ladies without any attendant cavalier belonged to "Boston's best," and that the friendly horse-car would carry them safe and unmolested almost to their very doors, he would scarcely believe the testimony of his ears! In New York, with its large foreign population, ladies do not like to go out in the evening without an escort; but in dear old Boston, thanks to the Puritans, and to the glorious system of radiating horse-cars, two or three ladies together can with perfect safety and propriety go to lectures, concerts, etc. It goes without saying that I am not now speaking of very young girls, who should always be under the charge of some older person.

Since we have this most desirable privilege of going out whenever we please to breathe the fresh air, we certainly ought not to abuse it. Few things are more distasteful than a party of young women making themselves conspicuous in public places by loud talk and laughter. If they are careless enough to attract attention in this way they must not be surprised if they bring upon themselves rude notice from some of the other sex.

There is a form of folly quite prevalent in New York which seems to be peculiar to the place. It is for women who are entirely respectable and well-behaved members of society to imitate the dress of a fast and loud class, because they think it is rather knowing to do so. Thus, one will often see a middle-aged, quiet-looking woman resplendent with gold-dyed hair and a very showy costume, the incongruity between the garments and their wearer being quite startling. It seems perfectly incredible that such a woman should imagine her theatrical appearance to be stylish, appropriate, and in "good form;" yet evidently this is her belief, for otherwise why should she array herself after this manner? No one intentionally makes a scarecrow of herself unless it be on the stage.

Great freedom of taste in the matter of street costume is certainly allowed in this country. Fifty years ago Charles Dickens commented on the bright colors and silk dresses worn by ladies in the streets of our cities. The same phenomena

may still be observed. Ladies of good taste and innate refinement, however, now avoid wearing showy costumes and brilliant colors when they go out, especially when on a shopping
tour, or to visit the business part of a city. For walking or
paying visits on Fifth Avenue in New York, or Beacon
Street in Boston, it is allowable to dress more handsomely;
but the tendency of fashion during the last few years has
been undeniably in the right direction, namely, toward
wearing quiet and simple attire in the street.

In this country a lady does not take a gentleman's arm
when walking with him in the daytime. The protection it
gives is unnecessary, and American women always prefer to
be independent as far as possible. It was formerly the custom for a married or betrothed couple to walk arm-in-arm;
but it is now thought old-fashioned to do so, especially for two
fiancés. In the evening, a gentleman should always offer his
arm to the lady he is escorting, and she may accept it or not,
as she chooses; in large cities, it is customary for her to
accept the courtesy. If a gentleman is walking with two
ladies, one only should take his arm, and both should walk
on the same side of him. The spectacle of a "Lynn couple,"
or a thorn between two roses, always makes people smile.
Where it is necessary for protection, however, or where the
ladies are infirm and elderly, or the walking very slippery, a
gentleman should not hesitate to offer an arm to each of them,
even if it may make him appear rather ridiculous to do so.
An English contemporary gravely remarks that no lady
should ever take the arms of two gentlemen at once, — we
might add, unless she were learning to skate. When walking
with a lady, a gentleman takes the curbstone side of the
street and offers to carry any parcels she may have in her
hands. In a crowded thoroughfare he takes the left side,
to shield her from the elbows of passers-by. If she bows to
any lady or gentleman, he bows also, and removes his hat,

19

even if it be to salute a person with whom he is entirely unacquainted. He does this as a token of respect to his companion and her friends. A gentleman should always remove
his hat when bowing to a lady. He should do so with his
left hand in order to leave the right hand free, where he has
reason to expect that she will shake hands with him. If he
has no such expectation, he will take off his hat with the
hand that is farthest from her, unless it is especially inconvenient to do so.

A lady always bows first in this country, as in England.
On the continent of Europe the reverse is the case. Where
a lady and gentleman know each other very well, the recognition is of course practically simultaneous; but in the case of an
ordinary acquaintance the gentleman always waits until the
lady bows. It has been suggested that young men should
recall themselves to recollection by bowing first to ladies who
have entertained them, and who are older than themselves.
This might perhaps be permissible as an acknowledgment of
past hospitality; but if the lady were young, it would be
considered a great liberty. If a gentleman has a cigar in his
mouth, he always removes it before bowing to a lady, or if
he is very polite he throws it away. If his hands happen
to be in his pockets (a most ungraceful attitude) he will, of
course, take them out.

A gentleman should never stop a lady and keep her standing in the street while he talks with her. If he has something he wishes to say, and if he knows her sufficiently well
to warrant his doing so, he may turn and walk with her in
the direction in which she is going. This does not oblige
him to accompany her to her destination. On parting with
a lady, a gentleman must always raise his hat.

There is said to be an old and particularly dead law in
Boston which forbids smoking in the streets! We have
changed all that many years ago; but it is still considered bad

form for a gentleman to smoke on streets that are used as promenades, at the hours in which he will be likely to meet many ladies. The same is true of public drives. It is very uncommon to meet a gentleman smoking on Bellevue Avenue at Newport. A gentleman should never smoke while walking with or talking to a lady in the street. Indeed, he should never smoke anywhere in the presence of ladies, unless he has received especial permission to do so.

It is very rude to "cut" people, and one should never do it without very serious reasons. To return another person's bow with a blank stare is simply inexcusable, unless that person has committed some grave misdeed. It costs very little to make a civil bow, and does not necessarily involve even a calling acquaintance. Young people are sometimes unnecessarily sensitive regarding street salutations, and imagine themselves to have been slighted when they have only not been seen. Absent-minded and near-sighted persons frequently "cut" their friends without the least intention of so doing. Particularly is this the case in the crowded streets of a great city, where, unless one recognizes a person beforehand, one often does not look at him as he passes, and therefore his bow, if he makes one, goes unseen. It is a great mistake to fancy one's self "cut" when one is simply not recognized. On all these accounts it is well to bow in a decided manner, so that there may be no doubt about it. Some people have a way of making such a slight movement of the face — it can hardly be called of the head — that they virtually do not bow at all; and this is not always done from haughtiness, but often from extreme shyness.

When bowing in the street, the head only is bent and not the body, according to modern usage, unless one wishes to show great respect, or more than ordinary attention, to some person. One should always return the salutations of servants or tradespeople whom one meets in the street. It is not usual to recognize in this way the clerks or salesmen of dry-goods stores, nor would it indeed be considered proper for a young lady to do so.

A gentleman can never, under any circumstances, "cut" a lady. If he does not wish to continue her acquaintance, his only resource is to avoid meeting her eyes; even this would be very ungentlemanly conduct, unless he should have some very strong reason for it. He would have no excuse for thus treating a lady who behaved and dressed as a lady should. If a gentleman escorts a lady to her house he should wait until she has been admitted before taking leave of her, especially if it is after dark, and should not be content with seeing her to the foot of the steps only.

When walking or driving on a public walk or promenade, where the same people pass and repass each other many times, it is not necessary to bow every time one meets a friend or acquaintance. It is sufficient to bow once. One gentleman does not usually remove his hat in bowing to another gentleman, unless the latter is much older than himself, or is accompanied by a lady, when he removes it out of respect for her. Young men should always be careful that their greetings to men older than themselves are sufficiently respectful. You may nod to a contemporary in age, who is also your equal in position, if you know him well; but to one who is your superior in social or official position, or who is your elder, it would be decidedly improper to do so.

Gentlemen keep on their hats when they are in shops or at the entrance of a theatre, etc., because they are supposed to be passing through these places, or at best, making a very short sojourn there. The etiquette in regard to the hat, therefore, is like that of the street, and the same is true of the corridors of a hotel. But in an elevator where there are ladies, a gentleman must always remove his hat, because the elevator is so small that it is like the room of a private house, — where no one would think of keeping his hat on.

Ten or twenty years ago there were still many elderly gentlemen who saluted their friends and acquaintances by touching the hat instead of by removing it; but the grace with which they performed this quasi-military salute, and the respect expressed by the motion, made the salutation far more deferential than the stiff bow of the modern dude, even though the latter is always careful to remove his hat. Sometimes these elderly gentlemen do not even touch their hats, but make instead a graceful gesture with the hand.

The question whether or not gentlemen should give their seats to ladies who are standing in the horse-cars, is such a vexed one, and one that is so often discussed in print, that it is not worth while to enter into it here in all its length and breadth. Suffice it to say, that there are few, if any, truly polite men who are satisfied to sit while women are standing around them. They may argue against being obliged to give up their seats, but in practice they do it. It would seem as if there ought to be a little mutual forbearance and politeness on both sides in this matter. Young men, unless they are very tired after a hard day's work, have little excuse for keeping their seats; old men should not be expected to leave theirs under ordinary circumstances. A man should always offer his seat to an old woman, or to one who has an infant in her arms. If he does not, he may feel rather ashamed to see some woman show the politeness which it was his place and privilege to extend. Women should never seem in any way to claim a seat where there is none vacant. It is very impolite to look at a man in such a way that he shall feel compelled to offer his seat. Unless one is ill or very much fatigued, it is better to accept the situation cheerfully, and wait till some one gets out. If there is a small boy in the car, a bribe of a few pennies will usually secure his seat. A lady should always be careful to thank a gentleman audibly when he offers her his place. No gentleman should think of taking a seat that becomes vacant in a car, until all the ladies who are standing are provided with seats. A Boston woman, young and handsome, was riding in a New York car recently, patiently awaiting her turn to sit down. A seat was vacated, and she was on the point of taking it, when a young man dexterously slipped past her and into it, smiling at the girls who were with him, as if he had done a very clever thing. The Bostonian said to her friend, "I would n't have believed that ; but then, we are in New York in the nineteenth century !" The rude youth heard her words, turned scarlet, and looked sheepish enough.

A great deal of selfishness is shown on our railroads in the matter of taking up an undue amount of room. Two or three people will turn over seats, thus converting them into a sort of private box, and will be very much provoked if some other person claims the empty place, though there may not be another one in the car. Others fill up the vacant half of a seat with bundles, and look daggers when asked whether the seat is engaged. If conductors would make it a rule that people should pay for all the seats they occupy — personally or with bundles — it would be an excellent thing. " Is this seat engaged?" said one woman to another. " No ; but there are plenty of seats in the *next car*," said the seated one, in a disobliging tone, calmly ignoring the fact that the train was already moving! Commuters have a cheerful way of taking up a whole seat for each man through the length of an entire car. A party of ladies will enter, but it will seldom occur to these gentlemen to change their places and allow the ladies to sit together.

It is very difficult to ventilate a car in a way that will suit everybody. Some people feel that they must have fresh air, while others are at the same time shivering with cold. Any one who wishes to have a window open should always remember that, owing to the current made by the rapid motion of the car, the person in the seat behind feels the draught much more severely than the one sitting beside the open window. It is neither polite nor right to expose another person to the imminent danger of catching cold in this way, without first asking him whether he objects to having the window opened. The forward part of the car is always better ventilated than the rear, because the fresh air is constantly drawn in there by the motion, and the bad air is driven to the farther end of the conveyance.

A friendly correspondent says : "I can usually infer the breeding of a man or woman by the way in which either takes a seat in a street-car. The individual who sits down carelessly, pushing those on either side, and with no avoidance of such part of their clothing as may be within sitting distance, is underbred. The person who, on entering or leaving a railroad car, neglects to close again the door which he finds closed, is wanting in that consideration for others which is at the bottom of true politeness. Aggravated (and aggravating) instances of this are seen in cold weather, when people will sometimes walk through a car leaving the door at either end open."

CHAPTER XXXI.

PRIDE AND PARVENUS.

IF one circle of society is really better than and superior to another, why is it not a laudable ambition for a man or woman to wish to rise to that which is best? Why does the world laugh, good-naturedly or bitterly, according to its mood, at those who strive to ascend the social ladder? The world does not laugh at people who try to improve their fortunes or strive to remedy the defects of their early education; but for the social aspirant — the *parvenu* — it always has a scornful word!

This attitude of society seems a very unjust and illogical one to many ambitious persons, and they bewail long and bitterly the snobbishness, the injustice, the overweening pride which distinguishes the demeanor of the "ins" toward the "outs." It is never safe, however, for the pot to call the kettle black; and if the attitude of society is illogical, is that of the social climber any less so?

"If one set of people is just as good as another, why are n't you satisfied to stay where you are, and to remain in the circle where you were born and bred? We grant you that all men are free and equal, and we therefore consider that we have a right to choose our own associates, and leave you to choose yours. We regard society as a great club, where the right of the blackball is sacred. Society would not be worthy of the name if it possessed no safeguards against the intrusion of uncongenial persons; it would degenerate into a mere mob. The parties to a trial by jury have a right to challenge peremptorily those whom they do not wish to have for jurors; we claim the same right, and the same privilege of with-holding our reasons." In such words might the members of the charmed circle reply to those who knock for admission; and if one asks why the parvenu is smiled at, the reasons are not far to seek.

A parvenu, in the first place, is not a soldier who has been promoted from the ranks for merit; he is rather a deserter from his own friends and belongings. He is a renegade, and the world despises renegades and turncoats. Parvenus have been defined as those who do not want to belong to their own people, and do not in reality belong to any other.

Thus it will be seen that a man who rises in the social scale because he deserves to rise, is not necessarily a parvenu. The man of high talent, the great general, the successful poli-tician, need make no effort to go into society. Society comes to them, and is only too happy to secure their presence at all fêtes. Such men are no parvenus, and are not considered in that odious light. The parvenu is the man who has succeeded in society, — succeeded because of his own efforts. He has been the active agent of his own elevation; he has sought it, and sought it at the expense of old ties, old friendships. Like the woman in the story, who flung her children to the wolves to save her own life, the parvenu will sacrifice not only his wife's relations, but most of his own, to the Moloch of gentility. His conduct is virtually that of Trabb's boy; he says "I don't know you" to every one save the few peo-ple whom he considers it desirable to know.

Your true parvenu is not a man who wishes to raise all mankind to the same high level, or even to pull them down to a lower level. He is no democrat — very far from it. All that he wishes is to raise himself, and when he has once

attained the coveted position, he instantly reverses his tactics.
His efforts then are all directed downward instead of upward.
He wishes to push away the ladder by which he has himself
climbed, and to prevent any one else from following in his
footsteps. The parvenu is wondrously exclusive; he knows
by his own experience that social barriers can be forced, and
it grieves him excessively if others leap in through the gap
which he has made!

He is usually a bold, persistent person, who has taken the
social world by storm; he stands where he has longed to
stand; he has conquered all weapons employed against him,
save that last unconquerable weapon, the defence of all intel-
lect against brute strength, — ridicule. Satire has ever been
the dread of tyrants, the refuge of oppression. With its lash
Horace, Juvenal, and Persius scourged the wickedness and
folly of their times, while Rabelais and Chaucer attacked
with it the rottenness and corruption of the Church, whereof no man durst then openly complain. Nay, why else was
Socrates put to death, save because he wielded the flashing
blade of ridicule as no one has been able to do before or
since?

In the words of the little Queen Anne's man : —

> Yes, I am proud; I must be proud to see
> Men not afraid of God, afraid of me :
> Safe from the bar, the pulpit, and the throne,
> Yet touch'd and sham'd by ridicule alone.
> O sacred weapon ! left for truth's defence,
> Sole dread of folly, vice, and insolence !
> To all but heav'n-directed hands deny'd,
> The Muse may give thee, but the gods must guide.
>
> POPE : Epilogue to the Satires.

Therefore when society has been conquered by some ruth-
less invader, what wonder if it falls back on its last resource,
a smile, and thus declares that the conqueror shall never

win its respect, though he may have succeeded in forcing himself into an undesired fellowship!

The stories that are related at the expense of parvenus show the esteem in which they are held,—how this one "drew the line" at his own brother, when making out a list of invitations for a great ball; how that one "cut" all his old friends as soon as he had safely secured a position among more advantageous acquaintances.

Shakspeare, in "A Winter's Tale," gives us a bit of his delightful and inimitable satire, at the expense of those who have been suddenly elevated by a freak of fortune.

"*Clown.* You denied to fight with me this other day, because I was no gentleman born. See you these clothes? say you see them not and think me still no gentleman born: you were best to say these robes are not gentlemen born: give me the lie, do, and try whether I am not now a gentleman born.

"*Autolycus.* I know you are now, sir, a gentleman born.

"*Clown.* Ay, and have been so any time these four hours.

"*Shep.* And so have I, boy.

"*Clown.* So you have: but I was a gentleman born before my father; for the king's son took me by the hand, and called me brother; and then the two kings called my father brother; and then the prince my brother and the princess my sister called my father father; and so we wept, and there was the first gentlemanlike tears that ever we shed."

Thackeray, in his "Diary of C. Jeames de la Pluche," has followed out somewhat the same train of thought, but at greater length, and with more elaboration. The following account of Jeames's presentation at court hides a keen thrust at the toadyism and snobbishness of mankind in general, while it pretends to attack only the folly of the poor silly footman, who has completely lost his head in his sudden exaltation.

"You, per'aps, may igspect that I should narrait at lenth the suckmstanzas of my hawjince with the British Crown. But I am not one who would gratafy *imputtnint curaiosaty.*

Rispect for our reckonized instatewtions is my fust quallaty. I, for one, will dye rallying round my Thrown.

"Suffise it to say, when I stood in the Horgust Presnts — when I sor on the right & of my Himperial Sovring that Most Gracious Prins, to admire womb has been the chief Ohjick of my life, my busum was seased with an imotium which my Penn rifewses to dixcribe — my trembling knees halmost rifused their hoffis — I reckleck nothing mor until I was found phainting in the harms of the Lord Chamberling. Sir Robert Peal apnd to be standing by (I knew our wuthy Primmier by Punch's pictures of him, igspecially his ligs) and he was conwussing with a man of womb I shall say nothink, but that he is a Hero of 100 fites, *and hevery fite he fit he one.* Nead I say that I elude to Harthur of Wellingting? I introjuiced myself to these Jents, and intend to improve the equaintance, and per'aps ast Guvmint for a Barnetcy."

While we laugh at the absurd airs and ridiculous affectations of the footman turned gentleman, Thackeray takes good care to show us the greater worldliness, the more unpardonable folly, of those who receive the parvenu into their society solely because of his wealth, and cater to the insolence of a low-bred lackey in the hope of furthering their own fortunes.

The parvenu could never succeed in forcing an entrance into the citadel of good society, were there not traitors among the garrison ready to aid and abet him, — people quite willing to barter the influence of their social position for the gold or the gifts of their new associate. Therefore the parvenu has quite as good a right to despise his new-found and mercenary acquaintances as they have to look down upon him. Indeed, his contempt is more justifiable than theirs, because he has forced these people to falsify their own traditions, abandon their own theories, and stoop from their own deliberately chosen position, — they, the men of culture, education, and high-breeding, — and all in favor of one whose advantages, save in the single point of money, have been far inferior to their own. The higher the sinner stands, so much the greater is his sin. Where a high-born family accept a rich boor for their son-in-law, who can pity them if he walks over their sensibilities and their prejudices rough-shod? They must have known that he would do so; and it is a part of their just punishment that they should become "doormats under the feet" of the coarse Crœsus whose ingots they basely coveted.

To do justice to the *nouveaux-riches*, it is not always they who make the first overtures to what is technically termed society. Society, or certain emissaries thereof, sometimes go to them, knocking at their gates and asking leave to come into their ample halls. In this case the newly rich man is not obliged to abandon his dignity, but merely yields gracefully to the force of circumstances.

No one would advise such a man to take up his abode in the good city of Boston, however, under the influence of any such delusive hope. If he had the wealth of the Rothschilds, the Vanderbilts, and the Astors all rolled into one, he might live to be as old as Methusaleh, but he would never be invited to join the fashionable set, unless he made the first advances himself, and made them, be it said, with the greatest circumspection. The fashionable society of the grand old Puritan city cannot but have something of the sternness which characterizes the native land of conscience; it is to be feared that they use that sternness chiefly toward outsiders, "and slay them with their noble birth."

New people have found their way into the most aristocratic circles of Boston, but they have got in through the back-door of Europe, or gone around by the way of Newport or Mount Desert. No one ever yet went boldly up to the front door of Beacon Street, and struck with the lance's-point on the shield which hangs there ever ready for the fray, — no one ever did this, and lived to tell the tale. At least, he never cared to tell the only tale which he could truthfully unfold, because it was full of sorrow and defeat.

But e'en the failings of the dear old city lean to virtue's side; she never *could* submit to conquest in the days of Bunker Hill and Lexington, and she does n't mean to now. On the whole, it is a proud boast of Boston, that she does not allow her most exclusive circles to be invaded as readily as do other cities; and more than one ambitious family has left her precincts in despair of ever achieving social success there.

But if it be legitimate for certain people to refuse to grant to others coveted social privileges, there are still various ways in which that refusal may be expressed, some courteous, and some just the reverse of courteous. "One would rather be trodden upon by a velvet slipper than by a wooden shoe," said some one *apropos* of the French Revolution; and there is a way of saying "no" that takes half the sting from that bitter monosyllable.

Among the weapons that exclusive people take to keep others at a distance, none is more aggravating, none is more unpleasant, than a species of haughty stare, a look of half-suppressed pride and disdain, with which many women — and especially many young women — disfigure their countenances. To do them justice, they probably are not aware of their own expression; but it is the hidden thought, the inward feeling of superiority, that betrays itself unbidden on the face. And the cruellest use of this weapon is when it is employed in a reckless and indiscriminating way against the innocent and the guilty alike.

A young lady will walk abroad, armed and protected by this Gorgon's-head expression of countenance, and during her progress she will distribute it right and left, bestowing it not only on people whom she does not know, but on people who do not know her, and do not even know who she is, save that she assumes the air of the Great Mogul himself.

How wise were the ancient Athenians when they set forth in their fable that only one of the Gorgons was mortal, but that the remaining two of the dread sisters *could not perish!* It has seemed to some of us, when walking the streets of our native Boston, that those two old Gorgons were indeed alive, — alive in modern Athens, and that their beautiful, cold, cruel faces, young but stony, still petrified the men and women whom they encountered!

Nor is it in Boston alone that one finds the sin of pride openly written on the human brow. Even in small towns and villages one may often observe persons whose air seems to say, " I own, if not the whole earth, certainly all that is worth speaking of." And to those who seriously contemplate assuming this high-toned expression of countenance, perhaps a word of warning may not come amiss. Do not try to look as if you owned " all creation " unless you are *perfectly sure* that you do. The least failure in this grand attempt, the least wavering in your look, will be fatal to your pretensions.

It goes without saying that the undisguised and therefore most offensive look of pride, what Dickens called the " turn-up-nosed peacock " expression, is seldom if ever seen, except on the face of some parvenu, or some newly rich person, whose recently acquired fortune has had an unhappy effect on the angle of his nasal elevation.

The true aristocrat, the man who has inherited from his ancestors a high social position, may not be lacking in pride, but he does not consider it necessary to express it constantly in his manner and bearing, to go about exasperating his fellow-mortals by a constant assumption of superiority over them. He is, on the contrary, indisposed both by nature and training to injure the feelings of any one else. "Noblesse oblige" is his motto, and it obliges, above all other things, to perfect civility of demeanor and speech. The true aristocrat is so sure of his own position that he does not need to bolster it up by haughty looks or words.

There are plenty of exceptions to this rule, in the case of men whose souls are little and mean, and who are vulgarians at heart, in whatever station in life they may happen to have been born; just as among those who are of the most humble birth and breeding there is occasionally to be found a man whose natural nobility of character and native refinement stamp him as one of nature's gentlemen.

Burns belonged to the latter class. The letters of this most unfortunate man of genius are full of just and bitter indignation at the neglect, the contempt with which he was too often treated. As Carlyle says, in his noble eulogium of the peasant poet, mankind could find nothing better to do with this wonderful man than to make a gauger of him!

In our own country we have no recognized aristocracy, no absolutely superior class, and we have reason to be devoutly thankful therefor. But our democratic form of society is attended with some evils, and one of these is the boundless self-assertion with which many people strive to eke out what else were very insufficient claims to social pre-eminence. They know, at the bottom of their hearts, that they have no real right to the superiority which they would fain assume; hence they strive, by an arrogant bearing, by an aping of the faults of the aristocracies of European countries, to put themselves on a level with these latter. They forget that the higher the station, the greater are its obligations. An hereditary nobility without refinement, grace, or a sense of duty and responsibility, with no claim to elevated rank save that of boundless pride, would not long be endured by any country. Its members may often be profligate and morally worthless ; but even such unworthy scions of a noble race know that amiability and graciousness are expected of them, why else the title "Your Grace"? When we come to royalty, it is very plain that even the puppet kings and queens of England pay dearly for their exalted station, by the sacrifice of their own time, tastes, and pleasures, by the wretched condition of dress parade, and the continual appearance in public, which is rigorously exacted of them.

Hence the spectacle of one set of people claiming to be like another simply because they have produced a fair imitation of the faults of the latter, is about as absurd as if a scarecrow should claim to be like a man because he too wore a coat and hat!

While pride, as a weapon of offence, is entirely out of place in civilized society, there is still a certain species of it,—what people call proper pride,—which a self-respecting man has a perfect right to use as a shield against impertinence or over-familiarity. There are persons in this world who will take advantage of the courtesy with which they are treated, to assume a familiarity that the acquaintanceship in no wise warrants, toward those whom they know very slightly. Such persons have only themselves to blame if they are snubbed. To be perfectly polite and courteous, and to be "hail fellow, well met" with everybody one meets, are two very different matters.

The rebuke of the young King Henry V. to the impertinent greeting of Falstaff is a famous instance of a richly-deserved reprimand,—not of vice only, but of undue familiarity as well. Yet the royal Harry was not filled with an overweening pride of place. He was the darling of his soldiery, not for his skill and bravery alone, but for his humane and generous temper as well. His oft-quoted epitaph on Falstaff,—

> " Poor Jack, farewell !
> I could have better spared a better man,"

20

shows his real appreciation of the wit and genial humor of his famous companion.

In the same way, when our friend Jeames is treated with hauteur by Captain George Silvertop, we feel that the gallant Captain is in the right, though our sympathies are with the eloquent Jeames.

"'Mr. De la Pluche,' here said a gintlemen in whiskers and mistashes standing by, 'had n't you better take your spurs out of the Countess of Bareacres' train?' 'Never mind mamma's train' (said Lady Hangelina), 'this is the great Mr. De la Pluche — let me present you to Captain George Silvertop.' The Capting bent just one jint of his back very slitely; I retund his stare with equill hottiness."

The man who goes about the world enraging everybody by his ill-concealed pride and arrogance, is like a householder who throws hot water out of the window on the inoffensive passers-by. But the man who only appears haughty when he is treated with unwarrantable familiarity, may be likened to the householder who knows that his house is his castle, and will not permit trespassers therein. "It makes my blood boil to be treated with the supercilious manner which Mr. —— puts on toward me because he is rich and I am poor," said an intelligent young man not long since.

Oh, men and women on whom fortune has smiled, do you realize how cruel you are to use the success which Providence has given you, as a two-edged weapon with which to stab and thrust back those who are less fortunate than yourselves? You do not, I am sure you do not; for if you did, you would remember that it is the arrogance of the victor which makes defeat bitter to the vanquished. Surely success should bring smiles and happiness, not frowns and arrogance. How well did the ancient Romans understand the weakness and pride of the human heart when they placed the slave, with his " memento mori," in the triumphal car of the conqueror!

Thackeray had a theory that snobbishness was universal; that every one was more or less of a snob at heart. It seems to me that the great satirist had studied this odious phase of human character so long, that his view had become somewhat jaundiced thereby. Might we not say more truly that snobbishness is a sort of fever which every one has at some period of his existence? Many people recover from it after one dreadful attack, which always occurs between the ages of fifteen and twenty-five. Others, again, are subject to an intermittent variety of snobbishness; while to some persons it clings with the persistence of a true malaria, and they are never wholly free from its malign influence.

Human nature is too full of varied emotions to be treated as if it were a one-stringed fiddle playing the same old tune everlastingly. We are not always under the dominion of the same faults, any more than we are always swayed by the same virtues. There were seven devils who entered the house spoken of in Scripture; and while Snobbishness is certainly a very large and powerful devil, it is not the only one of its tribe. Indeed, it may be considered in the light of a single manifestation of two evil forces, — selfishness and cowardice. A man is a snob — first, because he is afraid of what other people may say of him; and second, because he is selfish and wishes to advance his own way in the world.

It seems a little singular that youth should be the time of life which is more subject than any other to this form of moral cowardice; because in the mere matter of physical courage young people are very superior to their elders. But youth is very selfish in many ways, though full of noble and generous emotions if the right chords are only touched. The young man, newly released from the pleasant bondage of childhood, sees the whole world suddenly placed within his reach, as he thinks. At the same time it is revealed to him, as by a flash of light, that mankind attach great importance to the outward shows and forms of things, — a truth which is entirely concealed from the clear and beautiful vision of childhood. So the young man, filled with a desire to grasp the sum of earthly happiness, and over-estimating the importance of what we call "appearances," — because he has just found out that they are of any consequence at all, — becomes a good deal of a snob in minor and outward matters. He suffers tortures if he is obliged to do anything except "what everybody else does," or if he is obliged to appear in any way unlike other people. But a child never troubles its happy little heart about what people will think or say, or about its own appearance. A pretty little girl of twelve fell down on the ice some years ago and broke out one of her front teeth. Her relatives were very much troubled at this misfortune, and at the sad havoc that it made in the little lady's beauty. But she herself was perfectly serene as soon as the pain had subsided, and tried in vain to understand why her friends were troubled. She had plenty of teeth left, she said, and it did not hurt now!

The torments which parents endure from the extraordinary sensitiveness to appearances which afflicts their growing sons and daughters, would be pathetic were they not so universal. The young people suddenly discover that the charming roomy old mansion in which they have been brought up is shabby and old-fashioned. The family carryall, in which they have driven sleepily to church from their earliest infancy, is changed in the twinkling of an eye from an easy-going, delightful old vehicle, to a hopelessly decrepit rattle-trap. The horse is condemned, without appeal, as old, fat, and lame, and the driver is not half spruce enough, — he must have a tall hat, mutton-chop whiskers, top-boots, and livery, without delay.

As to the young lady and gentleman themselves, of course their raiment is found to be hopelessly out of style, and nothing but the services of the most expensive tailors for both sexes can make them feel in any degree satisfied with their own appearance. A domestic revolution takes place very promptly; poor paterfamilias puts on a very rueful face, and wishes that if young people must be discontented with their clothes, like Cinderella, that they would at least follow her example by providing their own fairy godmother.

The doctrine that fine feathers make fine birds seems to be a very old one. In a delightful ballad, which must be nearly as old as the wars between Stephen and Mathilda, and from which Shakspeare quotes, we find these verses :—

HE.

O Bell, my wiffe, why dost thou floute ?
    Now is nowe, and then was then :
Seeke now all the world throughout
    Thou kenst not clownes from gentlemen.
They are cladd in blacke, greane, yellowe, or gray,
    Soe far above their own degree :
Once in my life Ile doe as they ;
    For Ile have a new cloake about mee.

SHE.

King Stephen was a worthy peere,
    His breeches cost him but a crowne ;
He held them sixpence all too deere,
    Therefore he calld the taylor lowne.
He was a wight of high renowne,
    And thouse but of a low degree,
Itts pride that putts the countrye downe,
    Man, take thine old cloake about thee.

CHAPTER XXXII.

THERE IS NOTHING NEW UNDER THE SUN.

WHEN we read of the manners and customs of by-gone times, nothing pleases us so much as to come across some little trait of character or some observance which reminds us of our own day. We see demonstrated — perhaps for the thousandth time — the essential brotherhood of man, the oneness of human nature, ancient and modern. The imagination bridges over the intervening centuries between our own days and those of old with a rapidity which throws the operations of military bridge-builders far into the shade. We seem to walk and talk with spirits long vanished from the earth.

"One touch of nature makes the whole world kin," as Shakspeare undoubtedly said, though the humaritarian vanity of the nineteenth century has lately put it into the head of a writer to say that the great poet did not intend this famous passage to be read in the sense ordinarily ascribed to it — that Shakspeare builded better than he knew! Truly, in none but a conceited epoch like the present would any one dare to limit the imagination of a Shakspeare, or have the presumption to declare that the poet who understood human nature from A to Izzard, needed a lesson in its essential nobility from the era of penny-a-liners!

The antiquarian spirit within us certainly delights in odd discoveries, and in the bringing to light of curious facts in regard to by-gone days. When in these ancient legends we find the prototypes — or the origin — of things well known to ourselves, then is our historical happiness made perfect ; we revel in facts at once strange and familiar, and the archæ-ologist and philosopher in our breasts are both well satisfied. We feel as does the philologist who is studying some new language, and who rejoices greatly whenever he discovers an old familiar word masquerading under a new form.

Thus it is truly delightful to find eras of Jeffersonian sim-plicity constantly recurring throughout history, to be as con-stantly succeeded, alas ! by periods of profusion and prodigality. The reign of Philip Augustus of France (the contemporary of Richard Cœur-de-Lion) inaugurated a day of economy among kings and princes, made necessary by the enormous outlays for the machinery of war, — arrows, helmets, chariots, etc., — and for the pay of men-at-arms demanded by the crusades. Philip never made any considerable displays of magnificence save on occasions of state, and had only a few personal at-tendants, — a chancellor, a chaplain, an esquire, a cup-bearer, some knights of the Temple, and a few sergeants-at-arms comprising all the officers of the palace. The king and the princes changed their garments only three times a year, — at the Feast of Saint Andrew (the last day of November), on Christmas, and at the Feast of the Assumption. They wore simple raiment, the king's royal mantle of scarlet being ap-parently the one piece of genuine finery ; certainly it was the one jewelled garment that existed at court, and this was only worn on grand occasions. The royal children slept in sheets made of a species of serge, and their nurses wore dark robes made of a woollen material called "brunette."

Philip the Handsome was economical as long as his first wife, Jane of Navarre, lived ; an ordinance to the *maître d'hôtel* of his time empowers that functionary "to buy all the clothes and furs for the king, to keep the key of the wardrobes, to know how much cloth was given to the tailors, and to verify the accounts when the tailors were paid."

A much more modern instance of royal economy for wise purposes is found in Frederick the Great's melting into silver dollars the staircase of solid silver built by his grandfather. Indeed, the traditions of the house of Hohenzollern favor a rugged simplicity of life which would not be endured for a moment by any wealthy inhabitant of our luxurious republic. The narrow camp-bedstead, the simple wash-stand, etc., of the Emperor of Germany would be scorned by any American whose income was a thousand dollars a year!

Queen Victoria herself has been sometimes charged with penuriousness, although it seems impossible that any *very* mean person should put lace worth eighty thousand dollars (if I mistake not the figure) into the royal rag-bag, where it was discovered by the sharp eyes of her devoted youngest daughter. However, there is no doubt that the wax-candles from the Royal Palace are regularly sold to the outside world, since it is contrary to etiquette to light them a second time. Let us hope, however, that the Queen does not directly profit by the sale of the "palace ends," as they are called.

It is interesting to learn that Lord Chesterfield's celebrated Advice to his Son had a prototype as early as the end of the fourteenth century, in a book of instructions written by one Geoffroi de la Tour-landry, an Angevin nobleman, for the benefit of his three daughters. This anxious father, wishing his daughters to have prudence and wisdom as safeguards to their beauty, gave a number of rules for their conduct, interspersed with anecdotes by way of illustration.

One of these reminds us of the well-known story of General Washington and the negro. " I have seen a great lady take off her ' chaperon ' [a sort of hood] and salute a simple 'tail-landier' [edge-tool maker]; when some one expressed surprise at this proceeding, the lady replied, ' I prefer to have been too courteous to this man, rather than to have shown the least impoliteness to a chevalier.'" It seems a strange notion to us, that of a lady removing her head-gear when about to make a salutation. Knight says that the chaperon or hood of this period was of a most indescribable shape, and was sometimes worn over the capucium, or cowl; thus it may have been thrown back, to show the features of the wearer.

The eldest daughter of this discreet father lived an exemplary life, but the second one was much addicted to feasting and gayety, and arose in the middle of the night, like a naughty school-girl, to stuff herself with good things. Her husband followed and discovered her, and was so much enraged that he beat her with a stick, a fragment whereof flew off and injured her eye ; after which, the old chronicler naïvely says, he was less fond of her!

The chastisement of the young by their parents we know to have been highly approved of in King Solomon's time, and no doubt long before ; but there is a curious anecdote that deserves mention in regard to Anne of Austria, regent of France, and the frequent whippings which she bestowed on her son Louis Quatorze. The Queen always accompanied the floggings with profound reverences, which she considered as due to the future king of France, till one day he cried out, "Ah, Madame, not so many reverences or so many whippings!"

The modern *dîner à la Russe* seems to have existed in a rudimentary form as long ago as the time of Herodotus. That historian says of the Persians : "They are moderate at their meals, but eat of many after dishes, and those not served up together. On this account the Persians say that the Greeks rise hungry from table, because nothing worth mentioning is brought in after dinner, and that if anything were brought in they would not leave off eating."

It is pleasant to learn that the Yankees are not the only nation who connect the destruction of sticks with the making of a bargain. The Zulu does not, to be sure, whittle a stick while dickering with his savage brother; but he puts a piece of wood in his mouth and chews it, hoping by this symbolic act to soften the heart of the man from whom he wishes to buy oxen. In the same way stick-chewing constitutes a part of his wooing, and is thought to soften the hard heart of his dark-skinned lady-love. This is reversing the old Hebrew tradition in accordance with which the rejected lover broke a wand over his knee when his mistress wedded another man.

Many people consider that the witchcraft of ancient days was an early manifestation of modern spiritualism, and it is certainly rather startling to find in John Bale's sixteenth century interlude, an account of stools and earthen pots moving about, much after the fashion of our modern table-tipping.

> "Theyr wells I can up drye,
> Cause trees and herbes to dye,
> And slee all pultereye,
>   Whereas men doth me move :
> I can make stoles to daunce,
> And earthen pottes to praunce,
> That none shall them enhaunce,
>   And do but cast my glove."

N. B. It is evident from this passage that in the days of Elizabeth the Boston or broad pronunciation of "dance" and similar words existed in England. Witchcraft is said to have been known in Europe in the centuries preceding the tenth, but it had no especial prominence. Charlemagne anticipated the tolerance of the nineteenth century by more than a thousand years! This wise and powerful monarch, far from persecuting witches, like a Sewall or a Cotton Mather, enacted laws directed *against* such people as should put men or women to death on the charge of witchcraft.

Among the superstitions which still survive even in the minds of educated people, a notable one is the fear that the building a new house will cause a death in the family. This seems undoubtedly to be a survival of the old barbarian belief that a victim must be buried under a new building in order to make it stand. History gives numerous instances of varying forms of this belief, from the folly of which even highly-civilized people are not exempt.

The custom of consulting old women, and one's acquaintance generally, in cases of illness, is a very ancient one, though perhaps no nation save the Babylonians ever recognized this sort of quackery as the best mode of treatment for disease. Herodotus says: "They bring out their sick to the market-place, for they have no physicians; then those who pass by the sick person confer with him about the disease, to discover whether they have themselves been afflicted with the same disease as the sick person or have seen others so afflicted . . . and advise him to have recourse to the same treatment as that by which they have escaped a similar disease." He adds that no one was allowed to pass by a sick person in silence. This was certainly applying the doctrine of Molière's "Le Médecin malgré lui" to a whole nation!

Every one knows the delightful proposition made by a writer in our own century to shut up boys — in barrels or otherwise — during the odious period of hobbledehoydom; and it is both curious and instructive to find our all-wise Shakspeare expressing the same wish, though with greater mildness. He says in "A Winter's Tale": "I would there was no age between ten and three-and-twenty; or that youth would *sleep out the rest.*" Whence we may reasonably infer that the young fellows of that day were very much like the troublesome boys of our own time.

When we come to speak of amusements, we find that many of our games have been played for hundreds of years, and some were known to the ancient Greeks and Romans. Virgil describes a whipping-top, and Pliny tells about a rich woman who was very fond of playing chess. Bagatelle was played three or four hundred years ago under the name of Trou-madame, or Pigeon-holes. An old treatise on Buxton baths, in describing the amusements of the place, says: "The ladies, gentlewomen, wives, maids, if the weather be not agreeable, may have in the end of a bench eleven holes made, into the which to troule pummits, either violent or soft, after their own discretion; the pastime *troule in madame* is termed."

An illumination of the fifteenth century shows Louis XI. of France playing checkers with his courtiers. They are represented as sitting on hard wooden benches and playing on a bare wooden table. Despite the presence of the king, and the fact that the scene is apparently within doors, all wear their hats. These look like low-crowned Derbys, or soft felt hats.

Two centuries earlier we find gentlemen of quality amusing themselves with backgammon, checkers, and chess, "to which certain chevaliers consecrated all their leisure."

Playing-cards were used by Charles VI. of France, and an entry in the account-book of his treasurer, about the year 1393, mentions this item: "Fifty-six sols of Paris given to Jacquemin Gringonneur, painter, for three packs of cards, gilt and colored, and of different sorts, for the diversion of his Majesty." An old manuscript copy of "Renard le Contrefait" would seem to prove that cards were known in France about the year 1340, or six years before the battle of Cressy, where firearms were used for the first time.

The fact that gunpowder and the "Devil's pictured books" came into use at the same period might perhaps furnish an additional argument to those who contend that cards are an invention of the Evil One. "A youth of frolics, an old age of cards," said Pope. But Thackeray understood the matter much better. In his "Roundabout Papers" he says:—

"If I had children to educate, I would at ten or twelve years of age have a professor or professoress of whist for them, and cause them to be well grounded in that great and useful game. You cannot learn it well when you are old, any more than you can learn dancing or billiards. . . . A waste of time, my good people! *Allons!* What do elderly home-keeping people do of a night after dinner? Darby gets his newspaper, my dear Joan her 'Missionary Magazine,'— and don't you know what ensues? Over the arm of Darby's arm-chair the paper flutters to the ground unheeded, and he performs the trumpet obbligato *que vous savez* on his old nose. My dear old Joan's head nods over her sermon (awakening though the doctrine may be). Ding, ding, ding; can that be ten o'clock? It is time to send the servants to bed, my dear,— and to bed master and mistress go too. But they have not wasted their time playing at cards,— oh no! . . . Not play at whist? 'Quelle triste vieillesse vous vous préparez!' were the words of the great and good Bishop of Autun."

The art of dancing in the Middle Ages had not yet attained the degree of intricacy which marks our modern german. From miniatures of that period it would seem that ordinary dancing consisted simply of forming large rounds or circles, in which people turned around, and swayed themselves in cadence, observing the measure of the music.

Some curious dances also are illustrated in ancient books, such as the torch dance, and the famous dance of satyrs, which caused a fearful accident at the court of France in 1392. Froissart describes how a squire of Normandy devised six coats made of linen cloth covered with pitch, and thereon flax-like hair. The king and five noblemen put these on; "and when they were thus arrayed in these sad coats, and

sewed fast in them, they seemed like wild woodhouses
[savages] full of hair from the top of the head to the sole
of the foot." All the varlets holding torches were com-
manded to stand up by the walls, and none of them to
approach near to the woodhouses that should come thither
to dance. They were so disguised in flax that no man knew
them; five of them were fastened one to another; the king
was loose, and went before and led the device.

The Duke of Orléans was so anxious to find out who the
dancers were, that he placed a torch so near the satyrs that
the flax took fire; all were burned to death save the king
and one other, who fled to the "botry" and cast himself
into a vessel full of water wherein they rinsed pots, and
thus saved himself. "The Duchess of Berry delivered the
king from that peril, for she did cast over him the train of
her gown and covered him from the fire."

The boat-races of antiquity seem to have excited almost as
much contemporaneous interest as the international yacht-
races of our day. Virgil, in his account of the games at
the tomb of Anchises, describes how the owner of one of
the boats became so enraged at his pilot for not hugging the
turning-stake (in this case a rock) as much as he thought
proper, that he pitched the unfortunate man into the sea,
and every one laughed at the luckless navigator when he
finally succeeded in climbing on to the rock, panting for
breath, and dripping with sea-water. In the same account
Virgil describes the terrible *cæstus*, or ancestor of our modern
boxing-glove, which consisted of seven thicknesses of bull's
hide, strengthened with lead and iron, and sometimes adorned
with brass knuckles. The imagination shudders at the
thought of what the great John L. would be able to accom-
plish arrayed in these terrible gauntlets. In the Iliad they
are called "the gloves of death;" and so dangerous was
the contest with these "iron hands," that both Homer and

Virgil dwell on the difficulty of inducing heroes to enter the ancient prize-ring, where prizes were provided for the vanquished as well as for the victor.

There is not space enough left in this chapter to speak at length of the follies in dress of ancient times, or to solve the difficult problem of the date and origin of the first dude. Richard II. of England was perhaps the greatest fop of his century; and by a somewhat singular coincidence his reign was filled with labor troubles and commotions, very much as is our own Age of Dudes. The shoes, also, were worn with very long points or pikes, like an exaggeration of those we have lately seen. Richard " had a coat estimated at thirty thousand marks, the value of which must chiefly have arisen from the quantity of precious stones with which it was embroidered, such being one of the many extravagant fashions of the time." The wearing of enormous sleeves reaching almost to the feet was another foolish habit of this period, against which Chaucer and his contemporaries all inveighed. John of Gaunt, the founder of the house of Lancaster, did not yield to the follies of dress prevalent in his nephew's reign, but wore a sleeve tight to the wrist, with a sort of balloon above the elbow.

Foreign as well as native writers bear witness to the foppery of the English at or about this time. Paul Lacroix relates an anecdote of a French lord to whom some one had spoken disparagingly of the fashion of his wife's dress. " I wish my wife dressed like the good ladies of France, and not like those of England," replied the worthy gentleman. "It was the latter who first introduced into Brittany wide borders, bodices divided at the hip, and *hanging sleeves*."

In the reign of King John of England — a century earlier — the beaux curled and crisped their hair with irons. They seldom wore caps, but bound slight fillets around their heads. as they wished their " crimps " to be seen and admired.

CHAPTER XXXIII.

HINTS FOR YOUNG MEN. — WASHINGTON CUSTOMS.

It has been said that the aim of education should be to teach a person how to study. The young man who graduates from college has still no doubt much to learn, but the key of future knowledge has been put into his hand. He knows where to look for information on various points; he has been placed on the right road, and it will be his own fault if he does not keep to it. Herein he has a great advantage over the self-educated man, who wanders blindly and without compass over vast fields of (to him) unclassified information. It is wonderful what we can all find in books, pictures, or the face of Nature, when we have once learned what to look for. The diver cannot find the pearl unless he knows where the oyster lies.

It is with this hope — the hope that I may have been able to place the reader on the right track, to turn his face in the right direction — that I now prepare to bring this little volume to a close. No one ever learned the art of dancing, swimming, or fencing, or the secret of a courtly and polished manner, from the study of books alone. These can give but the theory, and practice must be added to theory to make it perfect. Carlyle points out, in a very striking passage, that in every art and trade there is much that has never been and never will be written down, but is transmitted from one generation of artists and mechanics to another, — a visible tradition, if I may be allowed the expression. Thus a lost art or trade can never in the nature of things be resuscitated, though it is sometimes rediscovered.

An additional difficulty in the way of fixing upon paper the open secret of what constitutes good manners is, that our manners, like our language, are constantly undergoing changes. The spirit alone of true courtesy remains always the same, and he who builds the edifice of his behavior on this foundation builds on a rock.

What are the qualifications that best fit a person for making himself agreeable in society? Are they not tact, wit, and good spirits? The most important of these — and perhaps the rarest — is tact. The man of tact is not of necessity false and insincere, although very downright people like to call him so. Say rather he is a person who possesses an infinite power of silence; a ready steersman, who can always dexterously change the helm of conversation when rocks or shoals are near. He can know or divine what are the skeletons in the closets of a whole roomful of people, and yet not once mention these disagreeable subjects, nor allow others to mention them if he can help it. This is his passive or negative virtue. His active and positive one is the knowledge that he possesses of what is agreeable to each individual, as well as what gratifies the world at large. He talks, or, better still, he listens to each man on the subject of which that man loves most to discourse. Tact means literally the act of touching. A person who possesses true tact may be said to resemble one of those radiates which have a thousand sensitive tentacles or feelers. By their help his mind comes in contact with the minds of his neighbors at an infinite number of points; but the contact is one of sympathy, and is never a violent collision. Ready sympathy is a very necessary element of tact, but it is not the only one. Sympathy without intellectual acuteness leads people into

21

frightful blunders.   Thus the sympathetic woman will often
read, by a sort of semi-mesmeric power, what is passing in
the mind of her interlocutor; but the latter may be dwelling
on some subject that is very painful to him, and if the sympathetic woman be lacking in intelligence, she will be very apt
to introduce this painful theme into the conversation, always
with the best intentions.   Absent-minded people are guilty
of the same mistakes, and are often celebrated for their in-
advertencies of this sort.   Thus if an absent-minded man is
talking to a person who has been insane, insanity will be
vaguely suggested to his mind; and forgetting the exact facts
of the case he will talk about crazy people, remembering,
when it is too late, the unkindness of which he has apparently
been guilty.

The man who is witty — and wise as well — is always a
favorite in society.   But his wisdom must teach him not to
be egotistical, and not to weary the company with too many
smart sayings.   Finally, the person who has good spirits
possesses that which all the world wants, and which every
man may borrow from him without impoverishing the lender.
He is like the sun; every one draws near him for warmth
and cheer.   One of the greatest charms of youth is its gay
good-nature, the brilliant spirits which result from vigorous
animal life and health, and from ignorance of the world and
its evils.   From a *blasé* young man or woman every one
prays to be delivered!

At the present moment brains, provided they be not too
heavy, are at a great premium in society.   The intellectual man
is the idol of the hour, and the man who can make his
hearers intellectual — at least in their own imagination —
is sought after and admired beyond all others.   It is therefore very desirable for young people to cultivate any talent
they may possess for reading aloud and reciting.   If a young
man has a thorough knowledge of any one subject, and can

discourse or lecture upon it clearly, intelligently, and in an interesting manner, he will find himself much more popular in society than the man who can do nothing for its instruction or amusement. But the cultivated man must strenuously avoid the temptation to display his talent continually ; he must be ready to do his part whenever he is called upon, but not otherwise.

The same is true of the person who can tell amusing stories, the woman who can play on the mandolin, the guitar, or the harp, and of many others.

The line which divides the most charming person in the world from the greatest bore is of a hair's width, — like the celebrated step which separates the sublime from the ridiculous. It is a gift of the gods to know when to stop ; and in the intoxication of success many people go far beyond the proper limit, when lo ! their popularity vanishes like a dream.

There is another very important qualification for making one's self agreeable in society, and that is the willingness to be generally useful. The obliging man or woman — especially if he or she have plenty of time at command — is found to be indispensable. But such a person, while secretly wielding great power, must beware of openly assuming social authority. The power behind the throne must remain ever in the shadow. If the man who holds it tries to sit upon the throne, he is sure to be kicked off.

If the greater portion of this volume — as of most books of the kind — is devoted to the consideration of the social duties of women rather than of men, it is not because the former stand in need of more instruction than the latter. Is it not rather that women are willing to give more thought to these subjects, and take a greater and more vital interest in them ? Howells's immortal saying, that "after two thousand years man is imperfectly monogamous" (I quote from memory), might have had as an addition that he is imperfectly civilized as well. Woman's intellectual position as compared with that of man may admit of dispute; but her position in civilization is certainly far ahead of his. Take a small community in our far West, where there are no women, and you will find the most highly civilized men relapsing into barbarism.

Even in our own part of the world young men are often found to be lacking in politeness, and in that deference toward their elders and toward women which is so becoming in a manly young fellow. To such an one the writer would like to offer a few words of advice in a friendly spirit.

A gentleman should always rise from his chair when a lady enters or leaves the room, and should not return to it until she has taken a seat or passed out, as the case may be. In the latter instance, he should open the door for her; in the former, he should bring a chair rather than suffer her to lift one for herself. The man who will allow a lady to carry a chair from one part of the room to another without offering to assist her, is wanting in good-breeding. Some very punctilious men always rise whenever a lady rises, and remain standing until she resumes her seat; but this may be rather embarrassing to her if she has occasion to go about the room often.

Gentlemen should avoid making very long or very late evening calls, which exhaust the patience of their entertainers. Many young men are voted bores because they make visits of two or three hours' length; whereas if they remained only an hour or an hour and a half, they would be considered as decidedly agreeable persons.

No doubt one reason for these interminable calls is that many men do not know how to get out of a room, and postpone the hour of departure because they dread it so much. When they rise to take their leave, they are easily persuaded to sit down again, although perhaps the invitation to do so is merely given by the hostess as a matter of form.

> "Stand not upon the order of your going,
> But go at once."

A lingering leave-taking is wearisome to host and guest alike; nor is it polite to the hostess, since she feels compelled to stand until the caller has left the room. When a gentleman takes his leave after making a call on several ladies, it suffices for him to make a decided bow to the lady of the house, with a slighter inclination to the other members of the family. Some men make a sort of final and general salutation as they pass out at the door of the room; but this custom does not prevail generally in America.

The custom of making evening calls, except upon intimate friends, is rapidly going out of fashion. Young men now call in the afternoon, after an invitation to dinner for instance, and make a visit of twenty minutes or half an hour in length. This change of hours is due in part to the imitation of English customs, and in part to the present fashion of dining late, which gives gentlemen an opportunity to make calls after business hours, and before the seven-o'clock dinner now so much in vogue.

A gentleman should never allow a lady to sit backwards in a carriage, but should himself take the seat the back of which is turned toward the horses, where it is necessary for some one to do so. In the same way a young lady should not permit an older or a married lady to ride backwards. According to strict etiquette, the lady who owns the carriage keeps her own seat; but she will usually surrender it to a married lady if she is herself unmarried, or to one who is much her senior.

As it makes some people positively ill to ride backwards, those who can do so without inconvenience or suffering should offer to take these undesirable places. A hostess enters the carriage after her guests, unless they are much younger than she is.

A gentleman should always get out of a carriage before the ladies do, taking care not to pass in front of them, but to get out at the door which is nearest to his seat. He should then help the ladies to get out, each in her turn. There are several ways of doing this, a lady requiring more or less assistance according to the height of the vehicle, her own age and activity. Perhaps the most approved way is where a gentleman offers his arm, the lady placing her hand upon it. He can then lend her additional assistance, if it is necessary, by supporting her elbow or forearm with his hand. At the same time he guards her dress from the wheel by holding his cane or umbrella in front of it, with his left hand.

Another method is for a gentleman to offer a lady one or both hands; or if she is descending from a very high vehicle, she may place both hands upon his shoulders, as he is thus enabled to support her arms. When a lady ascends a tally-ho coach, she goes first, a gentleman mounting the ladder one or two steps behind her and keeping her dress in place with his cane. In descending, he goes first, for the same reason, both of them coming down backward. The companion-ways on board ship are mounted and descended in the same manner.

The art of mounting a lady properly on horseback is one that many gentlemen do not understand. The lady should place her left foot in one or both of the gentleman's hands, her left hand on his shoulder, and her right hand on the pommel of the saddle. Then at a given word she springs upward, the gentleman at the same moment raising his hand so as to assist but not actually to lift her into the saddle. When accompanying a lady on horseback, a gentleman always keeps on the right side.

In dancing, he should offer his hand gracefully to a lady, where he has occasion to do so at all. The hand should be presented palm downward, taking care that the thumb does not project in an awkward way. To hold the hand vertically, with the thumb sticking up in the air, looks extremely awkward. A gentleman should also be careful not to shake hands with too much violence, and not to press a lady's hand so that her rings will hurt her fingers. *Per contra*, ladies should not shake hands as if those members were paralyzed or hopelessly limp; and if they should have occasion to take a gentleman's arm — in the evening or in some crowded street — they need not be afraid to lean some of their weight upon it. Most men rather enjoy the sense of protecting the weaker sex, and admire a woman who knows " how to take an arm " properly.

A gentleman should always offer to pass up a lady's fare in a stage or in a horse-car where there is no conductor, and should get off the steps of a car rather than allow a lady to be uncomfortably crowded as she enters or leaves it. And just here it is pleasant to be able to say that many of our countrymen in what might be called the humbler ranks of life offer these civilities in a way that is gratifying to see, and that reflects much credit upon them.

It has been said elsewhere that the custom of saying Madam and Sir is falling into disuse. There are still some occasions, however, when it is necessary to use these expressions; notably, when one addresses a stranger. If a gentleman offer to bring a lady any refreshment at an entertainment, to hand up her fare in a horse-car, or to call her attention to a parcel that she has left behind, he should in these and similar cases address her as Madam, and never as Miss, even though he may know that she is unmarried. A lady responding to any civility which may have been courteously offered to her by a *stranger*, uses " Sir " in speaking to him. But neither party should continue the conversation, for obvious reasons. Elderly ladies, whose experience of the world has given them knowledge of men and things, sometimes converse with their fellow-travellers, especially on long railroad journeys; but it is very undesirable and unsafe for a young woman to do so.

In conclusion, the writer would say that no young man should despair of social success because he does not speedily achieve it. It is no uncommon thing to see a young man much laughed at for his awkwardness or his ungainly figure when he first enters society; and then to see the same youth, by pluck, perseverance, and practice, become a fine dancer, an agreeable partner, and a leader of fashion. Women admire courage; and the man who perseveres in spite of defeat is pretty sure to win favor in their eyes.

It is more courteous to send a separate invitation to the young men of a family, and not to direct an envelope to " Miss Atwater *and bro.*" The latter form is of course allowable, and frequently employed; but some gentlemen object to it very much, especially where they have been in society for several years. A fashionable young man who is a social favorite complains bitterly that he never receives a separate invitation, but is always invited as a "bro," tacked on to his sister's name. Where there are several unmarried sons living at home, and they are no longer very young, it is more courteous to send an invitation to each by name, rather than include them under the general term " Messrs." It is always proper to invite two or more sisters as "the Misses Atwater," no matter what their ages may be.

The etiquette of Washington differs from that of other American cities; it is customary there for strangers to call first upon the members of the Government and on the wives of official personages. For this purpose receptions are held every afternoon, and a special day is set apart for each branch of the Government. Thus, Monday is Judges' day, and on that afternoon the justices of the Supreme Court remain at home and receive callers, assisted by the ladies of their families. Tuesday is the reception-day of members of the House of Representatives; Wednesday, of the Cabinet officers; Thursday, of the Senators; and Friday, of the Diplomatic Corps. The President's receptions are usually held on Saturday; and on that day the residents of Connecticut Avenue receive calls. The reason for this very catholic hospitality is an obvious one. It would be impossible for the wives of Congressmen, Cabinet officers, and others to call first upon every one who came to the National Capital; and yet according to our Republican theories every American citizen has a right to social recognition at the hands of the rulers whom his voice has helped to elect. Hence the wives of our public servants throw open their houses to visitors on one day of each week during the season, and any person who chooses, has a right to attend these informal receptions. According to Washington etiquette all these calls must be promptly returned; as their number and frequency are very great, they make the social duties of an official hostess extremely burdensome. Such a lady often employs a private secretary, whose duty it is to keep a record of the visits made, visits returned, and those still to be returned. The wives of the Cabinet officers recently rebelled against this slavery to the travelling public (for it is nothing else), and caused it to be known that they would not undertake to return calls personally, but that their cards would be sent instead. This course, however, gave rise to some bitterness of feeling among those who did not understand the exigencies of the situation, and who felt themselves insulted, forgetting that a public servant and his wife ought not to be made public slaves. The wife of one of our recent Secretaries of State is said to have seriously injured her health by her punctiliousness in returning all visits. As our country is increasing in population with such rapidity, and as the throng of visitors in Washington is in consequence growing constantly greater, it would seem as if some remedy must be found for this growing evil, and as if the course of the Cabinet ladies was the only one possible for them to pursue.

When the society in Washington was comparatively small, and the strangers who came to the city in the gay season comparatively few, all was very different; but matters have changed very much at our National Capital within five or six years. Transient visitors and excursionists now visit it in enormous numbers, and intrude themselves in houses where they have no right to go at all in some instances, and in others only on certain days of the week.

It would seem as if common-sense ought to teach people that to a card reception (that is, where the guests are all invited by card) no one save those specially invited would have a right to go ; but the Washington tourist is very unreflecting. His rule of conduct too often resembles that of the Irishman, — where you see a head, hit it. Where the Washington tourist sees a number of carriages standing before the door of a mansion, he immediately enters thereat ; and whether he is one, or whether he is two hundred, makes absolutely no difference in his view of the situation. The result of his theories is naturally disastrous. No private house can hold an unlimited number of people ; and where the uninvited throng in such numbers, the invited guests are unable to gain admission. A Washington lady received cards for a reception given by an official person. It was a little late when she started, and upon her arrival in —— Avenue she found a surging throng of people in and around the door of the house where the reception was to be held. After striving with the crowd for an hour or more, and reaching only the vestibule of the mansion, she and her escort gave up the attempt to gain further admittance, and went home without having been to the party at all! It transpired afterward that an excursion of two hundred people had arrived in Washington on that day, and had attended Mr. ——'s reception *en masse!*

Thus it is evident that the public abuses its privileges, and if less democratic customs should be adopted, the people themselves would be to blame. All public libraries and parks are conducted on the theory that the public will respect their own possessions; the moment that they cease to do so, that they begin to abuse the books or deface the beauty of the grass and trees, the free system becomes impossible. It is the same with the freedom of entrance in Washington society. It can only continue while the public are " upon honor," and behave like ladies and gentlemen.

No doubt the tourists are less to blame in regard to their conduct in Washington than might at first sight be supposed. Being strangers in the land, they naturally believe whatever is told them, forgetting that hotel-keepers, agents for excursions, hack-drivers, and others may, through interested motives, offer them more opportunities of sight-seeing and visiting than they have a legitimate right to do. It is to be feared also that mankind have a tendency to be less careful about their behavior when they are in foreign lands than they would be in their native place, where habit, and the desire to appear well in the eyes of their fellow-townsmen, act as restraining influences. One should always remember that travelling is the severest test of good-breeding; the man who does not forget his politeness among strangers, people whom he never expects to see again, will not be likely to forget it anywhere. It is a dangerous matter, too, to imagine that one's behavior in another city or country will not be known at home. This world is a very small place;

Printed in the United States
145003LV00007B/51/A

9 780548 904015